MCSE TestPrep

Internet Explorer 4

Andy Ruth
Kurt Hudson

New Riders
201 West 103rd St. Indianapolis, IN 46290

MCSE TestPrep: Internet Explorer 4

International Standard Book Number: 0-7897-1654-2

Library of Congress Catalog Card Number: 98-85229

Printed in the United States of America

First Printing: July 1998

00 99 98 4 3 2 1

Trademarks

All terms mentioned in this book that are known to be trademarks or service marks have been appropriately capitalized. New Riders Publishing cannot attest to the accuracy of this information. Use of a term in this book should not be regarded as affecting the validity of any trademark or service mark.

Warning and Disclaimer

This book is designed to provide information about Microsoft's "Implementing and Supporting Microsoft Internet Explorer 4.0 by Using the Internet Explorer Administration Kit" (70-079) exam. Every effort has been made to make this book as complete and accurate as possible, but no warranty or fitness is implied.

The information is provided on an "as is" basis. The authors and New Riders Publishing shall have neither liability nor responsibility to any person or entity with respect to any loss or damage arising from the information contained in this book or from the use of the discs or programs that may accompany it.

New Riders Publishing is an independent entity from Microsoft Corporation, and is not affiliated with Microsoft Corporation in any manner. This publication may be used in assisting students to prepare for Microsoft Certified Professional Exams. Neither Microsoft Corporation, its designated review company, nor New Riders Publishing warrants that use of this publication will ensure passing the relevant Exam. Microsoft is either a registered trademark or trademark of Microsoft Corporation in the United States and/or other countries.

Executive Editor
John Kane

Acquisitions Editor
Steve Weiss

Development Editor
Howard Jones

Technical Editors
Jim Cooper
Gerry High

Managing Editor
Sarah Kearns

Project Editor
Tom Dinse

Copy Editor
Alice Martina Smith

Indexer
Craig Small

Production
Steve Balle-Gifford
Pamela Woolf

About the Author

Andy Ruth is a vice-president with Hudlogic Corporation, a company that provides worldwide training, documentation, and consulting to the high-tech industry. Andy started his career in the U.S. Navy, where he worked with flight simulators. In private industry, Andy has worked on equipment ranging from desktop devices to mainframe computers, large and small networks, in most facets of the industry.

Dedication

To Jaylene, my love, my life.

Acknowledgments

First and foremost, thank God. Also, I'd like to thank the folks at Macmillan Publishing for standing behind this group of books that can be so helpful to the aspiring MCSE. In particular, thanks to Steve Weiss for assembling a team that is second to none, of which my three mentors were:

Howard Jones—development editor

Gerry High—technical editor

James Cooper—technical editor

All three did a fantastic job of making sure this book delivered what was intended—a preparation guide for the Internet Explorer 4.0 test, as well as a reference for understanding the purpose and theory behind the IEAK product.

Special thanks to Rich Thorp who wrote chapters 5 and 6 (and searched out great sources of information), and Bob Collier, who wrote the two quizzes found at the end of the book.

Thanks to my wife, Jaylene, and two kids, Zandy and James, who gave me up while this book was being written, along with my parents for giving me the "stick" to start and finish this project. Thanks to Dianea for providing stress relief in the form of losing at pinochle to Pete and I. Dora for being the other half of that losing team and providing me with a role model to pattern my career after (you'll have to get published now). Jimmy for being a big brother, and Cheri for always laughing at my jokes (at least I hope you're laughing at my jokes).

Contents at a Glance

Table of Contents

Introduction

The information in this study guide provides vital information on the Internet Explorer Administration Kit (IEAK) product and brief summaries on the operation of the product, while highlighting information that is imperative for passing the IEAK certification exam.

> **This book was developed to help you pass the certification exam for the IEAK. It is designed to be a resource for information on the product, but it is not to be considered a comprehensive product guide.**

This book is structured topically, in the same manner as the certification exam, and attempts to cover the same knowledge base you will be tested on in the actual exam. Several questions have been developed to help you determine your level of expertise with the IEAK.

The authors of this book know the product. They have taken the exam and worked with the IEAK extensively. This book is not simply a regurgitation of the limited documentation on the Internet Explorer Administration Kit. Instead, this book seeks to provide the information you have to learn to pass the exam and beyond.

Prerequisites

This book assumes that you have current knowledge of Windows NT Workstation, Windows NT Server, TCP/IP, Domain Directory Services, and Windows 95/98. It also assumes that you have knowledge of Internet Explorer 4.0 and the IEAK and are simply looking for a study guide to strengthen your knowledge.

About This Book

This book is divided into six chapters that reflect the six areas on which the Microsoft certification exam will test your skill level.

Chapter 1, "Planning"

Planning is one of the most important aspects of a successful deployment of Microsoft Internet Explorer 4.0 (IE 4.0). The IEAK is a valuable tool for deploying the IE 4.0 product to the user's desktop. Here are several areas you should especially consider:

- Upgrading from previous versions of Internet browsers, mail and news clients, and plug-in components
- Upgrading the user's hardware and software to support Internet Explorer 4.0 and associated applications
- Selecting the Web sites and channels to which users will subscribe
- Selecting the plug-in components that will be deployed to the user's desktop, and what functionality to allow the user.
- Selecting the methods used for deploying the custom IE 4.0 package you create with the IEAK

Chapter 2, "Installation and Configuration"

After you create and write a good deployment plan, you need to install and configure IE 4.0 and any associated components.

Chapter 2 provides insight into the hardware and software requirements for installing the IEAK and the platforms for which support is offered. The three modes in which the IEAK can run are discussed, as are the configuration capabilities you have in each mode.

The installation process of the IEAK is detailed, as is the configuration of the browser, Active Desktop components, Outlook Express, NetMeeting, and channel and site subscriptions.

Chapter 3, "Configuring and Managing Resource Access"

In this chapter, you take a closer look at the Corporate Administrator mode, particularly the zone security settings and the proxy server support settings. You also learn to use the Profile Manager to modify settings in a custom package, rather than creating a new custom package.

Chapter 4, "Integration and Distribution"

This chapter deals with upgrading clients that already have browsers configured, upgrading clients that already have mail clients configured, configuring and limiting Microsoft NetMeeting, and configuring distribution media.

This chapter provides a more in-depth look at the upgrade and implementation topics covered in Chapter 1.

Chapter 5, "Monitoring and Optimization"

Chapter 5 details how to customize Active Desktop items and Active Channels. You learn how to configure Web site subscriptions, channel subscriptions, and Active Desktop components.

With the capabilities offered when IE 4.0 is installed and the capability to receive Web site updates automatically, you have to know how to use the available desktop and network resources.

This chapter details the ability of the network administrator to configure these features to best use the network's resources without placing too much of a burden on those resources.

Chapter 6, "Troubleshooting"

Even with the best planning and implementation of IE 4.0 using the IEAK, you are still bound to run into problems.

This chapter looks at some of the tools available for troubleshooting problems. It also details some of the common problems that arise and provides resolutions to those problems.

Practice Exams

Two exercises at the end of the book test your overall knowledge of the IEAK product. Each exam contains 75 questions, evenly distributed to cover the content of the entire book. These exams are meant to test your overall understanding of the material; they do not provide you with the actual questions from the exam.

Appendix A, "Review of Additional Concepts"

The IEAK exam can be one of the most brutal Microsoft certification exams you are likely to take. The subject matter of the exam covers not only the use of the IEAK, but the use of IE 4.0, proxy server configuration, and TCP/IP configuration and troubleshooting tools.

This appendix is a useful look at some of the topics you are expected to know and should have learned from previous studies. Domain structure, user accounts, group accounts, and computer accounts are discussed, as are basic proxy and TCP/IP concepts. Some TCP/IP troubleshooting tools are detailed.

Glossary

The glossary provides definitions of the terms used throughout this book and can provide further information on some of the subject matter. For more information about the terms listed, open the IEAK Help. At the bottom of the left pane is an Index tab; select it. A list of the terms pertinent to IEAK and IE 4.0 appears. The definitions provided there are a bit more detailed than the definitions supplied in this book.

About the Exam

The Internet Explorer Administration Kit is used to automate the installation of Internet Explorer 4.0, its built-in components, and third-party programs.

In large networked environments, where several thousand client machines must be configured to take advantage of currently available Internet technology (and constantly changing products), a definite need exists for a tool that can ease client configuration.

The IEAK was designed to do just that. Tasks that generate considerable amounts of administrative overhead can be quickly and efficiently automated. Custom settings can be designed to limit the capabilities of machines that offer public access (such as public kiosk computers); these setting options are flexible enough to allow freedom to users who need more generous access rights.

The Microsoft certification exam for the IEAK has been designed to test your knowledge not only of the IEAK product and its capabilities, but also other components and skills required to support and secure a large Internetwork.

The certification is provided by Microsoft tests and ensures that you have knowledge of, and are qualified to support, a large network using the Microsoft tools.

Exam Difficulty

This may be the most difficult exam Microsoft has created yet. The requisite knowledge base is quite extensive. For example, you are expected to show an aptitude for using the IEAK and to display a high level of knowledge on the Internet Explorer 4.0 product. You are also expected to be knowledgeable in TCP/IP protocol and the other Microsoft products that provide Internet connectivity and troubleshooting capabilities.

Do not attempt to take the certification exam until you have a high level of competence using the newer components of IE 4.0, including the NetMeeting utilities, Web site subscriptions, channel subscriptions, and the configuration of each. Before attempting this exam, it is imperative that you run the IEAK Wizard in all three operational modes; explore every configuration option available. Then use the IEAK Profile Manager to view and modify configuration options. After setting options, view the information stored in the `Install.INS` file.

Why Certify?

One of the big questions always asked before a person starts the long, tedious, expensive quest to obtain a Microsoft certification is "Why certify?" The easiest answer to that question is to say that it's well worth the effort.

For years, a four-year college degree opened the door for young and talented people to join the workforce. Employers have traditionally used the four-year degree as a base requirement for an applicant to be considered for a position. A master's degree generally ensured that a new employee would receive higher compensation and a chance to move up the corporate ladder.

Microsoft certification provides an employer with some measurement of the technical ability of the potential employee; in many cases, it acts as a master's degree did in the past. This certification provides additional opportunities for many by opening more corporate doors and increasing compensation offers.

Which Certifications Are Available?

Several certifications are available, and more certifications are being developed. As the need for a more precise skill set is defined, certifications are developed to ensure each skill set. The following sections list available Microsoft certifications and the exams that must be passed to obtain them. The exams mentioned are the latest exams currently available for each server-based application. In some cases, there may be three versions of certain product exams out, one for each version of the software. In these cases, I have listed only the most current exam available at the time this book was written. For a complete list of exams available, visit the Microsoft Certification Web site at `http://www.microsoft.com/train_cert`.

MCP

The Microsoft Certified Professional (MCP) is obtained by passing one operating system exam. This is the easiest—and the first—certification obtained. The following exams apply:

- **70-073**: Implementing and Supporting Microsoft Windows NT Workstation 4.0
- **70-067**: Implementing and Supporting Microsoft Windows NT Server 4.0
- **70-064**: Implementing and Supporting Microsoft Windows 95
- **70-098**: Implementing and Supporting Microsoft Windows 98
- **70-160**: Microsoft Windows Architecture I
- **70-161**: Microsoft Windows Architecture II

MCP+Internet

The Microsoft Certified Professional + Internet (MCP+Internet) is an interim certification you can obtain on the way to becoming an MCSE or MCSE+Internet. The requirements for this certification are higher those for the MCPS, yet lower than those for the MCSE. To become an MCP+Internet, you must pass the following exams:

- **70-059**: Internetworking Microsoft TCP/IP on Microsoft Windows NT 4.0
- **70-067**: Implementing and Supporting Microsoft Windows NT Server 4.0
- **70-087**: Implementing and Supporting Microsoft Internet Information Server 4.0

MCSE

The Microsoft Certified Systems Engineer (MCSE) is probably the most widely sought after Microsoft certification. This certification ensures employers that you have a well-rounded knowledge of the Microsoft product line, and that you should be qualified to support a large, diverse Internetwork. The track you'll follow to obtain your MCSE is the 4.0 track. When Microsoft Windows NT 5.0 comes out, there will most likely be a 5.0 track to follow. There are four core exams and two elective exams needed for this certification. The 4.0 track is detailed here:

- **70-058**: Implementing and Supporting Microsoft Windows 98: Networking Essentials
- **70-067**: Implementing and Supporting Microsoft Windows NT Server 4.0
- **70-068**: Implementing and Supporting Microsoft Windows NT Server 4.0 in the Enterprise
- **70-073**: Implementing and Supporting Microsoft Windows NT Workstation 4.0

  or

  70-064: Implementing and Supporting Microsoft Windows 95

  or

  70-098: Implementing and Supporting Microsoft Windows 98

  plus any two of the following:

- **70-085**: Implementing and Supporting Microsoft SNA Server 4.0

  or

  70-086: Implementing and Supporting Microsoft Systems Management Server 2.0

  or

  70-028: System Administration for Microsoft SQL Server 7.0

  or

  70-029: Implementing a Database Design on Microsoft SQL Server 7.0

  or

  70-037: Microsoft Mail for PC Networks 3.2-Enterprise

  or

  70-059: Internetworking with Microsoft TCP/IP on Microsoft Windows NT 4.0

  or

  70-081: Implementing and Supporting Microsoft Exchange Server 5.5

  or

  70-087: Implementing and Supporting Microsoft Internet Information Server 4.0

  or

  70-088: Implementing and Supporting Microsoft Proxy Server 2.0

  or

  70-079: Implementing and Supporting Microsoft Internet Explorer 4.0 by Using the Internet Explorer Administration Kit

The exams listed for each product represents the latest exam released or about to be released. For a complete list of available exams, visit the Microsoft Web site. They are listed on the MCP page.

MCSE+Internet

The newest gem in the certification crown is the Microsoft Certified System Engineer + Internet (MCSE + Internet). On your way to obtaining this certification, you will become an MCSE. For the MCSE + Internet certification, you must complete seven core exams and two elective exams. The core and elective exams are as follows:

- **70-058**: Implementing and Supporting Microsoft Windows 98: Networking Essentials
- **70-059**: Internetworking with Microsoft TCP/IP on Microsoft Windows NT 4.0
- **70-067**: Implementing and Supporting Microsoft Windows NT Server 4.0
- **70-068**: Implementing and Supporting Microsoft Windows NT Server 4.0 in the Enterprise
- **70-079**: Implementing and Supporting Microsoft Internet Explorer 4.0 by Using the Internet Explorer Administration Kit
- **70-087**: Implementing and Supporting Microsoft Internet Information Server 4.0

- **70-073**: Implementing and Supporting Microsoft Windows NT Workstation 4.0

  or

  70-064: Implementing and Supporting Microsoft Windows 95

  or

  70-098: Implementing and Supporting Microsoft Windows 98

  plus any two of the following:

- **70-028**: System Administration for Microsoft SQL Server 7.0

  or

  70-029: Implementing a Database Design on Microsoft SQL Server 7.0

  or

  70-081: Implementing and Supporting Microsoft Exchange Server 5.5

  or

  70-085: Implementing and Supporting Microsoft SNA Server 4.0

  or

  70-088: Implementing and Supporting Microsoft Proxy Server 2.0

MCSD

The Microsoft Certified Solution Developer (MCSD) certification can be considered a "programmer" certification. This is a certification for software support. To receive this certification, you must pass two core exams and two elective exams. The required exams are as follows:

- **70-160:** Microsoft Windows Architecture I
- **70-161:** Microsoft Windows Architecture II

  plus any two of the following:

- **70-029**: Implementing a Database Design on Microsoft SQL Server 7.0

  or

  70-024: Developing Applications with C++ Using the Microsoft Foundation Class Library

  or

  70-024: Implementing OLE in Microsoft Foundation Class Applications

  or

  70-165: Developing Applications with Microsoft Visual Basic 5.0

  or

  70-069: Microsoft Access for Windows 95 and the Microsoft Access Developer's Toolkit

  or

70-052: Developing Applications with Microsoft Excel 5.0 Using Visual Basic for Applications

or

70-054: Programming in Microsoft Visual FoxPro 3.0 for Windows

MCT

The Microsoft Certified Trainer (MCT) certification allows a trainer to teach Microsoft Official Curriculum (MOC) material at Authorized Technical Education Centers (ATECs). To view the current requirements to become a Microsoft Certified Trainer, visit the Microsoft Certified Trainer 1998 Guide Web site at `http://www.microsoft.com/train_cert/mct`.

The Certification Process

To gain certification, you need not attend any courses, read any books, or even use the software the certification exam covers. However, it is recommended that you pursue any and all education channels available to you.

All you have to do to become certified is register to take an exam and make a passing score in the time allotted. The exams have traditionally been multiple choice, but are starting to introduce actual task simulators that test your ability to perform specific tasks.

The newer exams are also employing an adaptive testing method, in which the questions you are asked are based on the answers you have given in previous questions. Most of the elective exams cover not only the knowledge base for the product for which you are being tested, but also standard knowledge an MCSE is expected to have.

Registering for and Taking an Exam

Testing is done at Sylvan Prometric Testing Centers and must be scheduled in advance. The first time you register for an exam, you are assigned an identification number. You must provide your Social Security Number or Social Insurance Number, which becomes your identification number.

If you prefer, you can have Sylvan assign you a Sylvan identification number. This number is then the number you use for all your exams. If you get a new number each time you test, the exams will not be credited to you properly.

You must also provide your mailing address, phone number, email address, company name, and method of payment. You are required to pay for an exam in advance; the cost is $100 US for each exam. Testing prices are subject to change and are based on current exchange rates. There may be additional taxes applied in some countries.

Certain weekdays, such as Fridays, seem to fill up rather quickly, so schedule your exams well in advance to get the time and day you want.

When you show up to take the exam, you must provide two forms of identification. You are not allowed to take anything inside the testing room except scratch paper and pencil, which are provided by the testing center.

The following chart lists phone numbers for registering to take an exam:

Country	*Telephone Number*
Australia	1-800-808-657
Austria	0660-8582
Belgium	0800-1-7414
Canada	800-755-3926
China	10800-3538
France	1-4289-8749
Germany	0130-83-9708
Guam	001-61-800-277583
Hong Kong	800-6375
Indonesia	011-800-61571
Ireland	1-800-626-104
Italy	1-6787-8441
Japan	0120-347737
Korea	007-8611-3095
Malaysia	800-2122
Netherlands	06-022-7584
New Zealand	0800-044-1603
Philippines	1-800-1-611-0126
Puerto Rico	800-755-3926
Singapore	800-616-1120
Switzerland	155-6966
Taiwan	008-061-1142
Thailand	001-800-611-2283
UK	0800-592-873
United States	800-755-3926
Vietnam	61-2-9414-3666

Tips for Passing an Exam

Make sure that you get a good night's rest before you take an exam. If you are a morning person, make sure that you schedule the exam for the morning. If you are an afternoon person, schedule the exam for later in the day. Don't attempt to "cram" for the test on the day you are scheduled to take the exam.

Make Notes

Although you cannot take notes in to the exam, notepaper is provided when you take an exam. When you take the exam, write down any notes you may find useful for test items that tend to be confusing to you or that require a lot of thought on your part.

If you are unsure about the answer to a question, go with your first thoughts on what the correct answer might be—and then don't change your mind or any answers.

Mark Questions

As you take the exam, you have the ability to mark questions. You can either mark questions you are unsure of, or mark questions you are absolutely sure of. Any questions you do not answer before you end the exam are marked as incomplete after you have gone through the questions. The review phase of the exam gives you the opportunity to review incomplete and marked questions.

If you think you may have difficulty finishing the exam on time, select an answer on the first pass, marking the ones you question. If you have time, you can go back and review marked items near the end of the exam. Any unanswered questions are considered incorrect.

Read the Question

It is very easy to read a portion of the question, think that you know what is being asked, and go directly to the answers. Do not do this with the Microsoft certification exams.

Typically, one word in the question changes the answer, and is buried in useless information. Make sure that you read the question completely before answering the question.

For scenario-based questions, read the required results and the solution before looking at the desired optional results. Make sure that the required results are satisfied before even attempting to see whether the optional results are satisfied.

Exam 70-079: What to Expect

The exam is broken into six main categories. Sometimes, it is difficult to decide which questions are meant to test the knowledge base for which area. The six categories are described in the following sections, with a brief explanation of what might be expected in each area, as well as some of the non-IEAK–specific subject matter that might also be tested.

Planning

Planning can cover myriad facets of knowledge about the IEAK product. Several of the scenario questions will challenge your knowledge of the product and your ability to plan product deployment.

You are expected to know which IEAK operational mode you need to use to configure various components of Internet Explorer 4.0. In addition, you must know what levels of security are available for different types of clients, and how to customize the backgrounds and taskbars during installation.

Finally, you need to know how to upgrade current users of previous versions of Internet Explorer or Netscape Navigator and how to upgrade users who currently use previous versions of Internet mail software.

Installation and Configuration

Installation and configuration tests your knowledge of what client support is offered, what methods of distribution are available under each operational mode, and what components can be installed.

You have to know how to configure Active Setup components, customize the client browser and Internet mail installation, and configure built-in components of Internet Explorer 4.0.

Configuring and Managing Resource Access

The questions that deal with this portion of the exam will challenge your knowledge of the Profile Manager and the use of Microsoft JScript, autoproxy, `.INS` files, and `.ADM` files to modify client settings.

Integration and Distribution

The *integration and interoperability* section of the exam tests your understanding of the IEAK and how it is used to update and upgrade browser settings, upgrade or replace Internet mail programs, and configure the NetMeeting features for the server and the client.

Monitoring and Optimizing

The questions on *monitoring and optimization* test your ability to customize Active Desktop components and Active Channels.

You also need to prove that you understand how IEAK can monitor and update site subscriptions, channel subscriptions, and the Active Desktop settings for clients.

Finally, you have to understand how caching can be tuned to better performance.

Troubleshooting

The *troubleshooting* questions on the certification exam not only measure your knowledge of troubleshooting problems with IEAK configuration and use, but also test your knowledge of basic TCP/IP utilities you may need to use to troubleshoot client-side problems.

Scenario questions lay out a specific problem and offer a solution that may or may not provide the required results.

You have to know what basic TCP/IP utilities can be used to verify specific TCP/IP configurations.

Non-IEAK–Specific Topics

There will be questions on the exam that cover Internet-based products that, although not directly related to the IEAK, can be combined with, and play a role in, your rollout of Internet Explorer 4.0.

A good example is Microsoft Proxy Server 2.0, and how Internet Explorer 4.0 has to be configured to properly interface with the Proxy Server product. The Proxy Server product affects the installation of Internet Explorer for clients that gain Internet access through the Proxy Server.

Chapter 1

Planning

To plan for a deployment of Internet Explorer 4.0 on any scale, you must take a lot into consideration. You have to discover and document what browsers, mail and news clients, and add-on components are in use. You also have to decide whether you will force users to upgrade all or only some of those components. You must decide whether you want to import current information, such as URL bookmarks, email messages, and address books.

Internet Explorer 4.0 provides much more robust functionality than some of its predecessors, but that capability requires more desktop and network resource to operate. You have to plan for upgrades to hardware and software, and then determine what components of IE 4.0 you want to implement—and what components your network can support.

Although the Internet Explorer Administration Kit (IEAK) is free of charge, you must register to use the IEAK. When you register, you will be provided with a customization code (a keycode) that is embedded into every copy of IE 4.0 you deploy using the IEAK. The type of customization code you request determines the operational modes in which you can run. To get a customization code, you must agree to register on a quarterly basis the number of times you deploy IE 4.0 using the IEAK.

Most importantly, you must know what capabilities are available, how to configure those capabilities, and what type of training your staff and users will need to support the IE 4.0 deployment and use the product.

This chapter covers these certification test objectives:

- In Corporate Administrator or Internet Service Provider operational mode, choose the appropriate installation of Internet Explorer 4.0, with or without the Windows Desktop Update.
- Develop custom installation strategies for Internet Explorer 4.0.
- In Corporate Administrator mode, develop appropriate security strategies for using Internet Explorer 4.0 for various sites, including public kiosks, end users, and business sites.
- Choose Active Desktop items and develop Active Channels.
- Develop strategies for replacing other Internet browsers, including Microsoft Internet Explorer 3.x and Netscape Navigator.

- Develop strategies for replacing other Internet mail clients, including Internet Mail and News, Netscape Mail, and Eudora.
- Choose the appropriate configuration strategy for Microsoft Outlook Express.
- Choose the appropriate configuration for Microsoft NetMeeting, including settings and restrictions.
- Choose the appropriate configurations for the NetMeeting client, including Internet Locator Service (ILS) server connectivity, IP connectivity, peer-to-peer networking, proxy server settings, and proxy server client settings.
- In Corporate Administrator mode or Internet Service Provider mode, choose the strategies for managing automatic configuration by using the IEAK Profile Manager, including Microsoft JScript autoproxy and `.INS` files.
- Develop a configuration plan for Active Setup components.
- Develop strategies for using the Internet Connection Wizard in Internet Service Provider mode, including modem detection, stack installation, and configuration of dial-up connections.

1.1 Installation/Operational Modes

The Internet Explorer Administration Kit (IEAK) is used to create custom deployment packages that install Internet Explorer 4.0 and support applications on a user's desktop. With the IEAK, you can configure custom setup screens, configure plug-in components, and place limits on the user's ability to use some components that might pose a security threat or drain network resources. There are three operational modes in which the Internet Explorer Administration Kit (IEAK) can be run:

- Internet Content Provider/Developer mode
- Internet Service Provider mode
- Corporate Administrator mode

Each mode offers different capabilities to perform tasks. For example, the Internet Service Provider mode allows you to create a single-floppy deployment package; you can also configure an Internet Connection Wizard profile and include it in the deployment package. The Corporate Administrator mode doesn't have either of those capabilities, but allows more detailed control over a user's abilities to use some of the more advanced features of IE 4.0.

1.1.1 Internet Content Provider/Developer (ICP) Mode

Internet Content Provider/Developer operational mode can be used to create custom deployment packages for customers who have already established Internet accounts. This mode offers the ability to create custom IE 4.0 deployment packages and add custom title bars and bitmaps to the Active Setup screen. Internet Content Provider mode allows you to do the following:

- Customize the IE 4.0 Setup program
- Customize the IE 4.0 browser and channels
- Use the IE 4.0 logo on your packaging and promotional materials

In Internet Content Provider mode, you can create custom deployment packages that can be placed on CD-ROM or multiple floppy disks. In this mode (as well as in ISP and CA operational modes), a download deployment package is also created. There is no Outlook Express configuration capability in this mode. The system policies and restrictions you can access in this mode are listed here:

- Microsoft Chat
- Internet settings including colors, fonts, languages, modem settings (in IE 4.0), programs (calendar, contacts, Internet call), and advanced settings for browsing, multimedia, security, Java VM, printing, searching, toolbars, and HTTP 1.1 settings

1.1.2 Internet Service Provider (ISP) Mode

Internet Service Provider operational mode can be used to create custom deployment packages for customers, whether they currently have Internet accounts or not. This mode is meant to be used by Internet Service Providers to provide new clients with deployment media for installing IE 4.0.

The deployment media can be customized to configure the client's Internet connection and Internet Explorer. The Active Setup screens can be configured with custom title bars and bitmaps. Internet Service Provider mode allows you to do the following:

- Customize the Setup program
- Customize the browser and channels
- Control how customers sign up for your service
- Use the IE 4.0 logo on your packaging and promotional materials

Several capabilities are common to all three operational modes, but some capabilities can be found only in one of the three modes. The ISP mode allows you to do the following:

- Create single-floppy deployment media.
- Use a custom profile created with the Internet Connection Manager Administration Kit (CMAK) to configure an Internet account.
- Select an Internet sign-up method and custom sign-up files. These methods include an Internet sign-up server, serverless sign up, and no sign up.
- Configure Outlook Express for deployment. You can specify type and name of the mail and news servers, as well as set Outlook Express to be the default mail and news reader. A small infopane can be configured to be displayed at the bottom of the Outlook Express screen.
- Configure Lightweight Directory Access Protocol (LDAP) settings and authentication method.
- Configure Microsoft NetMeeting and Outlook Express settings and limitations in addition to the Microsoft Chat and Internet settings available in ICP mode.

Single-Floppy Distribution

Internet Service Provider is the only mode that provides the capability to create single-floppy deployment media. The floppy contains all the information needed to attach to the ISP and download the rest of the IE 4.0 custom package over the Internet.

Modem and Stack Detection

Automatic modem and stack detection are available as part of the Active Setup capabilities. Active Setup interrogates the computer on which IE 4.0 is being installed for a valid modem, dialer, and TCP/IP stack. If any or all of these components are not available, Active Setup installs the missing components, establishes a connection to the server you specify, downloads the necessary IE 4.0 `.CAB` files, drops the connection, and continues the IE 4.0 deployment. The utilities to accomplish these tasks can be placed on a single floppy, which is one of the deployment methods available while running the IEAK in the ISP operational mode.

1.1.3 Corporate Administrator (CA) Mode

Corporate Administrator operational mode is meant to be used by network administrators of a company's intranet. This mode offers the greatest degree of customization capability of the three operational modes. In Corporate Administrator mode, you can do the following:

- Customize the Setup program
- Customize the browser and Windows Desktop Update
- Manage security and ratings
- Configure the Active Desktop
- Configure IE 4.0 to install silently (without user intervention)
- Configure the user for automatic updates
- Configure Internet restrictions, Web desktop, and subscriptions as well as Microsoft Chat, Microsoft NetMeeting, Internet settings, and Outlook Express settings and limitations

This mode does not offer the capability of creating single-floppy deployment media, using a CMAK profile, or selecting an Internet sign-up method. CA mode does offer the network administrator the ability to set security levels for sites and configure the rating system.

There are four security levels: low, medium, high, and custom. The low security level provides the least security and most capability when accessing URLs; the high security level provides the greatest level of security with the least capability when accessing URLs. The medium security level balances safety and functionality, while the custom level allows you to configure your own capabilities.

The four security levels are applied to each of four zones. A *zone* is a group of URLs. The zones are listed here:

- **Internet zone:** Contains all sites accessed across the Internet. The default security level is set to medium. These sites typically have a period in the site name (for example, `http://site.domain.com`).
- **Local Intranet zone:** Contains all sites accessed on the local intranet. Typically, these sites do not contain a period in the site name (for example, `http://site`).
- **Trusted Sites zone:** You add site to this zone that you "trust" won't damage your users' software or attempt to breach security. The default security level for this zone is set to low.

- **Restricted Sites zone:** You add sites to this zone that you do not "trust" and that could damage your users' software or attempt to breach security.

Corporate Administrator mode provides the capability to install silently (that is, no user intervention is required), as well as configure the user's Active Desktop and set IE 4.0 for automatic configuration. Automatic configuration allows the corporate administrator to make changes to a master configuration and have that configuration automatically implemented on all the users' desktops.

1.1.4 Questions

1. You want to create single-floppy deployment media, but only multiple floppy deployment media is available as a selection. How would you fix this?

   A. Start the IEAK Wizard in Internet Content Provider (ICP) mode.

   B. Start the IEAK Wizard in Internet Service Provider (ISP) mode.

   C. Start the IEAK Wizard in Corporate Administrator (CA) mode.

   D. Do nothing. Single floppy deployment media is automatically created when multiple floppy deployment media is created.

2. What operational modes are available with the IEAK? (Select all that apply.)

   A. Internet Content Provider/Developer (ICP) mode.

   B. Network Administrator (NA) mode.

   C. Corporate Administrator (CA) mode.

   D. Internet Service Provider (ISP) mode.

3. You are running in Content Provider (ICP) mode. Which statements below are true? (Select all that apply.)

   A. You cannot customize the IE 4.0 browser and channels.

   B. You can customize the IE 4.0 browser and channels.

   C. You can set system policies and restrictions for Microsoft Chat.

   D. You cannot set system policies and restrictions for Microsoft Chat.

4. For Internet Service Provider (ISP) mode, which statements are true? (Select all that apply.)

   A. The IE 4.0 browser and channels are configurable.

   B. You can configure the Active Desktop.

   C. You can create single floppy deployment media.

   D. You can configure how customers sign up for your service.

5. What does the IEAK Wizard allow you to do when running in ISP mode? (Select all that apply.)

   A. Configure the Active Desktop.

   B. Create single floppy deployment media.

   C. Use a custom profile created with the CMAK.

   D. Configure LDAP.

6. You want to create a custom deployment package that can run automatic modem and stack detection. What mode must you run in?

   A. These capabilities are available in all operational modes of the IEAK Wizard.

   B. Internet Content Provider/Developer mode.

   C. Internet Service Provider mode.

   D. Corporate Administrator mode.

7. You want to provide Internet access to a group of users that currently have no Internet access. You want to provide them with a custom deployment package that will automatically configure their connection to your service. What mode must you be in when creating the custom deployment package?

   A. Internet Content Provider/Developer mode.

   B. Corporate Administrator mode.

   C. Internet Service Provider mode.

   D. This capability is available in all three operational modes.

8. You want to be able to manage security and ratings. What operational mode must you be running in?

   A. Internet Content Provider/Developer mode.

   B. Corporate Administrator mode.

   C. Internet Service Provider mode.

   D. This capability is available in all three operational modes.

9. You want to be able to configure the Active Desktop. What mode must you be running in?

   A. Internet Content Provider/Developer mode.

   B. Corporate Administrator mode.

   C. Internet Service Provider mode.

   D. This capability is available in both Content Provider and Service Provider modes.

10. Which statement best describes zones and security levels? (Select the best answer.)

    A. There are four zones that can be applied to each of the four security levels.

    B. There are three security levels that can be applied to each of the three zones.

    C. There are four security levels that can be applied to each of the three zones.

    D. There are four security levels that can be applied to each of the four zones.

11. What zone would an IIS server on your local network be placed in by default?

    A. Internet zone

    B. Local Intranet zone

    C. Trusted Sites zone

    D. Restricted Sites zone

12. What zone would `www.microsoft.com` be placed in by default?

    A. Internet zone

    B. Local Intranet zone

    C. Trusted Sites zone

    D. Restricted Sites zone

13. You created a custom deployment package and selected CD-ROM as the deployment media, but when you looked at the directory structure of the deployment package, you noted that `CD-ROM` and `Download` directories had been created. Why is this?

    A. The `Download` directory is always created, no matter what deployment media you elect to have created.

    B. You inadvertently selected download as a media you wanted to create.

    C. The `Download` directory is created only when CD-ROM is the deployment media.

    D. The directory structure is created, but no actual files are placed in the structure; they are placed on the CD-ROM when the IEAK Wizard finishes running.

1.1.5 Answers

1. **B** Single-floppy deployment media can be created only when running in ISP mode. You must be licensed to run in this mode.

2. **A, C, and D** Network Administrator is the only operational mode that is not valid with the IEAK.

3. **B, C** You can customize the IE 4.0 browser and channels, as well as set restrictions for Microsoft Chat in Internet Content Provider mode.

4. **A, C, and D** You can create single floppy deployment media in ISP mode, but you can configure the Active Desktop only in Corporate Administrator mode.

5. **B, C, and D** All the items listed are configurable in ISP mode with the exception of the Active Desktop, which is available only in Corporate Administrator mode.

6. **C** Internet Service Provider operational mode provides automatic modem and stack detection.

7. **C** ISP mode provides the capability to configure an Internet sign-up method.

8. **B** Security and ratings can be configured only when running in Corporate Administrator mode.

9. **B** Active Desktop configuration is available only in Corporate Administrator mode.

10. **D** There are four security levels that can be configured for each of the four zones.

11. **B** Sites on your local network are placed in the Local Intranet zone by default.

12. **A** The site listed is an Internet URL and is therefore placed in the Internet Zone by default.

13. **A** The `Download` directory is always created, no matter what deployment media you elect to create.

1.2 Deployment Media

The IEAK can create three different types of deployment media: floppy disk, CD-ROM, and a `Download` directory. The `Download` directory deployment media is created whenever a custom IE 4.0 deployment package is created. The other two methods can be selected while running the IEAK Wizard. The only deployment not available in all three modes is the single-floppy deployment media, which is available only while running in ISP mode.

1.2.1 Floppy Disk

Floppy disk as a deployment media is available in all three operational modes. You can create a multiple-floppy deployment package, in which all the files necessary for completely installing your custom deployment package of IE 4.0 are placed in `.CAB` files and stored in directories under an `Mfloppy` directory. Under that directory are subdirectories `Disk1` through `Disk`*X* for each floppy you must create for the custom deployment package. You can then copy the information stored in the directories to floppy disk to create the multiple-floppy disk set.

When running the IEAK Wizard in ISP mode, you can also create single-floppy deployment media. In this case, all the files needed to establish a connection with your server are placed in a directory named `Floppy`. The files in this directory fit on one floppy and can be given to customers. When the floppy starts the installation process, the client computer establishes a connection with your server and retrieves the remainder of the deployment package. The connection is terminated, and the installation process continues as it would with the other deployment methods.

1.2.2 CD-ROM

CD-ROM can be selected as a deployment method. This deployment media is available in all operational modes; it creates a CD-ROM directory that stores the deployment data. If you selected CD-ROM as a deployment method in the IEAK Wizard, you have the opportunity to customize the starting autorun screen by adding a custom title bar, bitmap, and buttons.

1.2.3 Download Directory

The `Download` directory is created automatically any time a custom IE 4.0 deployment package is created. The data is stored in a directory named `Download`. Figure 1.2.1 shows the directory structure created for the custom download deployment package.

Figure 1.2.1 shows the deployment directory as being named `Deploy`, and the language for the installation as English (`EN`). Had the language been Spanish, the directory would have been the `SP` directory.

1.3 Client Configuration

When creating a deployment package, you can control the user's capabilities when using IE 4.0. If the computer on which you are deploying IE 4.0 is a public or community computer that must be able to provide Internet access—but in a limited fashion—you can minimize the capabilities a user will have. If you are the network administrator, you can configure the abilities a user will have while using IE 4.0. If you're an ISP or content provider, you can customize a deployment package to provide the tools you want to provide to your customers.

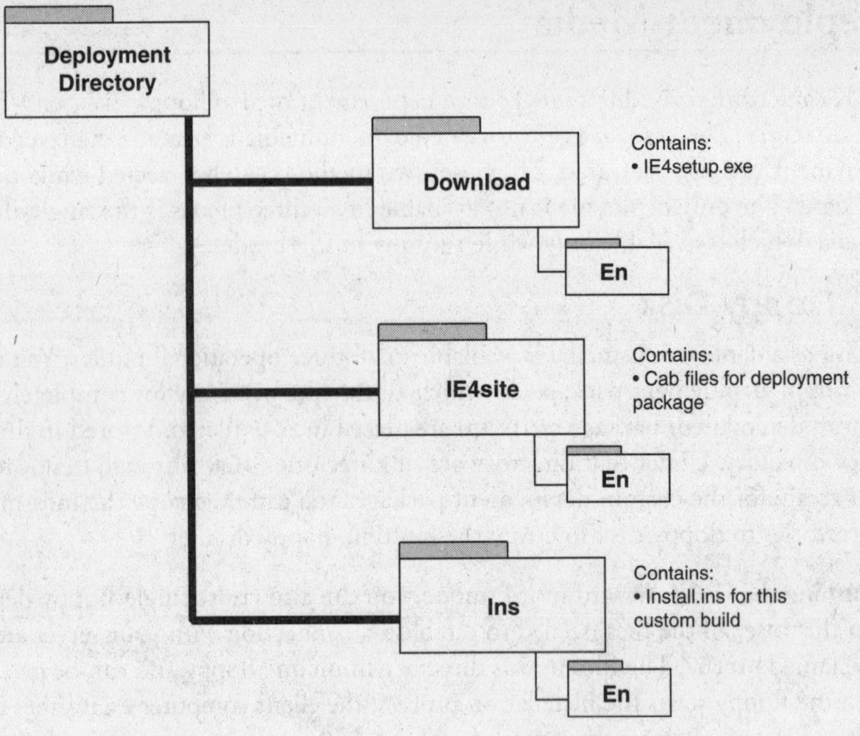

Figure 1.2.1 Directory structure for deployment media.

1.3.1 Public Kiosk

A *public kiosk computer* is typically located in an open, public area, and is used by the general public to obtain specific information. For example, if you are in an office building, a kiosk computer might provide the directory listing for all the inhabitants of the building. In a corporation, a kiosk computer might be used to review the employee's benefits package.

This type of computer would have limited functionality and limited access to Internet objects. A custom deployment package can be created to provide limited capability to perform tasks and allow the user to operate inside a very stringent set of guidelines. This mode is typically associated with the Content Provider mode.

1.3.2 End User

The end user typically is associated with running in ISP mode. The service provider usually does not want to limit a user's ability to access Internet objects, but wants to provide the IE 4.0 package and associated components to the end user. With this type of deployment package, the ISP can configure custom title bars and bitmaps, and use the Internet Connection Manager Administrator Kit (CMAK) to configure a user connection to the ISP providing the deployment media. Examples of this deployment method are America Online and CompuServe, which provide a custom CD-ROM for installing a dialer and configuring an Internet connection on the end user's desktop.

1.3.3 Business

With business computers, the network administrator is typically tasked with enforcing company policy when users access the Internet. The network administrator also typically governs the use of network and desktop resources. This type of configuration is typically associated with the Corporate Administrator mode of the IEAK Wizard, providing the most control over user capabilities and configuration.

With CA deployment packages, the user's IE 4.0 deployment can be updated by modifying one master copy of the deployment package. Then all the users receive the update. The update interval is configurable.

1.3.4 Questions

1. What operational mode allows you to select CD-ROM as deployment media? (Select all that apply.)

    A. Internet Content Provider/Developer mode

    B. Internet Service Provider mode

    C. Corporate Administrator mode

    D. All the operational modes allow you to use CD-ROM as a deployment media

2. You are running the IEAK Wizard and get an Autorun configuration screen, which you don't remember getting any other time you ran the IEAK Wizard. What does this indicate?

    A. You are running in Content Provider mode.

    B. You selected multiple floppy as a deployment media.

    C. You selected CD-ROM as a deployment media.

    D. You are running in Corporate Administrator mode.

3. You created a deployment package and selected Japanese as the language and multiple floppy, single floppy, and CD-ROM as the deployment media. When you attempt to look in the `EN` directory for the `Ie4setup.exe` file, you find that the `EN` directory wasn't created, but a `JA` directory was. What does this indicate?

    A. This indicates that just applications are available in this directory.

    B. This indicates that Japanese was selected as the deployment language for IE 4.0.

    C. This indicates the deployment package had errors when it compiled.

    D. The directory the files are placed in is a randomly generated two-character folder name created by the IEAK Wizard.

4. Your company mandates that all users will have limited capability in NetMeeting and a specific Active Desktop configuration. Which operational mode would you run the IEAK Wizard in to create the custom deployment package?

    A. Intranet Service Provider mode

    B. Internet Content Provider/Developer mode

    C. Internet Service Provider mode

    D. Corporate Administrator mode

5. You need to be able to create a custom IE 4.0 deployment package that can detect the modem in a user's computer and determine whether the protocols installed on the user's computer need to be installed or modified to connect to your service. What mode must you run in to create this package?

    A. All operational modes of the IEAK provide this capability

    B. Internet Content Provider/Developer mode

    C. Internet Service Provider mode

    D. Corporate Administrator mode

1.3.5 Answers

1. **D** All three operational modes allow you to use CD-ROM as a deployment media.

2. **C** You have selected CD-ROM as a deployment media. This configuration option is only available when you are creating CD-ROM media.

3. **B** The directory the files are stored in indicates the custom deployment's language.

4. **D** You would create the package in Corporate Administrator mode, which provides you with the greatest capabilities for user configuration.

5. **C** The ISP mode is the only mode that provides the capability to detect the user's modem and stack.

1.4 Active Channels

Active Channels provide a vehicle for the user to subscribe to a Web site or multiple Web sites and receive periodic updates for the sites. The amount of data received and the frequency of the updates can be configured and stored in a Channel Definition File (CDF). If bandwidth is a consideration on the network, you can configure the Web site updates to occur only during non-peak hours, such as from midnight to 5:00 a.m., thus limiting the impact that channel updates have on your network.

1.5 Active Desktop

The Active Desktop is new to IE 4.0. The Active Desktop can be automatically implemented on the user's desktop, the user can choose to run the Active Desktop, or the user will not be provided the Active Desktop functionality. The Active Desktop is part of the Windows Desktop Update, which provides the Active Desktop function and a different desktop toolbar, Control Panel, and My Computer window.

The changes are supposed to provide the user with a better-integrated desktop that provides the same user interface whether accessing local resources or Internet-based resources. The Active Desktop should allow the user to learn one interface and therefore become more productive.

1.5.1 Questions

1. One of your users has to get updates to your company's two internal inventory URLs on a regular basis so the information displayed is current. How can you accomplish this? (Select the best answer.)

   A. Write a batch file that causes the user's IE 4.0 to update those two sites regularly.

   B. Write a script file that causes the user's IE 4.0 to update those two sites regularly.

   C. Add an Active Channel subscription for the sites to the user's IE 4.0 Active Channels.

   D. Add two Active Channel subscriptions to the user's IE 4.0 Active Channels.

2. One of your users is running IE 3.01 and is complaining that his desktop doesn't have the same features as his friend's desktop. After further investigation, you determine that the friend is running IE 4.0 with Active Desktop activated. How could you provide your user with that functionality? (Select the best answer.)

   A. Upgrade the user's computer to IE 4.0 and enable the Active Desktop.

   B. Enable Active Desktop in IE 3.01.

   C. Add an Active Channel subscription for the sites to the user's IE 4.0 Active Channels.

   D. Add two Active Channel subscriptions to the user's IE 4.0 Active Channels, one for each site.

3. Which of the following best describes an Active Channel? (Select two.)

   A. Part of the Windows Desktop Update that provides the Active Desktop and a different desktop toolbar, Control Panel, and My Computer window.

   B. Provides a vehicle to allow the user to subscribe to a site or sites, and get regular updates automatically.

   C. The subscription information is stored in a `.CDF` file.

   D. The information is stored in a `.INS` file.

4. Which of the following best describes the Active Desktop? (Select two.)

   A. Part of the Windows Desktop Update that provides the Active Desktop and a different desktop toolbar, Control Panel, and My Computer window.

   B. Provides a vehicle to allow the user to subscribe to a site or sites, and get regular updates automatically.

   C. The Active Desktop was introduced in IE 3.01.

   D. The Active Desktop was introduced in IE 4.0.

1.5.2 Answers

1. **D** You can add a subscription to a channel that will update both sites at regular intervals.

2. **A** The user could be upgraded to IE 4.0 and the Active Desktop activated. The Active Desktop is new to IE 4.0.

3. **B, C** Channel subscriptions allow a user to subscribe to multiple Web sites and receive regular updates to the Web site. This information is stored in a `.CDF` file.

4. **A, D** The Active Desktop was introduced with IE 4.0 and is part of the Windows Desktop Update.

1.6 Upgrading Browsers

An upgrade path is provided for IE 3.x and Netscape Navigator that allows configuration information for those versions of Web browser to be imported into the Internet Explorer 4.0 package being installed. Plug-in and add-on components are not imported into IE 4.0; they must be reinstalled or included as part of the deployment package.

1.6.1 Upgrading from Internet Explorer 3.x

An upgrade path is provided from IE 3.x to IE 4.0. When IE 4.0 is installed, IE 3.x is uninstalled, but configuration information such as proxy server settings, cookies, and Favorites folders can be imported into IE 4.0. After an upgrade, the user is prompted to import the favorites information during the first use of IE 4.0.

1.6.2 Upgrading from Netscape Navigator

An upgrade path is available from Netscape Navigator 3.0 and Netscape Communicator. As with IE 3.X, the proxy server setting is imported. Netscape Navigator Bookmarks are also imported. The Bookmark in Netscape Navigator provides the same function as the Favorites folder in IE 4.0. Figure 1.6.1 shows the information imported when upgrading from other Web browsers.

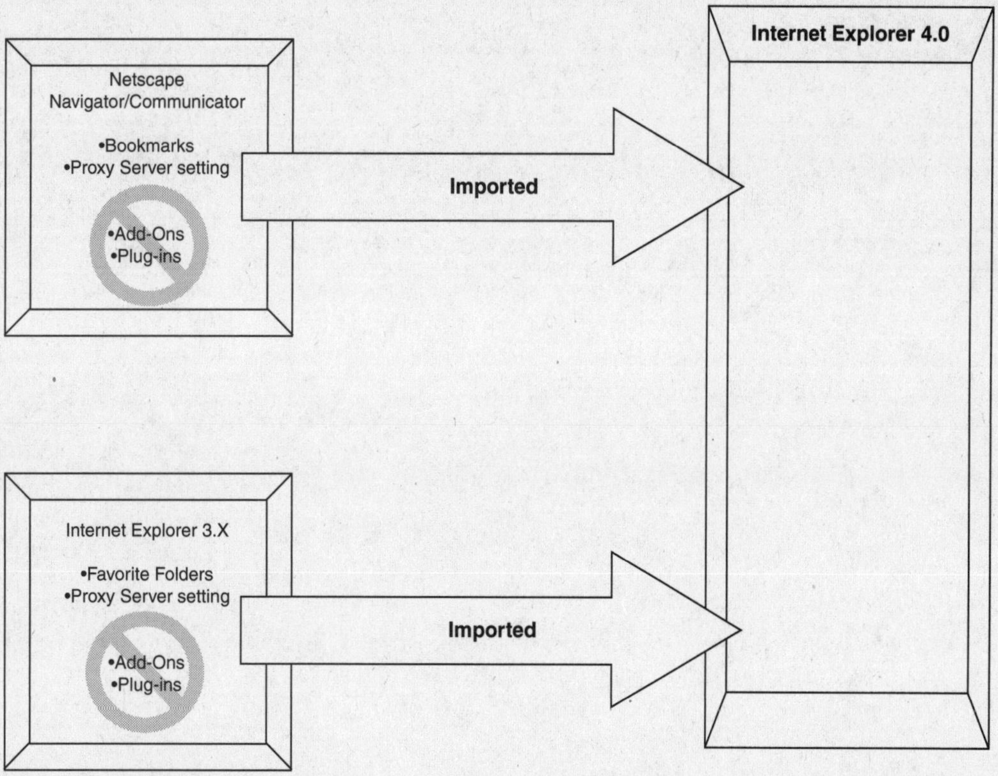

Figure 1.6.1 Information imported from IE 3.x and Netscape Navigator.

When IE 4.0 is installed, it imports the configuration and bookmark information as it does with IE 3.x, but Netscape Navigator is not uninstalled when IE 4.0 is installed. Both browsers can be configured on the same desktop.

1.6.3 Questions

1. What will be imported when upgrading from IE 3.1 to IE 4.0? (Select all that apply.)

   A. Proxy server settings

   B. Favorites folders

   C. Plug-in components

   D. Add-on components

2. What is the result when you upgrade from IE 3.0 to IE 4.0?

   A. Both IE 3.0 and IE 4.0 are on the computer the upgrade was performed on.

   B. Only IE 4.0 is on the computer the upgrade was performed on.

   C. Both IE 3.0 and IE 4.0 are on the computer the upgrade was performed on, but IE 4.0 becomes the default browser.

   D. The upgrade will fail. You have to uninstall IE 3.0 and then install IE 4.0.

3. What will be imported when upgrading from Netscape Navigator to IE 4.0? (Select all that apply.)

   A. Proxy server settings

   B. Bookmarks

   C. Plug-in components

   D. Add-on components

4. What is the result when you upgrade from Netscape Navigator to IE 4.0?

   A. Both Netscape Navigator and IE 4.0 are on the computer the upgrade was performed on.

   B. Only IE 4.0 is on the computer the upgrade was performed on.

   C. Only Netscape Navigator is on the computer the upgrade was performed on. You have to uninstall Netscape Navigator and then reinstall IE 4.0.

   D. Netscape Navigator is removed from the computer and IE 4.0 is not installed. After Netscape Navigator is removed, you can proceed with the installation of IE 4.0.

1.6.4 Answers

1. **A, B** Favorites folders and proxy server settings are imported from IE 3.1 when an upgrade is performed. Any plug-ins or add-ons must be reinstalled.

2. **B** When an upgrade is performed from IE 3.x to IE 4.0, IE 3.x is removed from the system.

3. **A, B** Bookmarks and proxy settings are imported from Netscape Navigator. Any plug-ins or add-ons must be reinstalled.

4. **A** Both Netscape Navigator and IE 4.0 will be on the computer. IE 4.0 does not uninstall Netscape Navigator.

1.7 Upgrading Mail Support

An upgrade path is available from most major mail clients to Outlook Express. The information that can be imported includes messages from any folder, address book entries, and mail account settings. Figure 1.7.1 shows some of the information that can be imported when Outlook Express is installed as part of the IE 4.0 deployment.

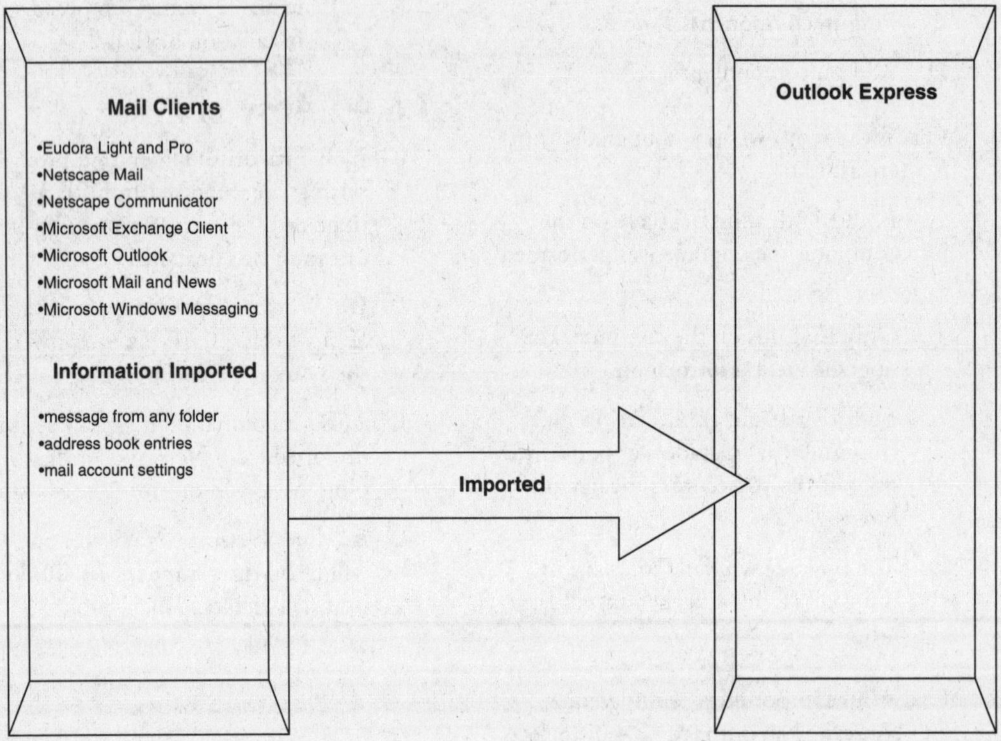

Figure 1.7.1 Information imported from mail clients.

Some of the mail clients from which you can import this information include Eudora Light and Pro, Netscape Mail, Netscape Communicator, Microsoft Exchange Client, Microsoft Outlook, Microsoft Mail and News, and Microsoft Windows Messaging.

When creating a custom deployment package using the IEAK Wizard, you have the option of making Outlook Express the default mail and news reader; you can also customize the Outlook Express configuration.

1.7.1 Questions

1. You are creating a custom deployment package and are configuring Outlook Express as the default mail and news client. What will be imported from Eudora Pro? (Select all that apply.)

   A. Mail account settings

   B. Messages from any folder

   C. Favorites folders

   D. Address Book entries

2. Outlook Express provides an upgrade path from which of the following mail clients? (Select all that apply.)

   A. Eudora Light and Pro

   B. Netscape Mail and Communicator

   C. Microsoft Exchange client

   D. Microsoft Outlook

1.7.2 Answers

1. **A, B, and D** Favorites folders are part of IE, not Outlook Express. Mail messages from any folder, Address Book entries, and mail account settings are imported.

2. **A, B, C, and D** An upgrade path exists from all of the listed mail clients.

1.8 Outlook Express

When deploying Outlook Express using the IEAK Wizard, or when modifying existing installations, you can configure various Outlook Express items, such as the following:

- The POP3 or IMAP mail server name
- User name and account
- Email address
- Signature files to attach to mail and news messages
- LDAP settings
- Outlook Express infopane and welcome message

The *infopane* is a small window at the bottom of the Outlook Express window that can display an HTML or bitmap file. The infopane can be used by customer support to provide help desk numbers and helpful hints and reminders. The IEAK Wizard allows you to designate Outlook Express as the default mail and news client when IE 4.0 is installed.

1.8.1 Questions

1. What configuration options for Outlook Express are available when running the IEAK Wizard? (Select all that apply.)
   - A. Maximum news messages to download
   - B. Infopane configuration
   - C. User name and account information
   - D. POP3 or IMAP mail server name

2. You are creating a custom deployment package using the IEAK Wizard and want to have the name and address of your company appended to the bottom of each email message. How would you do this?
   - A. Have the user run a script file before mailing each new email message.
   - B. Cannot. The signature cannot be configured using the IEAK Wizard.
   - C. While creating the custom deployment package, configure the signature settings to add a custom signature to every mail message.
   - D. Add the company name and address to the POP3 mail server name.

1.8.2 Answers

1. **B, C, and D** The only optional information that is not imported is the maximum mail messages download.
2. **C** You can add custom signatures for all outgoing mail or news messages.

1.9 NetMeeting Configuration: Server-Side

NetMeeting provides very useful peer-to-peer functionality, using components such as Microsoft Chat, a whiteboard, and collaboration techniques. An Internet Locator Service (ILS) server can be configured. When users log on to an ILS server, they are listed in a directory that includes their names, email addresses, and the functionality they have (for example, audio and video support). Users can contact each other and communicate using Internet technology to pass files, share information, and collaborate on files so that all users can work on one file simultaneously. If the hardware is in place, multiple users can connect together and hold audio and video meetings across the Internet or an intranet.

1.9.1 Settings

The NetMeeting capabilities can create potential security problems and can overload network resources. The IEAK Wizard and IEAK Profile Manager provide the network administrator with the capability of controlling users' NetMeeting settings.

The network administrator can set initial capabilities for a user and can also limit the user's ability to modify settings.

1.9.2 Restrictions

The network administrator can limit the user's NetMeeting capabilities (such as the capability to send files or video or the capability to receive files or video). The administrator may want to restrict these capabilities because video transfer can place a heavy burden on network resources, and file transfer can pose a serious security risk.

1.9.3 Questions

1. What is the best description of an Internet Locator Service (ILS) server?

   A. It keeps a list of all the other users logged on to the Internet.

   B. Acts as an Outlook Express mail server to help back up the primary mail server.

   C. Keeps a list of users logged on to the ILS to help establish communications for use with the NetMeeting functions.

   D. Used to configure NetMeeting capabilities for the end user.

2. What can potentially happen to your network if the end user's NetMeeting settings are not configured properly? (Select the two best answers.)

   A. The user can send or receive files through NetMeeting, creating a potential security risk.

   B. The user cannot send and receive files through NetMeeting, so no potential security risk exists.

   C. The user can communicate using streaming audio and video technology, possibly using too much network bandwidth.

   D. The user can communicate using streaming audio and video technology, but the new technology is so efficient that there is no possibility of using too much network bandwidth.

3. What can be said of the network administrator's ability to limit a user's capabilities while using NetMeeting?

   A. The network administrator has no control over the end user's NetMeeting capability.

   B. The administrator can configure the end user's NetMeeting capabilities.

   C. The network administrator can limit access to the ILS, but can't control a user's NetMeeting settings.

   D. The end user, not the network administrator, has complete control over NetMeeting settings.

1.9.4 Answers

1. **C** When NetMeeting initializes, the end user can log on to an ILS server; the information provided by the user is listed in a "white pages" type listing.

2. **A, C** If NetMeeting is not configured to meet your network security standards, a potential security hazard exists. Although audio and video technology has advanced over the last few years, the cost in bandwidth to support this technology can be prohibitive.

3. **B** The network administrator can limit an end user's NetMeeting settings, including his or her ability to modify the settings.

1.10 NetMeeting Configuration: Client-Side

Client-side NetMeeting settings are configured during the final stage of the IEAK Wizard and can also be configured with the IEAK Profile Manager. If the client's IE 4.0 has been configured for automatic configuration updates, the network administrator can provide or limit user functionality from one centrally located master file and that functionality will be implemented on all the client's computers. Figure 1.10.1 shows Microsoft NetMeeting.

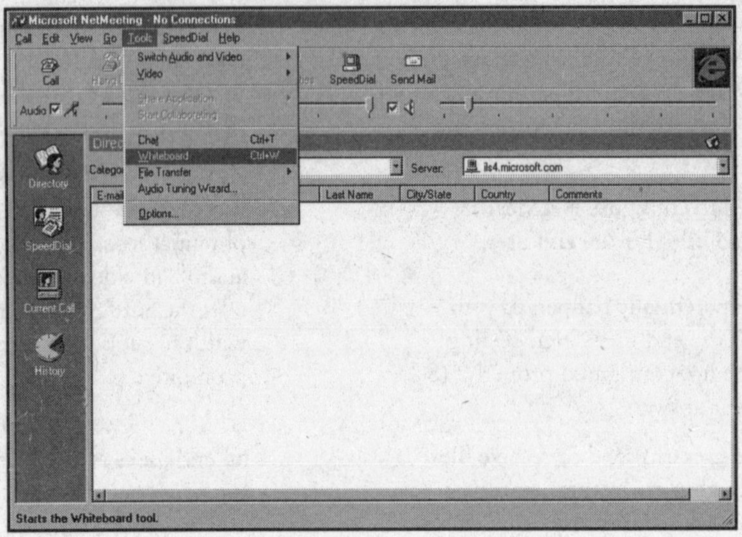

Figure 1.10.1 Microsoft NetMeeting.

Some of the NetMeeting settings you can configure with the IEAK Wizard or IEAK Profile Manager include setting the default directory server, Exchange Server properties for NetMeeting, NetMeeting home page, and the protocols used for NetMeeting.

Some of the limits that can be configured in NetMeeting include restricting file transfer capabilities, application sharing capabilities, collaboration capabilities, access to the Options menus, and use of video.

1.10.1 Internet Locator Service (ILS) Connectivity

The end user of NetMeeting can connect to a directory listing of other NetMeeting users after the fashion of a white pages telephone book. The Internet Locator Service (ILS) server acts as the white pages in this example.

When configuring NetMeeting functionality, you have the capability of setting the ILS server. When the end user comes online, he or she registers with the ILS and can access the ILS database.

1.10.2 IP Connectivity

The use of the TCP/IP protocol for NetMeeting is optional. The limitation is not set under the TCP/IP protocol in the Network Properties page, but can be configured in the Advanced options of NetMeeting. The IEAK Wizard and IEAK Profile Manager allow you to disable the use of TCP/IP for NetMeeting.

1.10.3 Peer-to-Peer Networking

Peer-to-peer communication through the NetMeeting components can be greatly limited. The peer-to-peer capabilities that are provided with NetMeeting include the following:

- **Microsoft Chat:** Opens an interactive chat window on all computers that join the chat session and displays updates to the dialog box on all computers simultaneously.
- **Whiteboard:** Opens an interactive whiteboard session on all computers that join the whiteboard session. This is a paintbrush-type session that allows a user to "draw" in the whiteboard area; the drawing is displayed on all other whiteboards simultaneously.
- **File Transfer:** One of the built-in capabilities of NetMeeting is to transfer files with other NetMeeting users. This capability can be limited to just sending files, just receiving files, or not having the capability to transfer files through NetMeeting.
- **Audio/Video Support:** Audio and video sessions can be conducted across the Internet or intranet through NetMeeting. If the hardware is in place, users can conduct audio and video meetings through NetMeeting. Because these capabilities can use tremendous amounts of bandwidth, you can disable the use of these features or limit the amount of bandwidth that can be used by these features.

1.10.4 Proxy Server Settings

The proxy server settings for an IE 4.0 client can be configured through the IEAK Wizard and the IEAK Profile Manager. The proxy server settings you can configure are the IP address or the host name. The use of proxy scripts can also be configured.

If the client is being upgraded from a previous version of Internet Explorer, or if Netscape exists on the client computer, proxy server settings can be imported to IE 4.0.

1.10.5 Questions

1. Of the items listed, which can be configured with the IEAK Wizard? (Select all that apply.)
   - A. Default directory server
   - B. NetMeeting home page
   - C. Default mail server
   - D. The protocols NetMeeting can use
2. Of the items listed, which can be configured for limited capability with the IEAK Wizard? (Select all that apply.)
   - A. Root directory of the shared folder
   - B. File transfer capabilities
   - C. Collaboration capabilities
   - D. Use of video in NetMeeting
3. Of the items listed, which can be configured with the IEAK Wizard? (Select all that apply.)
   - A. Exchange Server properties for NetMeeting
   - B. Streaming capabilities
   - C. Application sharing capabilities
   - D. Access to the NetMeeting Options menus
4. What does configuring the NetMeeting user for an ILS server provide to the user? (Select the best answer.)
   - A. The user will be able to "listen" to the Internet for select people to log on to the Internet.
   - B. When the user starts NetMeeting, the user will log on to the ILS server and be provided with a list of all the users logged on to that ILS server.
   - C. The user is automatically logged on to his or her mail server.
   - D. The user will be able to use the collaboration features of the whiteboard by logging on to the ILS.
5. Choose the statement that best describes NetMeeting's use of TCP/IP.
   - A. Use of the TCP/IP protocol for NetMeeting is mandatory.
   - B. NetMeeting operates only over the TCP/IP protocol.
   - C. NetMeeting can only operate over the NetBEUI protocol.
   - D. Use of the TCP/IP protocol for NetMeeting can be disabled.
6. Which are integral components of NetMeeting? (Select all that apply.)
   - A. Outlook Express
   - B. Microsoft Chat
   - C. Microsoft Whiteboard
   - D. FTP
7. What is needed to use the audio/video capabilities of NetMeeting? (Select all that apply.)
   - A. Audio/video hardware
   - B. Proper permissions configured in NetMeeting
   - C. An Internet connection
   - D. TCP/IP protocol installed
8. Select the statements that are true of proxy client support that can be configured with the IEAK Wizard.
   - A. The client can be configured to use a proxy server by IP address or host name.
   - B. The client can be configured to use proxy script files.
   - C. Proxy server support has to be configured manually.
   - D. The client cannot be configured to use a proxy script file.

1.10.6 Answers

1. **A, B, and D** The IEAK Wizard provides the capability to configure the default directory server, NetMeeting home page, and the protocols NetMeeting can use.
2. **B, C, and D** The IEAK Wizard provides the capability to limit file transfer capabilities, collaboration capabilities, and the use of video in NetMeeting.
3. **A, C, and D** The IEAK Wizard provides the capability to configure the Exchange Server properties for NetMeeting, application sharing capabilities, and access to the Options menu.
4. **B** The user will log to the ILS server, which maintains and provides a list of all the users logged on to that ILS.
5. **D** NetMeeting can be configured to use or not be allowed to use the TCP/IP protocol.
6. **B, C** Microsoft Chat and Microsoft Whiteboard are both components of NetMeeting.
7. **A, B** NetMeeting does not require Internet access or the TCP/IP protocol.
8. **A, B** The IEAK Wizard allows for configuration of the proxy server and proxy script files.

1.11 IEAK Profile Manager

The IEAK Profile Manager is a tool that can be used to modify a custom installation package or settings on users' computers. The users can be configured for automatic update and the IEAK Profile Manager can be used to modify settings to a master configuration file. The users then receive the updated configuration after a configurable time period. Figure 1.11.1 shows the IEAK Profile Manager.

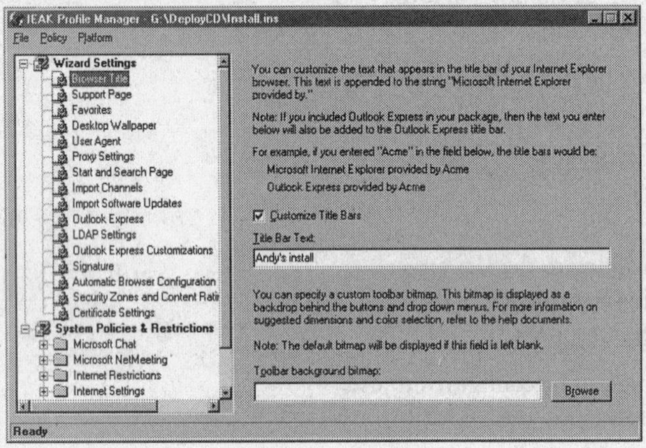

Figure 1.11.1 IEAK Profile Manager.

1.11.1 Microsoft JScript Autoproxy

Microsoft JScript is a scripting language used to write proxy scripts. Using the IEAK Wizard, the client can be configured to use not only proxy servers, but proxy scripts to determine whether a URL will be contacted directly by the client or through a proxy server. When a client requests a URL, the proxy script is run to determine which communications path the user will take. Proxy server scripts can be used to customize client/server communications to a proxy server.

1.11.2 `.INS` Files

Internet Setup (`.INS`) files contain the custom deployment settings configured when the IEAK Wizard is run. The IEAK Wizard automatically creates the file `Install.INS`, which stores the information needed to set up Internet access and service for the end user. During the IE 4.0 installation process, a unique `.INS` file is created and stored on each user's computer by taking the information from the `Install.INS` and incorporating it into the user's `.INS` file.

The `.INS` file format is an extension of the Dial-Up Networking file format, which is actually a Microsoft Windows `.INI` file.

1.11.3 `.ADM` Files

Administration (`.ADM`) files are used to hold system policy information that allows or restricts a user from performing tasks. The `.ADM` files used and created by the IEAK Profile Manager follow the same format as the `.ADM` files created by the System Policy Editor for Windows NT 4.0.

The .ADM files used with IE 4.0 can be used to provide or deny the user access to some advanced features (such as the capability to transfer files in NetMeeting).

.ADM files can be stored on a central server to provide roaming rights to users who work on different computers in the same manner as the server-based or roaming user profile in Windows NT 4.0. Some settings are available to restrict certain functions on specific computers rather than users.

1.11.4 Questions

1. Select the statement that best describes the IEAK Profile Manager.

   A. Used to configure system policies when the System Profile Manager is unavailable.

   B. Used to create profiles that provide the user's information when accessing the Internet.

   C. Used to modify custom installation package settings or settings on users' computers.

   D. Used to configure user proxy settings.

2. What statement best describes Microsoft JScript?

   A. A scripting language used to write proxy script files.

   B. A file named `JScript` that contains proxy scripts.

   C. A tool used to modify a custom installation package.

   D. A file used to hold system policy information.

3. What file is automatically created by the IEAK Wizard that contains setup information?

   A. Install.INF

   B. Install.CAB

   C. Install.INS

   D. Install.PAC

4. What statement best describes an `.ADM` file?

   A. Contains the custom deployment settings configured by the IEAK Wizard.

   B. Used to hold system policy information that allows or restricts a user from performing tasks.

   C. A scripting language file that stores proxy routing information.

   D. A file that stores the user's SID.

1.11.5 Answers

1. **C** The IEAK Profile Manager can be used to modify custom deployment package settings or user settings after IE 4.0 has been deployed.

2. **A** JScript is a scripting language used to write proxy scripts.

3. **C** The IEAK Wizard automatically creates a setup file called `Install.INS`.

4. **B** An `.ADM` file stores policy information that allows or restricts a user from performing a certain task.

1.12 Active Setup

The installation program for IE 4.0 is based on the ActiveX engine and is called Active Setup. Because the installation is modular, the files needed to start the installation process can fit on a single floppy. In this case, the bulk of the files needed for installation are stored on a server and are accessed and downloaded to the user's computer after dial-up and protocol stack configuration are complete, and communications are established.

Active Setup allows the user to download only the files necessary to complete the user's custom IE 4.0 configuration. With this arrangement, less time is spent in the installation process.

1.12.1 Custom Title Bar and Bitmaps

With the IEAK Wizard, custom Active Setup title bars and bitmaps can be incorporated into the custom deployment package.

When the user starts the installation process, the title for the installation window and bitmap displayed is whatever is configured during the configuration of the deployment package. The bitmap is limited to 120 × 239 pixels × 256 colors.

While running the IEAK Wizard, you can configure the custom autorun setting if you are creating CD-ROM media. You can also configure a custom IE 4.0 title bar and bitmap for behind the IE 4.0 toolbar.

1.12.2 Automatic Component Updates

Changes to the user's desktop IE 4.0 configuration can be made from a central location by creating centrally located `.INS` files and setting the user for automatic configuration. When the centrally located file is modified, all the clients receive the change to the package. This approach allows a network administrator to quickly and effectively implement changes to the IE 4.0 operating environments of all users without having to reinstall IE 4.0.

1.12.3 Download Sites

With the IEAK Wizard, you can specify up to 10 download sites. This allows the IE 4.0 installation workload to be evenly distributed across several servers, rather than one server, as was the case with earlier versions of the IEAK Wizard.

1.12.4 Questions

1. Select the statement that best describes Active Setup.

    A. The installation program for the IEAK that is based on the ActiveX engine.

    B. The program used to set up ActiveX support.

    C. Provides automatic component updates.

    D. The installation program for IE 4.0 that is based on the ActiveX engine.

2. You need to add a custom bitmap for Active Setup, but you keep getting an error stating that the bitmap is the wrong size. What size does the bitmap have to be?

    A. 120×240×256

    B. 120×239×256

    C. 240×120×256

    D. 239×120×256

3. While running the IEAK Wizard, you configured the employees for automatic configuration. What effect will this have on the user?

    A. The user will receive IE 4.0 configuration updates when a centrally located configuration package is changed.

    B. The user will receive IE 4.0 configuration updates when a centrally located custom package is updated, if the user reinstalls IE 4.0.

    C. The user will receive IE 4.0 configuration updates when a centrally located custom package is updated and IE 4.0 automatically reinstalls.

    D. The user will receive notifications when the centrally located IE 4.0 custom deployment package changes.

4. How many download sites can be configured with the IEAK Wizard?

    A. 1

    B. 4

    C. 10

    D. Unlimited

1.12.5 Answers

1. **D** Active Setup is the installation program used to install IE 4.0; the installation program is based on the ActiveX engine.

2. **B** The Active Setup bitmap must be 120 pixels × 239 pixels × 256 colors.

3. **A** Automatic configuration will update IE 4.0 when a centrally located configuration file is modified.

4. **C** Up to 10 download sites can be configured with the new IEAK.

CHAPTER 2

Installation and Configuration

The actual installation of the Internet Explorer Administration Kit (IEAK) and the configuration of custom packages for deployment is, like most Microsoft installations, easy—as long as proper planning has been done.

In the last chapter, you looked at the various planning considerations for deploying Internet Explorer 4.0. Now that you have an idea of how you will deploy IE 4.0, you simply have to install the IEAK, run the IEAK Wizard, and provide your customers with access to the selected media.

The actual steps from conception to deployment are given here:

1. Plan a deployment
2. Install IE 4.0
3. Install IEAK
4. Run the IEAK Wizard
5. Provide users with a distribution method

To upgrade from a previous deployment of IE 4.0, there is only one step:

- Run the IEAK Profile Manager

If the deployment has been done properly, updates are as simple as modifying the package configuration using the IEAK Profile Manager. The clients can be configured to update automatically, on a timed basis, or when the system is restarted.

If you need different configurations for different groups of clients, you can use the Profile Manager to customize or modify settings for each group.

2.1 Hardware Requirements

The hardware requirements for installing the IEAK are the same as those for installing Microsoft Internet Explorer 4.0 without Windows Desktop Update. The exception is that additional free disk space is required for the IEAK. Also, if the computer on which the IEAK is loaded is also used to store the custom packages, additional space to hold the custom packages is required. The hardware requirements for installing the Microsoft Internet Explorer Administration Kit 4.01 are as follows:

- A 486/66 processor or greater
- For Windows 95: 8M of RAM
- For Windows NT: 16M of RAM
- 45M to 60M of free disk space for the kit installation
- 40M to 100M for each custom package
- An active connection to the Internet

2.2 Software Requirements

This version of the IEAK runs on Windows 95 (or newer) with the latest service pack, Windows NT 4.0 Server (or newer) with Service Pack 3, and Windows NT 4.0 Workstation (or newer) with Service Pack 3.

Internet Explorer 4.0 must be installed before the IEAK Wizard can be run, and an active connection to the Internet must be established for the IEAK Wizard to run properly. If IE 4.0 is not installed, the wizard may appear to run, but it will not build the customized packages correctly.

2.3 Client Support

IEAK 4.01 is limited to configuring and deploying IE 4.0 to Windows 95 and Windows NT 4.0 computers. IEAK 4.01a allows configuration and deployment for Windows 95, Windows NT 4.0, Windows 3.x, Windows NT 3.51, and UNIX computers.

2.3.1 Windows NT Server and Workstation 4.0

The minimum requirements for Windows NT Server computers as of this writing are as follows:

- 486/66 processor (or greater)
- 16M of RAM, 24M for the Active Desktop
- 43M to 78M (56M to 98M during installation) of free disk space
- Service Pack 3 applied

2.3.2 Windows 3.x

The minimum requirements for Windows 3.1, Windows 3.11, Windows for Workgroups 3.11, and Windows NT 3.51 computers are as follows:

- 486/66 processor (or greater)
- 12M of RAM (16M with Java applications)
- 25M to 62M (34M to 74M during installation) of free disk space
- All available service packs applied

2.3.3 Windows 95

The minimum requirements for Windows 95 computers are as follows:

- 486/66 processor (or greater)
- 12M of RAM (16M with Windows Desktop Update)
- 43M to 78M (56M to 98M during installation) of free disk space
- All available service packs applied

2.3.4 Macintosh

Macintosh client minimum requirements for running Microsoft Internet Explorer 4.0 are listed here. There is an IEAK for configuring and deploying Macintosh clients that must be run on a Macintosh computer.

- A Macintosh with 68030 or later processor or a Macintosh PowerPC processor
- System 7.1 or later (System 7.6 recommended)
- 8M of RAM with virtual memory on (12M recommended)
- 7M to 37M of free hard disk space
- MacTCP or Open Transport 1.1.1 or later (extension)

2.3.5 UNIX Computers

The minimum requirements for UNIX computers are as follows:

- A SparcStation 2 (or greater)
- 32M of RAM (64M recommended)
- 65M of free disk space
- English Solaris 2.5.1 or 2.6

For the latest postings for minimum requirements to run Internet Explorer, visit the following site:

```
www.microsoft.com/ie/download/sysreq.htm
```

2.3.6 Exercise

This exercise is a paper-based scenario. You have been tasked with deploying IE 4.0 on all the machines in your department. You have to provide the IS department with a list of computers that have to be upgraded before IE 4.0 can be implemented. Most of the computers in your area are Pentium-based computers with 32M of RAM and at least 200M of free disk space, all running Windows NT Workstation or Windows 95, both with the latest service packs installed.

You have six machines that do not fit this category, and you have to determine what upgrades, if any, are needed. Use the information in the preceding sections to determine what upgrades, if any, must be performed on the following machines:

- Pentium 75 with 16M of RAM and 40M of free disk space, running Windows NT Workstation
- 486/33 with 8M of RAM and 50M of free disk space, running Windows for Workgroups 3.11
- Macintosh PowerPC with 12M of RAM and 40M of free disk space, running System 7.1
- UNIX SparcStation 2 with 32M of RAM and 2 gigabytes of free disk space, running Solaris 2.5
- 386/25 with 8M of RAM and 20M of free disk space, running Windows 3.1
- Pentium 90 with 12M of RAM and 30M of free disk space, running Windows 95

2.3.7 Practice Problems

1. You are deploying Microsoft Internet Explorer 4.0 on a Windows 3.1 computer. The computer has an Intel 386/25 processor, 8M of RAM, and 100M of free disk space. Select the components that must be upgraded before you can install IE 4.0.

   A. Processor subsystem

   B. RAM memory subsystem

   C. Hard drive subsystem

   D. Nothing needs to be upgraded

2. A user on your network wants to upgrade to Internet Explorer 4.0 and wants to know if the computer she uses is capable. She tells you she has a Pentium 90 with 16M of RAM and a 1-gigabyte hard drive with 100M of free space running Windows 95. What components must be replaced to perform the upgrade?

   A. Processor subsystem

   B. RAM memory subsystem

   C. Hard drive subsystem

   D. Nothing needs to be upgraded

3. A UNIX user wants to install Internet Explorer 4.0 and asks if a SparcStation 2 with 64M of RAM and 40M of free hard disk space will be adequate. What components would you tell him are sufficient to support IE 4.0?

   A. Processor subsystem

   B. RAM memory subsystem

   C. Hard drive subsystem

   D. None of the above

4. Your company is preparing to deploy Internet Explorer 4.0 and your management team has asked you which computer meets the minimum requirements to run the IEAK Wizard. A download server will be used to deploy the custom packages. Select the computer that the IEAK can be run on with no modifications.

   A. A 486/66 computer with 16M of RAM and 70M of free disk space running Windows 95 with the most current service packs applied

   B. A SparcStation 2 with 128M of RAM and 2 gigabytes of free disk space

   C. A Pentium 200 computer with 128M of RAM and 500M of free disk space running Windows NT Workstation with no service packs applied

   D. A 486/33 computer with 16M of RAM and 60M of free disk space running Windows for Workgroups

5. You are attempting to run the IEAK Wizard on a Pentium computer with 64M of RAM and 1 gigabyte of free disk space. The computer has a fresh install of Windows NT 4.0 Server, and Service Pack 3 has been applied. The IEAK Wizard appears to run properly, but the custom packages don't work. What would you try doing first to fix this problem?

   A. Install Proxy Server 2.0

   B. Install IIS 2.0 or newer

   C. Install IE 4.0

   D. Reinstall the IEAK

6. One of your Macintosh users wants to install IE 4.0 on his computer. He has a Macintosh PowerPC running System 7.1 with 12M of RAM and 50M of free disk space. He wants to know what he needs to upgrade before he can install IE 4.0. What would you tell him to upgrade?

   A. Processor subsystem

   B. RAM memory subsystem

   C. Hard drive subsystem

   D. Nothing needs to be upgraded

2

7. You are attempting to install the IEAK on a Pentium 133 computer with 24M of RAM and 80M of free disk space, running Windows NT Server 3.51, but are having problems. Of the items listed here, what would need to be upgraded to allow the IEAK to be installed?

   A. Processor subsystem

   B. RAM memory subsystem

   C. Hard drive subsystem

   D. Operating system

8. You are deploying Microsoft Internet Explorer 4.0 on a Windows 95 computer. The computer has an Intel 486/66 processor, 12M of RAM, and 100M of free disk space. Select the components that must be upgraded before you can install IE 4.0 with the Windows Desktop Update.

   A. Processor subsystem

   B. RAM memory subsystem

   C. Hard drive subsystem

   D. None of the above

9. You are deploying Microsoft Internet Explorer 4.0 and will have to configure four different custom packages for your users. How much free disk space should you plan on having on your download server? Select the best answer.

   A. 400M

   B. 65M

   C. 160M

   D. 320M

10. You are deploying Microsoft Internet Explorer 4.0 on a Windows NT 3.51 computer. The computer has an Intel Pentium 75 processor, 12M of RAM, and 100M of free disk space. Select the components that must be upgraded before you can install IE 4.0.

    A. Processor subsystem

    B. RAM memory subsystem

    C. Hard drive subsystem

    D. None of the above

11. A user wants to install Microsoft Internet Explorer 4.0 on a Windows NT 4.0 workstation. The computer has an Intel 486/33 processor, 16M of RAM, and 90M of free disk space. Select the components that must be upgraded before you can install IE 4.0.

    A. Processor subsystem

    B. RAM memory subsystem

    C. Hard drive subsystem

    D. None of the above

12. Your company is preparing to deploy Internet Explorer 4.0, and you have to select a computer on which to run the IEAK Wizard. A download server will be used to deploy the custom packages, and you will install a fresh copy of Windows 95 on the computer that will run the IEAK. Select the computers on which you can run the IEAK without upgrading the hardware.

    A. A 486/33 computer with 16M of RAM and 70M of free disk space running Windows 95 with the most current service packs applied

    B. A SparcStation 2 with 128M of RAM and 2 gigabytes of free disk space

    C. A Pentium 200 computer with 128M of RAM and 500M of free disk space running Windows NT Workstation 3.51

    D. A 486/66 computer with 32M of RAM and 75M of free disk space running Windows NT Workstation 4.0 with Service Pack 3 applied

13. You are attempting to install the IEAK on a Pentium 133 computer with 64M of RAM and 200M of free disk space running Windows NT Server 3.51, but are having problems. Of the items listed here, which component is most likely causing the problem?

    A. Processor subsystem

    B. RAM memory subsystem

    C. Hard drive subsystem

    D. Operating system

14. You are attempting to run the IEAK Wizard on a 486/66 computer with 24M of RAM and 200M of free disk space. The computer has a fresh install of Windows NT 4.0 Workstation, and Service Pack 3 has been applied. The IEAK Wizard appears to run properly, but the custom packages don't work. What would you try doing first to fix this problem?

    A. Upgrade the processor subsystem

    B. Install IE 4.0

    C. Upgrade the RAM memory

    D. Reapply Service Pack 3

15. You are attempting to run the IEAK Wizard on a Pentium computer with 64M of RAM and 1 gigabyte of free disk space. The computer has a fresh install of Windows NT 4.0 Server, Service Pack 3 has been applied, and you have installed IE 4.0. This is your notebook computer, and you are attempting to configure the IEAK Wizard from your house. You have a modem and can attach to your network at work, which provides you with Internet access. When running the IEAK Wizard, you do not have any Web sites to select from for component synchronization, and the wizard fails. What would you try doing first to fix this problem?

    A. Use the modem to connect to your network at work

    B. Remove IE 4.0

    C. Reapply the service pack

    D. Reinstall the IEAK

16. One of your Macintosh users wants to install IE 4.0 on her computer. She has a Macintosh 68030 processor running System 7.1. She has 4M of RAM and only 50M of free disk space. She wants to know what she has to upgrade before she can install IE 4.0. What would you tell her to upgrade?

    A. Processor subsystem

    B. RAM memory subsystem

    C. Hard drive subsystem

    D. Nothing has to be upgraded

17. You are deploying Microsoft Internet Explorer 4.0 on a Windows for Workgroups 3.11 computer. The computer has an Intel 486/33 processor, 162M of RAM, and 25M of free disk space. Select the components that must be upgraded before you can install IE 4.0.

    A. Processor subsystem

    B. RAM memory subsystem

    C. Hard drive subsystem

    D. None of the above

18. A UNIX user wants to install Internet Explorer 4.0 and asks whether a SparcStation 2 with 16M of RAM and 70M of free hard disk space will be adequate. What components would you tell the user must be upgraded to support IE 4.0?

    A. Processor subsystem

    B. RAM memory subsystem

    C. Hard drive subsystem

    D. All of the above

19. You are deploying Microsoft Internet Explorer 4.0 on a Windows 3.1 computer. The computer has an Intel 486/66 processor, 12M of RAM, and 100M of free disk space. The user has to be able to run Java applications through IE 4.0. Select the components that must be upgraded before you can install IE 4.0.

    A. Processor subsystem

    B. RAM memory subsystem

    C. Hard drive subsystem

    D. Nothing has to be upgraded

20. You are deploying Microsoft Internet Explorer 4.0 and have to configure two different custom packages for your users. How much free disk space should you plan on having on your download server? Select the best answer.

    A. 200M

    B. 300M

    C. 400M

    D. 80M

21. You are deploying Microsoft Internet Explorer 4.0 on a Windows 95 computer. The computer has an Intel Pentium 75 processor, 16M of RAM, and 25M of free disk space. Select the components that have to be upgraded before you can install IE 4.0 with the Windows Desktop Update.

    A. Processor subsystem

    B. RAM memory subsystem

    C. Hard drive subsystem

    D. None of the above

22. You are deploying Microsoft Internet Explorer 4.0 on a Windows 3.11 computer. The computer has an Intel 486/33 processor, 12M of RAM, and 75M of free disk space. Select the components that have to be upgraded before you can install IE 4.0.

    A. Processor subsystem

    B. RAM memory subsystem

    C. Hard drive subsystem

    D. Nothing has to be upgraded

23. You are attempting to run the IEAK Wizard on a Pentium computer with 64M of RAM and 1 gigabyte of free disk space. The computer has a fresh install of Windows NT 4.0 Server, Service Pack 3 has been applied, and you have installed IE 4.0. This is your notebook computer and you are attempting to configure the IEAK Wizard from your house. You do not have a modem and are not attached to your network, which provides you with Internet access through your company proxy server. When running the IEAK Wizard, you do not have any Web sites to select from for component synchronization, and the Wizard fails. What would you try doing first to fix this problem?

    A. Install Proxy Server 2.0

    B. Gain Internet access

    C. Upgrade the operating system

    D. Reinstall the IEAK

24. A user wants to install Microsoft Internet Explorer 4.0 with the Windows Desktop Update on a Windows NT 4.0 workstation. The computer has an Intel 486/66 processor, 32M of RAM, and 90M of free disk space. Select the components that must be upgraded before you can install IE 4.0.

    A. Processor subsystem

    B. RAM memory subsystem

    C. Hard drive subsystem

    D. Nothing has to be upgraded

25. A user on your network wants to upgrade to Internet Explorer 4.0 with Windows Desktop Update and wants to know

whether the computer he uses is capable. He tells you he has a Pentium 90 with 12M of RAM and a 1 gigabyte hard drive with 100M of free space. The computer is running Windows 95. What components have to be replaced to perform the upgrade?

A. Processor subsystem

B. RAM memory subsystem

C. Hard drive subsystem

D. Nothing has to be upgraded

26. One of your Macintosh users wants to install IE 4.0 on her computer. She has a Macintosh PowerPC running System 6.8 with 12M of RAM and 40M of free disk space. She wants to know what she has to upgrade before she can install IE 4.0. What would you tell her to upgrade?

A. Operating system

B. RAM memory subsystem

C. Hard drive subsystem

D. Processor subsystem

27. Your company is preparing to deploy Internet Explorer 4.0, and you have to select a computer on which to run the IEAK Wizard. A download server will be used to deploy the custom packages. Select the computers on which the IEAK cannot be installed.

A. A 486/100 computer with 32M of RAM and 70M of free disk space running Windows 95 with the most current service packs applied

B. A SparcStation 2 with 128M of RAM and 2 gigabytes of free disk space

C. A Pentium 200 computer with 128M of RAM and 500M of free disk space running Windows NT Workstation 3.51

D. A 486/66 computer with 24M of RAM and 75M of free disk space running Windows NT Workstation 4.0 with Service Pack 3 applied

28. A user wants to install Microsoft Internet Explorer 4.0 with the Windows Desktop Update on a Windows 95 system. The computer has an Intel 486/66 processor, 12M of RAM, and 30M of free disk space. Select the components that do not have to be upgraded before you can install IE 4.0.

A. Processor subsystem

B. RAM memory subsystem

C. Hard drive subsystem

D. All of the above

29. You are deploying Microsoft Internet Explorer 4.0 on a Windows for Workgroups 3.11 computer. The computer has an Intel 386/25 processor, 12M of RAM, and 20M of free disk space. Select the components that have to be upgraded before you can install IE 4.0 and be able to run Java applications.

A. Processor subsystem

B. RAM memory subsystem

C. Hard drive subsystem

D. None of the above

30. Your company is preparing to deploy Internet Explorer 4.0, and your management team has asked you what the minimum requirements are for a computer to run the IEAK Wizard. A download server will be used to deploy the custom packages. Select the computer on which the IEAK can run with no modifications.

A. A 486/66 computer with 16M of RAM and 40M of free disk space running Windows 95 with the most current service packs applied

B. A SparcStation 2 with 128M of RAM and 2 gigabytes of free disk space

C. A Pentium 200 computer with 16M of RAM, 500M of free disk space, running Windows NT Workstation with Service Pack 3 applied, and running IE 4.0

D. A 486/33 computer with 16M of RAM and 60M of free disk space running Windows NT 3.51 Server

31. Your company is preparing to deploy Internet Explorer 4.0, and you have to select a computer on which to run the IEAK Wizard. The system will also act as the download server and you will install a fresh copy of Windows NT 4.0 Server before installing the IEAK. Select the best computer to use.

A. A 486/33 computer with 16M of RAM and 70M of free disk space running Windows 95 with the most current service packs applied

B. A SparcStation 2 with 128M of RAM and 2 gigabytes of free disk space

C. A Pentium 200 computer with 128M of RAM, 500M of free disk space running Windows NT Workstation 3.51

D. A 486/66 computer with 32M of RAM and 75M of free disk space running Windows NT Workstation 4.0 with Service Pack 3 applied

2.3.8 Answers and Explanations: Practice Problems

1. **A, B** The processor must be a 486 or greater, and have 12M to 16M of RAM on a Windows 3.1 computer.

2. **D** Nothing. This machine does exceed the minimum requirements for installing IE 4.0.

3. **A, B** The hard disk subsystem's free disk space is the only minimum requirement that is not met.

4. **A** The only computer that meets the minimum requirements for installing the IEAK is the first computer.

5. **C** IE 4.0 must be installed on the computer before the IEAK Wizard will create packages.

6. **D** The computer listed meets the minimum requirements for installing IE 4.0.

7. **D** The IEAK can be installed only on a computer running Windows 95 or Windows NT 4.0.

8. **B** The minimum memory requirement for a Windows 95 computer when the Windows Desktop Update is implemented is 16M of RAM.

9. **A** You should plan on having 100M of free disk space for each custom package configured. The package size can range from 45M to 100M.

10. **D** This computer meets the minimum requirements for installing IE 4.0.

11. **A, B** The minimum processor requirement is a 486/66 with 16M of RAM.

12. **C, D** Both of these computers meet the minimum hardware requirements for installing the IEAK, because a fresh copy of Windows 95 is to be installed on the computer.

13. **D** The IEAK can be installed only on a computer running Windows 95 or Windows NT 4.0. The other minimum requirements are satisfied.

14. **B** You must have IE 4.0 installed on the computer on which the IEAK Wizard is running.

15. **A** You must have an active Internet connection for the IEAK Wizard to run properly.

16. **B** The minimum requirement for RAM of the computer described is 8M, with 12M preferred.

17. **A, C** The processor must be a 486/66 or greater with at least 56M of free disk space to perform the installation.

18. **B** A UNIX system must have a minimum of 32M of RAM, with 64M preferred.

19. **B** The minimum requirement if Java support is needed is 16M of RAM.

20. **A** 100M of free disk space should be reserved for each custom package that will be needed.

21. **C** The amount of free disk space needed to install IE 4.0 is at least 56M.

22. **D** The machine listed meets minimum installation requirements.

23. **B** You must be attached to the Internet for the IEAK Wizard to run properly.

24. **D** The machine listed meets the minimum requirements.

25. **B** The minimum RAM requirement for a Windows 95 computer if the Windows Desktop Update is needed is 16M.

26. **A** The minimum operating system that will support IE 4.0 is System 7.1, with System 7.6 preferred.

27. **B, C** The IEAK can be run only on a computer running Windows 95 or Windows NT 4.0.

28. **A** The processor is the only component that meets minimum requirements.

29. **A, B, and C** The computer listed meets none of the minimum requirements.

30. **C** The computer listed in answer C is the only computer that does not need modification.

31. **C** Because the operating system will be changed, the Pentium computer in answer C would be the best computer to use for the IE40 deployment.

2.4 IEAK Installation Procedure

The installation procedure used to install the Internet Explorer Administration Kit (IEAK) has five steps:

1. Gathering information
2. Specifying Active Setup parameters
3. Customizing the Active Setup screen
4. Customizing the browser
5. Customizing components (if applicable)

Each of these steps is detailed in the exercises in the remaining sections of this chapter. The following sections briefly describe the information configured in each of the steps.

2.4.1 Gathering Information

During the first stage of the IEAK installation, you are prompted to provide your company name and license number, as shown in Figure 2.4.1. The customization code is obtained by registering for the product at the Microsoft Web site.

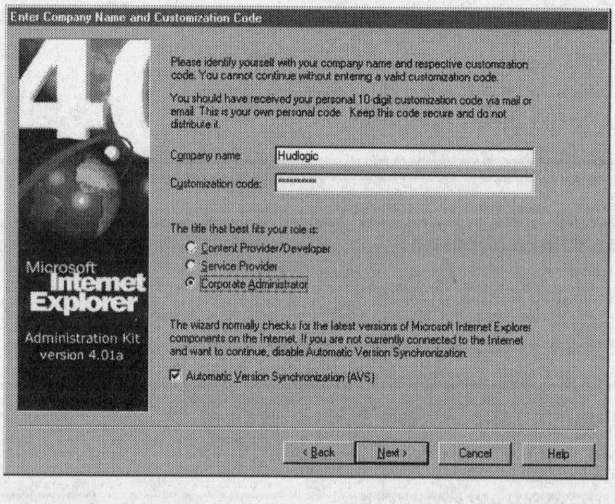

Figure 2.4.1 IEAK Wizard Stage 1: The user information screen.

You can request different types of licenses depending on how you will use the product. Not all codes allow access to all three roles for the product. Make sure that you register for the type of license that best suits your business. You can request several different licenses.

From this screen, you also select your role when using this product, and whether you want automatic synchronization of component versions. Based on the role you select, different options will be available during the installation and configuration of the IEAK.

If you select the Automatic Version Synchronization (AVS) check box, the IEAK can visit defined Web sites and update the version of all your Internet Explorer 4.0 components to the most current versions.

The next wizard screen allows configuration of the language used by IE 4.0. The language selected does not have to match the desktop's language—as long as no Active Desktop elements are being deployed. If you are running a newer version of the IEAK, such as IEAK v4.01a, you will see additional configuration screens, such as the Select a Platform screen. The newer versions of the IEAK are not covered on the certification exam, but for the purposes of using the product, you must be aware of the differences.

After selecting the language, you must provide a directory in which to store the deployment package created by the IEAK Wizard. The directory can be created on the computer you are running the Wizard on, or on a network share point. If the directory does not exist, the IEAK creates it for you.

The lower half of the screen allows you to select the deployment methods used, as shown in Figure 2.4.2. The options available are determined by the role you selected earlier in the wizard process. Three deployment methods are available:

- CD-ROM
- Multiple Floppy Disks
- Single Floppy Disk

The Single Floppy Disk option is available only if the role selected was Service Provider; it is not available otherwise.

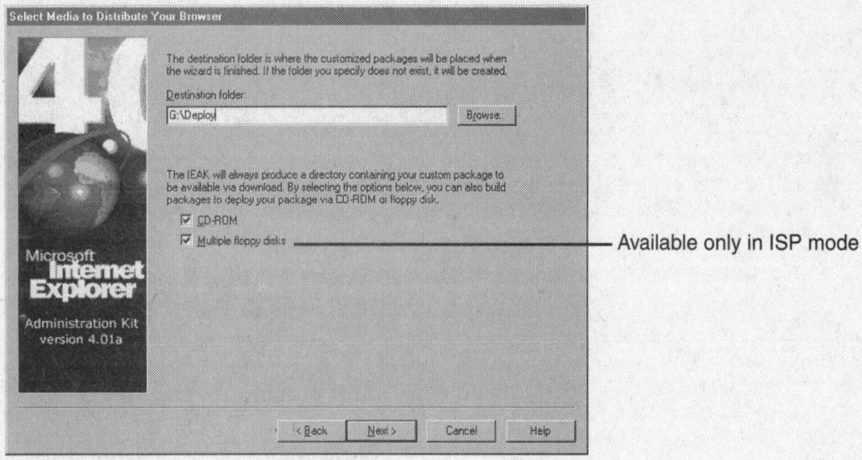

Figure 2.4.2 IEAK Wizard Stage 1: Selecting the media deployment method.

2.4.2 Exercise

In this exercise, you will complete Stage 1 of the IEAK Wizard. To perform this exercise, your computer must meet the minimum hardware and software requirements, you must have registered for a license at the Microsoft Web site, and you must have downloaded the IEAK.

Different versions of the IEAK are available. If you download the latest version of the IEAK (IEAK 4.01a), you will have additional configuration screens that are not covered in the exercises for this chapter. This exercise assumes that you have installed the IEAK and have a valid license.

At the end of this exercise, do not cancel the wizard configuration. You will continue running the wizard in later exercises throughout this chapter.

To run the IEAK Wizard Stage 1, follow these steps:

1. From the Start menu, select Programs|Microsoft IEAK and then select IEAK Wizard. This action starts the IEAK Wizard.
2. On the information screen that appears, type your company name in the Company field. In the Customization Code field, type the license number you received when you registered at the IEAK Web site. The license type you requested determines what roles are available to you. If available, select Corporate Administrator. Click Next.
3. Select English for the language. If you are not connected to the Internet, this box may appear blank.
4. For the destination folder, type the name of the directory in which you want to store the custom package. Note that the deployment options available to you depend on the role you selected.

This ends Stage 1. Stage 2 is covered in the following exercise. Do not stop the IEAK Wizard.

2.4.3 Practice Problems

1. You started the IEAK Wizard and selected the role of Corporate Administrator. When you reached the deployment media screen, you did not have the Single Floppy Disk option available. What would you have to do to have the Single Floppy Disk deployment method available?

   A. Install a floppy drive on the computer.

   B. Get a license for running the IEAK in ISP mode, start the IEAK Wizard using the ISP license, and select the ISP role.

   C. Change the destination folder to point to the floppy drive.

   D. Nothing. The Multiple Floppy Disk and Single Floppy Disk options do the same thing.

2. You started the IEAK Wizard, and when you arrive at the screen that asks what language you want to use, the download site list is blank. What might this indicate?

   A. The language is taken from the computer on which you are running the IEAK Wizard, and it is not English.

   B. You have to type in the language you want to use.

   C. You are not connected to the Internet.

   D. Nothing. The language option should be blank.

3. You entered your customization code, but the Corporate Administrator role is not available to you. What could be the problem?

   A. You are not running the IEAK on a fast enough computer.

   B. Restart the IEAK Wizard, this time using the `/CA` switch in the command line.

   C. The computer you are running the IEAK Wizard on does not have enough free disk space to allow you to store a custom package.

   D. You did not register for a license that provided the Corporate Administrator role.

2

4. You want to be able to specify the single floppy, multiple floppy, and CD-ROM deployment methods. What role must you select to have all these options available to you?

   A. Content Provider/Developer

   B. Service Provider

   C. Corporate Administrator

   D. None of these roles provide you with that capability. You must have the IEAK Extra to have all these options available.

5. Select the answer that best describes the function of the Automatic Version Synchronization (AVS) check box.

   A. When checked, a Microsoft-defined download site is used to verify that you have the most current version of each of the components of IE 4.0.

   B. When checked, a Microsoft-defined download site is not used to verify that you have the most current version of each of the components of IE 4.0.

   C. When checked, the versions of each of your components are recorded on the IEAK registration site for licensing registration.

   D. When checked, the versions of each of your components are not recorded on the IEAK registration site for licensing registration.

2.4.4 Answers and Explanations: Practice Problems

1. **B** The Single Floppy Disk option is available only when the wizard runs under the ISP role.

2. **C** You must be connected to the Internet for the IEAK Wizard to run properly.

3. **D** You can run the IEAK Wizard only in the roles for which you have requested the license.

4. **B** The ISP role allows you all these deployment methods.

5. **A** AVS verifies that you have the most current components available by comparing them with a Microsoft-defined Web site.

2.4.5 Specifying Active Setup Parameters

Stage 2, Specifying Active Setup Parameters, allows you to select the active components of IE 4.0 that will be available during the client's configuration.

Configuring the Active Setup components begins with Stage 2 of the IEAK Wizard. If AVS was selected during the first stage, you will be provided with a list of sites from which the IEAK can verify how current your components are, and from which it can retrieve the updated versions of each component, if needed. After you select a site, the next screen displays the active components available and displays one of three icons next to each component (see Figure 2.4.3):

- **Red X.** This icon indicates that you do not have the component.
- **Yellow Exclamation.** This icon indicates that you have a component, but not the most current version.
- **Green Check.** This icon indicated that you have the most current version of the component.

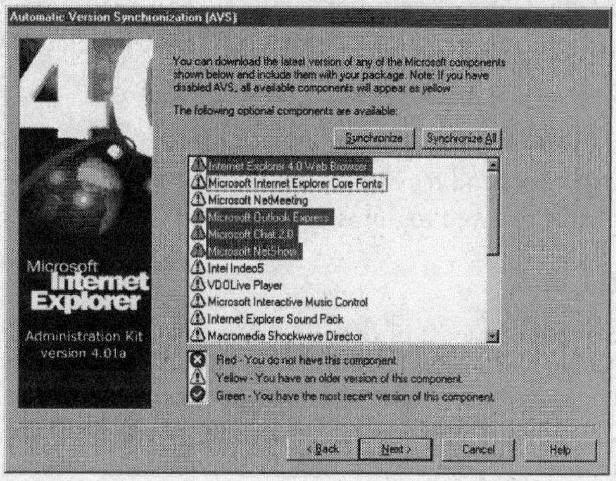

Figure 2.4.3 IEAK Wizard Stage 2: The component synchronization screen.

The Synchronize All button is available if AVS was selected during the first stage. The Synchronize button works like the Synchronize All button, but it checks only the highlighted items for synchronization. If AVS was not selected, the components are all displayed with a yellow exclamation icon.

The next wizard screen allows you to configure up to 10 additional custom components, as shown in Figure 2.4.4.

The custom components that are offered must exist in an executable (.EXE) or a compressed cabinet (.CAB) file. You must provide the path to each custom component added along with verification signature information, if used. The path provided includes the site URL and filename. Note that by default, IE 4.0 is configured to reject components that do not have a verification signature.

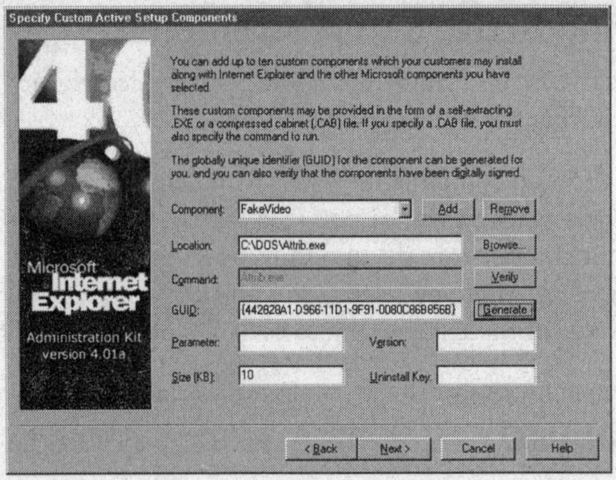

Figure 2.4.4 IEAK Wizard Stage 2: Selecting custom components.

You can provide a Globally Unique Identifier (GUID), which is an identifier used to distinguish one program or object from another. You can have the IEAK generate a GUID automatically for you.

You can also specify the size of your component, include any additional switches used during installation of the component, and register an uninstall program so that the component can be uninstalled from the Add/Remove Programs applet found in the Control Panel.

2.4.6 Exercise

In this exercise, you complete Stage 2 of the IEAK Wizard. This exercise assumes that you did not cancel the IEAK Wizard at the end of the last exercise.

1. From the Stage 2 description screen, click Next. From the download site item, select the site located nearest you. Note that if you did not establish an Internet connection before starting the Wizard, this box will be blank.
2. If AVS was selected, the wizard will take several minutes to verify the versions you have of each of the components listed. If AVS was not selected, all the items appear with a yellow exclamation icon. If you want to synchronize some of the components listed, select the component or components and click Synchronize. If you want to synchronize all the components listed, click Synchronize All. Click Next to continue.

> **CAUTION**
>
> **The synchronization process can take several hours. You cannot continue these steps until some version of the IE 4.0 Web browser is available.**

3. If desired, you can add up to 10 custom components. In this exercise, you do not add any custom components, but you should take the time to explore each of the options on this wizard page. Click Next to continue.

4. If one was available in the components listed in step 2 of this exercise, you can select a trusted publisher. Click Next to continue.

That ends the Stage 2 configuration and this exercise. Do not cancel the IEAK Wizard. Stage 3 is configured in the next exercise.

2.4.7 Practice Problems

1. You are starting Stage 2 of the IEAK Wizard. In Stage 1, you could not select any languages, and now no download sites are available. What could be the problem?

   A. You are running in Corporate Administrator role.

   B. You are running in ISP role.

   C. You didn't provide a language in Stage 1, so you cannot see the download information.

   D. You were not connected to the Internet when you started the IEAK Wizard.

2. Microsoft NetMeeting is showing up with a red check mark in the AVS window. What does this indicate?

   A. You do not have a sound card, and it is required.

   B. A valid copy of NetMeeting is not available on the download server you selected.

   C. You do not have a copy of NetMeeting available locally.

   D. You have a more current version of NetMeeting than is available on the download site.

3. You have a custom component you want to make available for your users, so you add it to the Custom Active Setup Components screen. You were told to register the uninstall key while configuring the component. What does the uninstall key do?

   A. Allows you to uninstall the custom component through the Add/Remove Program applet located in the Control Panel.

   B. Registers the custom component with Microsoft.

   C. Registers each user with the Corporate Administrator.

   D. When combined with the GUID, provides a password for access to the custom component.

4. Select the best definition for Globally Unique Identifier (GUID).

   A. The executable code for a custom component.

   B. A unique identifier that helps distinguish one program or object from another.

   C. The name of a custom component that a user selects to install that custom component.

   D. A .CAB file that, when expanded, contains the executable code for a custom component.

5. You are almost sure that at least some components listed on the AVS screen are current, but all the components show up with a yellow exclamation icon. What could be causing this?

   A. AVS was not selected in Stage 1 of the IEAK Wizard.

   B. AVS was selected in Stage 1 of the IEAK Wizard.

   C. You are running in CA role.

   D. You are running in ISP role.

2.4.8 Answers and Explanations: Practice Problems

1. **D** You must be connected to the Internet for the Wizard to run properly.

2. **C** You do not have any version of NetMeeting installed on the computer on which you are running the IEAK Wizard.

3. **A** Configuring the uninstall key registers an uninstall program in the Registry so that the component can be uninstalled with the Add/Remove Programs applet located in the Control Panel.

4. **B** A GUID is a unique identifier that helps identify programs or objects. An algorithm is used to help ensure uniqueness.

5. **A** If AVS is not selected during Stage 1 of the IEAK Wizard, all components show up with yellow icons because the Wizard cannot verify whether the versions are current.

2.4.9 Customizing Active Setup

In Stage 3 of the configuration process, you can customize the Active Setup Installation title bar and bitmap (must be 120×239×256), the Custom Component Installation title bar, the available installation options, and up to 10 user download sites.

The first few screens of Stage 3 allow you to enter custom text and bitmaps for the Active Setup Installation screen.

If you selected the Corporate Administrator role in Stage 1, you can select the Install Package Silently check box at the bottom of the wizard screen. If you configure the installation to install silently, you cannot configure more than one download site, and the user will not be prompted to provide any customization information. If you selected CD-ROM as a deployment method, you can also customize the autorun screen.

If the user is running a particularly large application while the installation is taking place, the installation could fail. Also note that after installation is complete, the system reboots, which could result in loss of user data. If you are running in ISP mode, you will be prompted to configure CMAK settings, which are used to configure the client's Internet connection.

The next wizard screen allows you to configure up to ten custom installation options in addition to the following three default installation options. Figure 2.4.5 shows the optional components installed during the standard installation. Here are the three default installation options:

- **Minimal Installation.** This method installs only the Microsoft Internet Explorer Web Browser 4.0. No add-on components will be installed.
- **Standard Installation.** This method is the default method; it installs the Microsoft Internet Explorer Web Browser 4.0, Microsoft Internet Explorer core fonts, Microsoft Outlook Express, VDOLive Player, Microsoft Interactive Music Control, and Microsoft Wallet.
- **Full Installation.** This method installs the Microsoft Internet Explorer 4.0 Web browser, Microsoft Internet Explorer core fonts, Microsoft Chat 2.0, Intel Indeo5, Microsoft Outlook Express, NetMeeting, Microsoft FrontPage Express, NetShow, Web Publishing Wizard, Microsoft Visual Basic Runtime, VDOLive Player, Microsoft Interactive Music Control, RealPlayer by Progressive Networks, and Microsoft Wallet.

After configuring any custom installation options you will need, you can configure up to ten download sites (by URL) from which the user can download your packages. You must configure at least one site. These sites are not checked by the IEAK.

After specifying at least one download site, you are prompted to provide a version number for the build. If you do not provide one, the system assigns one. Any subsequent changes made to the package increments the version number. The version number helps the client maintain the latest version of each component.

After configuring the version, you can configure the directory in which IE 4.0 will be placed on the client computer. The default is in the `Program Files` folder.

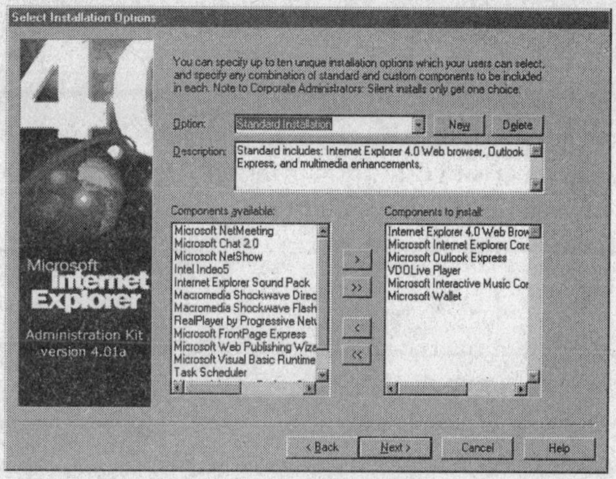

Figure 2.4.5 IEAK Wizard Stage 3: The installation type configuration screen.

The final screen in this stage determines whether and how the Windows Desktop Update will be implemented. The choices are as follows:

- Yes (Active Desktop will be on)
- No (Active Desktop will not be on)
- User Choice

The User Choice selection is not available if the silent installation option was selected.

2.4.10 Custom IE 4.0 Installations

In addition to the three default installations, you can define up to ten additional configurations that enable you to set up custom installation options for different installation needs. To configure a custom installation option, follow these steps:

1. Click the New button.
2. Select the components you want to install with this custom installation option. You can add a description to the custom installation if desired.

Note that you must always include the Internet Explorer 4.0 Web browser.

2.4.11 Exercise

This exercise takes you through Stage 3 of the IEAK Wizard. This exercise assumes that you did not cancel the IEAK Wizard at the end of the last exercise and are at the Stage 3 screen of the IEAK Wizard. The Stage 3 introduction screen has the title *Stage 3: Customizing Active Setup* and gives a brief explanation of what components will be configured.

1. Start at the *Stage 3: Customizing Active Setup* screen in the IEAK Wizard. Take a moment to read the screen and then click Next. The next wizard screen appears.
2. In the Title Bar text box, type a unique message. This message appears when the user is installing your custom package. For the Active Setup Bitmap path, click Browse to select a custom bitmap to

display during the client installation of IE 4.0. Note that the bitmap must be 120×239×256 colors (the first two measurements are in pixels). Click Next.

If you are running in ISP mode, you are also prompted to provide the path to a custom profile you can create using the Internet Connection Manager Administration Kit (CMAK), which sets up the client's Internet connection.

3. If you're running in Corporate Administrator mode, you can select the Install Package Silently option if you don't want the user to be aware that the installation is taking place. Click Next. The Installation Options screen appears.

CAUTION

If you select the Install Package Silently option, the user is not prompted to select any options and may lose data at the end of the installation process when the system reboots.

4. Take a moment to review the components installed with the Minimal, Standard, and Full installations. Create your own custom installation by clicking New. In the Description box, type `Custom Install Exercise`. Note that the IE 4.0 Web browser is automatically installed and cannot be removed. Press and hold the Ctrl key and select the Microsoft Outlook Express and Microsoft Wallet components. Both components should be highlighted. Click the arrow key that points to the Components to Install pane. The two selected components should now appear in the box of components to install. Click Next to continue. The Specify Download URLs screen appears.
5. You must specify at least one download URL to continue. The site you select is not checked by the IEAK Wizard, so it is important that you type the sites correctly. This field specifies the site at which the user can find your custom download package. Click Next to continue. The Version Information screen appears.
6. The Version Information screen allows you to create a version number for your custom package. Any changes made to the package cause the version number to increment. Click Next to continue. The Browser Path screen appears.
7. On this screen, you can select the path and folder in which you want to install IE 4.0. Click Next to continue. The Windows Desktop Update screen appears.
8. This screen gives you the options of having the user's desktop updated with the Active Desktop components, not having the desktop updated, or letting the user decide. If you selected the silent installation option, the User Select option is not available. If this option is installed, the minimum RAM requirements for the user go up. Select Next to continue.

You have now completed Stage 3 of the IEAK Wizard and this exercise. Do not cancel the wizard. The next exercise continues from this point.

2.4.12 Practice Problems

1. You want to add a custom bitmap for the Active Setup Installation screen, but you get an error message stating that the picture you selected is too large. What are the required dimensions for a custom bitmap for the Active Setup Wizard?

   A. 120×239 (pixels)

   B. 200×120 (pixels)

   C. 256×200 (pixels)

   D. 200×256 (pixels)

2. You want the user to be able to choose whether or not he or she uses the Windows Desktop Update, but the user is not being given the choice, and everyone gets the update. What is the most likely cause of the problem?

   A. You are running in the ISP role.

   B. You are running in the Corporate Administrator role.

   C. On the Integrate the Web Desktop Update screen, you selected Yes rather than User Choice.

   D. You are running in Content Provider mode.

3. Your management team wants all the computers on your network to have Internet Explorer installed in a folder called `Internet`. What is the easiest way to do this?

   A. Select Install in the specified folder within the Windows folder.

   B. From the Specify where you want your browser screen in the IEAK Wizard, select Specify Full Path of Custom Folder and type the path in which you want to install IE 4.0.

   C. Select Install in the specified folder within the Program Files folder.

   D. Give each of the users directions for installing IE 4.0 manually, and explain how to select the installation path.

4. You selected Install Package Silently during Stage 2. What options are available on the Windows Desktop Update screen?

   A. Yes, No, and User Choice

   B. Yes and User Choice

   C. No and User Choice

   D. Yes and No

5. You want to select the Install Package Silently option during Stage 3 of the IEAK Wizard, but it is not available. What is the most likely cause of the problem?

   A. The role you selected in Stage 1 was not Content Provider/Developer.

   B. The role you selected in Stage 1 was not Service Provider.

   C. The role you selected in Stage 1 was not Corporate Administrator.

   D. This option is only available with the IEAK Extra package.

2.4.13 Answers and Explanations: Practice Problems

1. **A** The custom bitmap must be 120×239 (pixels) with up to 256 colors.

2. **C** There are three options for Windows Desktop Update: Yes, No, and User Choice.

3. **B** You can specify the folder in which IE 4.0 will be installed while running the IEAK Wizard.

4. **D** User Choice is not available in silent installation mode because the user is not prompted for any information.

5. **C** You must be running in Corporate Administrator mode to have the silent installation option.

2.4.14 Customizing the Browser

Stage 4 of the configuration process allows you to customize the browser that will be installed on the client computer. The first screen allows you to add a name to the IE 4.0 Web browser and Outlook Express title bars and to provide a custom bitmap for the Web browser's toolbar.

The next several screens allow you to configure the default home page, the default search pane site, and the help page Web site. Then you can configure the default Favorites folders and decide whether you want to enable or disable the IE 4.0 Welcome page.

You then can customize channels and software distribution channels, as described in the following sections. You are then allowed to add one Active Desktop custom component and add a custom user agent string.

The next few screens are used to configure the automatic browser settings and basic proxy server settings. The automatic browser settings let you implement any changes you make to your custom packages automatically without reinstalling the client browser. You should use the Profile Manager to make any of these changes.

You can configure the changes to be implemented on a timed basis; if you leave these fields blank or set them to zero, the client update occurs whenever the client restarts his or her machine.

The final screens are used to configure security and zone information. The first screen in this group is used to configure which Certificate Authorities will be recognized; if Authenticode is enabled, the screens show the source of a program and verify that the program has not been modified. Both these options can be customized.

Channel Customization

Channel customization allows you to configure the channels that will appear on the client's desktop. You can add and delete channels from the channel bar or use the current channel configuration. To delete a channel, right-click the channel you want to delete and select Delete from the menu.

To add a channel, click Launch Channel Guide. Internet Explorer launches and connects you to an Active Channel search page. From the channel search page, you can select from the channels listed or search the Internet for new channels. Each channel provides a suggested update interval. If the client subscribes to the channel, updates occur automatically, based on the information stored in the `.CDF` file for each channel.

You have the option of not customizing the channels, or of importing the current channel and subscription configuration from the computer on which you are running the IEAK.

Software Distribution Channels

Software distribution channels allow you to enable automatic software distribution over your intranet or the Internet. When components such as Internet Explorer are updated, the new version can be placed on a server; users can then get the update, or the update can be "pushed" onto the user's computer.

If you are the corporate administrator, you can set up software distribution channels on your computer and import them into the IEAK Wizard; the changes will be implemented automatically. This can have a negative impact on network performance if all users are obtaining updates at the same time.

2.4.15 Exercise

This exercise takes you through Stage 4 of the IEAK Wizard. This exercise assumes that you did not cancel the IEAK Wizard at the end of the last exercise and are at the Stage 4 introduction screen.

1. Quickly read the *Stage 4: Customizing the Browser* screen and select Next to continue. The title bar and toolbar background customization screen appears.
2. If you want a custom title bar for IE 4.0 on all the computers being deployed, type what you want to appear in the title bar. You can also specify a bitmap for the toolbar background. Click Next to continue. The Start and Search customization screen appears.
3. From this screen, you can set the default home page and search the site for this custom package. After defining the default home page, click the Test URL button to verify that the site is up and active. Click Next to continue.
4. The next screen allows you to configure a custom URL for the Help button. The site you specify appears when the user clicks the Help button. Click Next to continue. The Favorites Customization screen appears.
5. Click the various Web sites and add and test your own URLs. The favorites you configure here will appear on every IE 4.0 computer that uses this custom package for installation. Click Next to continue.
6. From the next screen, you can configure the Welcome screen that appears, or configure a custom Welcome page. You can also disable the Windows Welcome message and set a default bitmap. Click Next to continue.
7. From the next screen, you can customize the channels that will appear in the Active Desktop. Click Launch Channel Guide; Internet Explorer launches a Microsoft channel search page from which you can add and search for channels. Exit IE 4.0. Click Next to continue.
8. The next screen allows you to customize software distribution channels. From this screen, you can select the time interval you want to use for software updates. Click Next to continue.
9. The next screen allows you to configure a custom agent string. Click Next to continue.
10. From the next screen, you can configure the browser for automatic updates using an `.INS` file. If the browser is configured for a proxy server, you can configure a site with `.JS` and `.PAC` files for updates. At the bottom of the page, you can set the time interval used to implement these updates. Click Next to continue.
11. From the next screen, you can enable a proxy server and configure the different protocols to use with specific proxy servers. You can also set certain addresses to bypass the proxy server. Click Next to continue.
12. From the next screen, you can configure Certificate Authorities and Authenticode security. Click Next to continue.

13. The next screen allows you to configure security zones and content ratings. Click Next to continue.

That completes Stage 4 of the configuration process and this exercise. Do not cancel the IEAK Wizard. The last exercise in this chapter starts at the point at which this exercise leaves off.

2.4.16 Practice Problems

1. You want to place a custom title in the title bar of IE 4.0 and add a custom bitmap that appears behind the toolbar. How can you do this?

   A. Configure a custom URL that has the information you want to display, and configure that as the home page for your custom package.

   B. Run the IEAK Wizard in Content Provider role and create a custom Web site in Stage 1 that has the information you want in the title bar.

   C. In Stage 4 of the IEAK Wizard, you can customize the title displayed in IE 4.0. You can also provide a path to a custom bitmap to be displayed behind the toolbar.

   D. This cannot be done from the IEAK Wizard.

2. You have created a custom Web page for users who click the Help button in IE 4.0. The Web page provides the number to your help desk. How can you configure your custom package to point to your custom help page?

   A. In the proxy server settings, set the Help selection to reflect your custom Web site.

   B. Set the search pane URL to point to your custom help Web page.

   C. Set the user's home page to point to your custom Web page.

   D. Set the support page URL to point to your custom site.

3. You do not want your users to see the default Welcome page when IE 4.0 is launched the first time. Where do you configure this in the IEAK Wizard, Stage 4?

   A. The Home Page Configuration screen

   B. The Welcome Message Customization screen

   C. The Support Configuration screen

   D. The Favorites Folder and Links screen

4. It has been requested that you delete the existing IE 4.0 channel configuration and create a custom channel selection for your company. How can you do this?

   A. From the Customize Active Channel Bar screen, select Delete Existing IE 4.0 Channels.

   B. From the Customize Active Channel Bar screen, select Do Not Customize Channels.

   C. Click the Launch Channel Guide button. From IE 4.0, remove the current channels from the channel search Web page.

   D. This cannot be done. By default, certain channels always have to be displayed.

5. You have a Web site that allows users in by reading the user agent string. You have to add a code to the end of the string. How can you do this?

   A. On the User Agent String Customization screen, add your custom string.

   B. From the Software Update Channels screen, select Security Codes and then add your custom string.

   C. On the Active Channel Bar customization screen, add a special access header string.

   D. This cannot be done from the IEAK Wizard.

6. You are deploying Microsoft Internet Explorer 4.0 and have to configure your clients to receive updates to their browser settings without having to reinstall constantly. How can you do this?

A. Select Enable Automatic Browser Configuration; under the autoproxy URL, provide the URL site on which the `.INS` file resides.

B. Select Enable Automatic Browser Configuration; under the autoconfiguration URL, provide the URL site on which the `.JS` or `.PAC` file resides.

C. Select Enable Automatic Browser Configuration; under the autoproxy URL, provide the URL site on which the `.JS` or `.PAC` file resides.

D. Select Enable Automatic Browser Configuration; under the autoconfiguration URL, provide the URL site on which the `.INS` file resides, including the filename for the `.INS` file.

7. You want the updates you configure through the IEAK Profile Manager to occur only when the user restarts the system. How can you do this? Select two answers.

 A. On the Automatic Browser Configuration page, leave the AutoConfig Every option blank.

 B. On the Automatic Browser Configuration page, set the AutoConfig Every option to -1.

 C. On the Automatic Browser Configuration page, set the AutoConfig Every option to Reboot.

 D. On the Automatic Browser Configuration page, set the AutoConfig Every option to zero.

8. You want to add a company information site to all your users' Favorites folder. How can you do this?

 A. From the Favorites Folder and Links Customization screen, click Add Folder and provide the URL to your company information site.

 B. From the Favorites Folder and Links Customization screen, click Add URL and provide the URL to your company information site.

 C. From the Favorites Folder and Links Customization screen, click Import and provide the URL to your company information site.

 D. From the Favorites Folder and Links Customization screen, click Test URL and provide the URL to your company information site.

9. You want all your users to use Lycos to perform searches by default. How can you do this?

 A. On the Customize the Start and Search Pages screen, type the name of the site under Home Page URL.

 B. On the Customize the Start and Search Pages screen, click the Test URL button.

 C. On the Customize the Start and Search Pages screen, type the name of the site under Home Page URL, type Search, and click the Test URL button.

 D. On the Customize the Start and Search Pages screen, type the name of the site under Search Page URL.

10. You are deploying Microsoft Internet Explorer 4.0 and need to configure your non-proxy clients to receive updates without having to reinstall constantly. How can you do this?

 A. Select Enable Automatic Browser Configuration; under Autoproxy URL, provide the URL site on which the `.INS` file resides.

 B. Select Enable Automatic Browser Configuration; under Autoconfiguration URL, provide the URL site on which the `.JS` or `.PAC` file resides.

C. Select Enable Automatic Browser Configuration; under Autoproxy URL, provide the URL site on which the .JS or .PAC file resides.

D. Select Enable Automatic Browser Configuration; under Autoconfiguration URL, provide the URL site on which the .INS file resides.

2.4.17 Answers and Explanations: Practice Problems

1. **C** In Stage 4 of the IEAK Wizard, you can configure custom IE 4.0 title bars and bitmaps for the toolbar.
2. **D** You would configure the support URL to point to your custom information site.
3. **B** The Welcome Screen Customization dialog box allows customization of the Welcome screen and messages.
4. **A** You can delete the current IE 4.0 channel setting by selecting Delete Existing IE 4.0 Channels.
5. **A** User agent string customization can be configured through the IEAK Wizard. The data is appended to the end of the string.
6. **D** Clients can be configured for automatic browser setting updates by specifying a site URL and a file in the Autoconfiguration box.
7. **A, D** By leaving the update interval blank or set to zero, updates occur only at system restart.
8. **B** You would add a URL to a folder. The entry would point to the site desired.
9. **D** To configure the default search page, you would provide the URL in the Search Page dialog box.
10. **D** Non-proxy clients use an .INS file for updates. The Autoconfiguration box points to the location of the .INS file.

2.4.18 Customizing Built-In Components

Stage 5 of the IEAK Wizard allows you to customize the components to be installed. Not all components are configurable, and not all options are available for each role you can select in Stage 1. Here is a list of some of the optional packages that can be configured and system policies that can be set in Stage 5:

- Mail
- LDAP
- Outlook Express
- Chat
- NetMeeting
- Internet settings
- Web desktop
- Subscriptions
- Internet restrictions

The configuration of each of these components is available only if it is included in the custom package being created. During the exercise later in this chapter, you can view the information configured for each of these components.

Outlook Express

If you are using Outlook Express as your mail and news server, you are prompted to provide configuration information. You can leave the fields blank (the user will have to provide the information), or you can specify the information for the user. Here is the information you can provide:

- Type of mail server
- Incoming mail server name
- Outgoing mail server name
- News server

You can also specify whether Outlook Express will be your default mail and new server, and whether Secure Password Authentication (SPA) will be used.

The next screen is used to set Lightweight Directory Access Protocol (LDAP) settings, which are used for Internet mail. You then have the option of using a custom pane along the bottom of the Outlook Express window, and can send an initial Welcome email message that will be at the top of the user's Inbox.

You can also configure a custom signature message that will be appended to the bottom of the user's outgoing email messages. You can set the signature to be appended only to new outgoing messages or to all messages.

NetMeeting

Microsoft NetMeeting allows a user to make audio and video calls and to share data over an intranet or the Internet. The user can transfer files, share applications, and share a whiteboard with others. System policies are used to define the abilities the user will have with each of the abilities listed above. The settings are divided into two main groups: NetMeeting Settings and NetMeeting Protocols. For NetMeeting Protocols you can select the following options:

- Disable TCP/IP
- Disable Null Modem

For NetMeeting Settings, you can configure the following main groups. For each of the groups, you can configure individual settings:

- File Transfer Restrictions
- Application Sharing Restrictions
- Options Dialog Box Restrictions
- Video Usage Restrictions
- Default Directory Server
- Exchange Server Property for NetMeeting Address
- Preset User Information Category
- Set NetMeeting Home Page
- Set Limit for Audio/Video Throughput

Site Subscriptions

By configuring subscription settings in the system policies, you can control the amount of information downloaded with updates and therefore the bandwidth used. Subscription settings allow you to better control the amount of network bandwidth that can be used to support subscriptions. The configuration settings allow you to set maximums for the following options:

- Site Subscription KB
- Channel Subscription KB
- Number of Site Subscriptions
- Minimum Minutes Between Scheduled Updates
- Beginning Time When Updates Will Not Be Allowed
- Ending Time When Updates Will Not Be Allowed
- Maximum Site Subscription Crawl Depth

The site crawl depth allows you to set how many levels down in the site's hierarchical structure you want to go for the update.

2.4.19 Exercise

This exercise takes you through the Stage 5 of the IEAK Wizard. This exercise assumes that you did not cancel the IEAK Wizard at the end of the last exercise and are at the Stage 5 screen.

1. Quickly read the *Stage 5: Component Customization* screen and select Next to continue. Depending on the options selected for this custom package, you may see the screens described in the following steps. If not, click Next to continue through the remainder of this exercise. While navigating through this section of the wizard, look at the various configuration options and the component being configured.
2. If the screen that appears is the Internet Mail and News Server configuration screen, note the options available for configuration. This is one of the screens used to configure Outlook Express. From this screen, you can make Outlook Express the default mail and news client. Click Next to continue.
3. The LDAP configuration screen should appear. From here, you can configure LDAP settings, including authentication type. Click Next to continue.
4. The Outlook Express customization screen should appear. From here, you can configure a custom pane that will appear at the bottom of the Outlook Express screen, and you can set a custom Welcome message that will be placed in the Inbox during setup. Click Next to continue.
5. From the next screen, you can configure a signature message that will be appended to the end of all messages or appended only to new messages. Click Next to continue.
6. The System Policies and Restrictions configuration screen should appear. Open each of the listed services and view the configuration changes you can implement on each service. Become as familiar with these settings as time allows. Click Next to continue.

The configuration portion of the IEAK Wizard is complete. If you click the Finish button at the bottom of the screen, the custom package you configured during the exercises in this chapter will be built. This process will take several minutes and will require enough disk space to store the custom package being assembled.

2.4.20 Practice Problems

1. You want all your users to use Outlook Express as their default mail and news client. How can you configure this?

   A. On the Specify Internet Mail Servers and News Servers screen, make Outlook Express your default mail client and news client.

   B. For the incoming mail server, configure the entry to use IMAP instead of POP3.

   C. For the incoming mail server, type **`Outlook.servername`**, where *`servername`* is your mail server's computer name.

   D. This must be configured at the mail server.

2. What authentication type selections are available for LDAP? Select all correct answers.

   A. Anonymous

   B. Clear Test

   C. Password

   D. Secure Password

3. You have to configure everyone to append the same signature to all new mail messages. How can you do this?

   A. From the Include a Signature screen, select Append the Following Signature to Each News Message.

   B. From the Include a Signature screen, select Append the Following Signature to Each Mail Message.

   C. From the Include a Signature screen, select Append the Following Signature to Each Mail Message, and add the signature.

   D. From the Include a Signature screen, select Append the Following Signature to Each News Message, and add the signature.

4. You want to prevent users from sending files with NetMeeting. How can this be configured?

   A. From the System Policies and Restrictions screen, select Microsoft NetMeeting and then select NetMeeting Protocols. Place a check in the Disable TCP/IP box.

   B. From the System Policies and Restrictions screen, select Microsoft NetMeeting and then select NetMeeting Settings. Place a check in the Prevent User from Sending Files box.

   C. From the System Policies and Restrictions screen, select Microsoft NetMeeting and then select NetMeeting Protocols. Remove the check from the Disable TCP/IP box.

   D. From the System Policies and Restrictions screen, select Microsoft NetMeeting and then select NetMeeting Settings. Place a check in the Prevent User from Receiving Files box.

5. What is the best definition of the site subscription crawl depth?

   A. How many levels down in the site's hierarchical structure you will update.

   B. How many levels up in the site's hierarchical structure you will update.

   C. How many levels across in the site's hierarchical structure you will update.

   D. How many levels down in the site's hierarchical structure you will not update.

2

2.4.21 Answers and Explanations: Practice Problems

1. **A** Select Outlook Express as Your Default Mail and News Server.
2. **A, C, and D** Clear Text is not a listed option.
3. **C** To include a signature on every mail message, select Append the Following to Every Mail Message. If you select this option, something must be typed in the signature box before you can continue.
4. **B** Under NetMeeting Settings, you can disable the user from sending or receiving files.
5. **A** The crawl depth is how many layers down that a site will update.

CHAPTER 3

Configuring and Managing Resource Access

In Chapter 2, "Installation and Configuration," you learned to run the IEAK Wizard and create a custom package of IE 4.0 for deployment. In this chapter, you take a closer look at the Corporate Administrator mode, particularly the security zone settings and proxy server support settings. You also learn to use the Profile Manager to modify settings in a custom package, rather than creating a new custom package.

The certification test topics covered in this chapter are listed here:

- In Corporate Administrator mode, create and assign various levels of security for security zones
- In Corporate Administrator mode, manage proxy server support for custom installations of Internet Explorer 4.0
- Manage automatic configuration by using the IEAK Profile Manager to modify JScript autoproxy
- Manage automatic configuration by using the IEAK Profile Manager to modify `.INS` files
- Manage automatic configuration by using the IEAK Profile Manager to modify `.ADM` files

3.1 Corporate Administrator Mode

Corporate Administrator mode is meant to be used by network administrators for a site, where the network administrator is responsible for implementing corporate policy.

With the IEAK running in Corporate Administrator mode, network administrators can customize the user's copy of Internet Explorer 4.0 to have preset subscriptions to Web sites and channels. Policies for add-on features of IE 4.0, such as Microsoft Chat and NetMeeting, can be configured to adhere to company policy and to not place excessive strain on available network resources.

The network administrator can also configure the user's IE 4.0 to access the Internet through a proxy server, and can set advanced proxy server settings so that the client bypasses the proxy server for intranet sites.

While running in Corporate Administrator mode, the IEAK Wizard doesn't provide the Single Floppy Disk deployment option; it also has no Connection Manager configuration, but it does offer more robust system policy configuration.

System policies allow you to configure the capabilities a user will have to perform a given task (for example, sending or receiving files through the NetMeeting interface). In Corporate Administrator mode, you have much more control over what your users can do than you have in ISP or Content Provider mode. In Corporate Administrator mode, you will notice differences in the wizard configuration options. Some of the more critical differences are listed here:

- No single-floppy installation option
- No Connection Manager configuration
- Windows Desktop Update options (not in ISP mode)
- More robust system policies

3.1.1 Exercise

In this exercise, you run the IEAK Wizard in ISP mode, taking note of the configuration screens available. Then you run the IEAK Wizard in Corporate Administrator mode, comparing and contrasting the differences between the two modes.

This exercise assumes that you have a valid copy of the IEAK and that you ran the exercises defined in Chapter 2.

To run the IEAK Wizard in ISP mode, follow these instructions:

1. From the Start menu, select Programs|Microsoft IEAK and then select IEAK Wizard. This action starts the IEAK Wizard.
2. In the Company field, type your company name. For the customization code, type the license number you received when you registered at the IEAK Web site. The license type you requested determines what roles are available to you. Select the Service Provider role and click Next.
3. Make note of each dialog box available for configuration. Notice that in ISP mode, you can create a single-floppy installation disk. Write down the configurable options available in the System Policies configured in Stage 5.
4. When you have worked through all the configuration screens, ***do not*** click Finish; instead, click Cancel to abort the custom package.

To run the IEAK Wizard in Corporate Administrator mode, follow these instructions:

1. From the Start menu, select Programs|Microsoft IEAK and then select IEAK Wizard. This action starts the IEAK Wizard.
2. In the Company field, type your company name. For the customization code, type the license number you received when you registered at the IEAK Web site. The license type you requested determines what roles are available to you. Select the Corporate Administrator role and click Next.

3. As you work through the configuration process, notice the different dialog boxes available and missing from the IEAK Wizard. Notice that the single-floppy installation media option is not available in Corporate Administrator mode. Pay particular attention to the System Policies items available for configuration.

4. When you have worked through all the configuration screens, ***do not*** click Finish; instead, click Cancel to abort the custom package.

3.1.2 Practice Problems

1. You are running the IEAK Wizard and are trying to create a single floppy disk to use for deployment, but that method is not available. What could the problem be? Select all that apply.

    A. You are running in ISP mode.

    B. You are not running in ISP mode.

    C. You are running in Corporate Administrator mode.

    D. You are running in Content Provider mode.

2. You have been tasked with deploying Internet Explorer 4.0 on all your company's computers. Your company has very stringent security requirements and you need to have as much control over the user's configuration as possible. What mode would you select?

    A. Content Provider

    B. ISP

    C. Corporate Administrator

    D. All modes provide the same configuration options

3. You are running the IEAK Wizard and have the capability of configuring proxy server settings. What mode are you running in?

    A. You are running in ISP mode.

    B. You are running in Corporate Administrator mode.

    C. You are running in Content Provider mode.

    D. The same proxy settings are available in all modes.

4. You are running the IEAK Wizard and must have the ability to create a single floppy for installation. What mode must you be running in?

    A. You must run in ISP mode.

    B. You must run in Corporate Administrator mode.

    C. That option is always available.

    D. You are running in Content Provider mode.

5. You have been tasked with deploying Internet Explorer 4.0 on all your company's computers. You need to be able to configure proxy settings. What mode must you run in?

    A. Content Provider

    B. ISP

    C. Corporate Administrator

    D. All modes provide the same configuration options

3.1.3 Answers and Explanations: Practice Problems

1. **B, C, and D** The only method that provides the single-floppy deployment method is the IPS mode.

2. **C** The Corporate Administrator mode provides the most flexibility in configuring user options.

3. **D** Proxy server settings are available in all IEAK modes.

4. **A** The single-floppy deployment method is available only in ISP mode.

5. **D** Proxy server settings are available in all IEAK modes.

3.2 Zone Security

Zone security is typically configured in Corporate Administrator mode to allow the administrator of an intranet to set security levels. Security zones are configured in Stage 4 of the IEAK and are modified in Stage 5.

As a network administrator, you can use site certificates and Authenticode settings to help secure your local network. With IE 4.0, you can also secure your network by using zone security, which allows you to add sites to different "zones," and to set different levels of capability for each of the zones. The predefined zones available with IE 4.0 are listed here:

- **Internet Zone.** This zone contains all Internet sites by default. The default security level for this zone is medium security.
- **Local Intranet Zone.** This zone is used for all sites that are local to your network, that are included in the list of sites that bypass the proxy server, or that are accessed using a UNC. IE 4.0 considers any site without a period in the name to be local. For example, `http://abc` is local but `http://abc.com` is in the Internet Zone. The default security level for the Local Intranet Zone is medium security.
- **Trusted Site Zone.** This zone is used to add sites considered "trusted" (that is, sites that are allowed to perform tasks on the local computer that could cause damage). The default security level for this zone is low security.
- **Restricted Sites Zone.** This zone is used to add sites that are considered not trustworthy. The default security level for this zone is high security.

You can apply one of three security level settings to each of the zones, or you can use the Custom setting to configure your own security level. The settings available are described here:

- **High (Most Secure).** Content that could corrupt your computer's software is not allowed.
- **Medium.** Content that could corrupt your computer's software is allowed, but you will be warned before proceeding.
- **Low (Least Secure).** Content that could corrupt your computer's software is allowed, and you are not warned.
- **Custom.** This setting allows you to create a security level that suits the needs of your network. When you select this option, the Settings button is activated; click the Settings button to set the levels of security for ActiveX functions, user authentication method, download capability, JavaScript running, and other potentially hazardous functions.

Although you cannot add sites to the Internet Zone, you can add them to the other three zones. This flexibility allows you to configure the capabilities your clients have on their computers when they connect to each site. The settings you can configure in the three security levels or by configuring the custom security are listed in Table 3.2.1.

TABLE 3.2.1 Security Zone Settings

Feature	Low Security	Medium Security	High Security
ActiveX Components			
Download Unsigned ActiveX Controls	Prompt	Disable	Disable
Script ActiveX Controls Marked Safe for Scripting	Enable	Enable	Enable
Initialize and Script ActiveX Controls Not Marked as Safe	Prompt	Prompt	Disable
Download Signed ActiveX Controls	Enable	Prompt	Disable
Run ActiveX Controls and Plug-Ins	Enable	Enable	Disable
User Authentication			
Logon	Automatic logon with current user name and password	Automatic logon only in Intranet Zone	Prompt for user name and password
Downloads			
Font Download	Enable	Enable	Prompt
File Download	Enable	Enable	Disable
Java			
Java Permissions	Low Safety	High Safety	High Safety
Miscellaneous			
Software Channel Permissions	Low Safety	Medium Safety	High Safety
Launching Applications and Files in an IFRAME	Enable	Prompt	Disable
Installation of Desktop Items	Enable	Prompt	Disable
Submit Nonencrypted Form Data	Enable	Prompt	Prompt

Feature	Low Security	Medium Security	High Security
Miscellaneous			
Drag and Drop or Copy and Paste Files	Enable	Enable	Prompt
Scripting			
Scripting of Java Applets	Prompt	Enable	Disable
Active Scripting	Enable	Enable	Enable

The settings listed in Table 3.2.1 are configured during Stage 4 of the IEAK Wizard. Profile Manager can be used to modify and implement changes to the settings after they have been configured in the wizard.

In Stage 5 of the IEAK Wizard, System Policies, you can disable the user's ability to make changes. You can also set the configuration so that the user has the right to change the zone security information on his or her computer.

3.2.2 Exercises

In the first exercise, you will run the IEAK Wizard in Corporate Administrator mode; in Stage 4, you will set zone security information. In the second exercise, you will use the System Policies to verify the user's right to modify security zone information.

To configure zone security, follow these instructions:

1. From the Start menu, select Programs|Microsoft IEAK and then select IEAK Wizard. This action starts the IEAK Wizard.
2. Select Corporate Administrator mode and navigate to Stage 4: Customizing the Browser. Navigate to the Security Zones and Content Ratings dialog box.
3. Select Customize Security Zones settings. This action activates the Modify Settings button. Click the Modify Settings button to open the Security dialog box. Select each of the four preconfigured zones and note the default security level for each. Click the Reset button when you look at the settings for each zone to make sure that you are looking at the default security levels.
4. For the Local Intranet Zone, select the Custom level. This action activates the Settings button. Click the Settings button to open the Security Settings dialog box. Select each of the four security levels and review the settings for each. Click the Reset button for each security level to view the default setting for each. Pay particular attention to the ActiveX settings, the user authentication settings, and the Java settings.
5. Note the various options that can be configured. Click Cancel to return to the Security dialog box. Click Cancel to return to the Security Zones and Content Ratings Customization dialog box in the IEAK Wizard.

To disable the user's right to reconfigure security options, follow these instructions:

1. Continue through the IEAK Wizard until you reach the System Policies and Restrictions dialog box. Click the + sign to the left of the `Internet Restrictions` folder. This action provides access to the contents of the `Internet Restrictions` folder.

2. Click the Security setting. The right pane of the dialog box displays three security level settings. Select the Do Not Allow Users to Add/Delete Sites from a Security Zone option. This action disallows the user from modifying the zone security settings.
3. Click the Help button at the bottom of the screen to open the online help and see further information on system policies and security settings.
4. Close the Help dialog box. Click the Cancel button to exit the IEAK Wizard without saving changes.

This exercise was meant to familiarize you with the settings available for security zones, with the system policies for the security zone, and with the IEAK online help feature. To effectively use this product and pass the certification exam, you must be comfortable with the interface and configuration settings. The security zones provided with IE 4.0 are not compatible with IE 3.02 settings; you must reconfigure the security settings if you are upgrading from IE 3.02.

3.2.3 Practice Problems

1. You are in Corporate Administrator mode configuring a custom package for deployment using the IEAK Wizard. You need to configure the security zone settings so that the user will not be prompted for a user name and password when accessing `http://monkey`, but will be prompted for this information for Internet-based sites. What security level would you use?

   A. High security

   B. Medium security

   C. Low security

   D. This is not configurable through the IEAK Wizard

2. You set the security zones using the IEAK Wizard, but your users can modify the settings you created. How could you have prevented users from changing security zone settings?

   A. In Stage 4 of the IEAK Wizard, select Disable Modifications in the Security Zone dialog box.

   B. In User Manager for Domains, remove the user from the Domain Users global group.

   C. During Stage 3 of the IEAK Wizard, set the browser for Read Only.

   D. During Stage 5 of the IEAK Wizard, set the System Policies for Internet Restrictions, Security, to Do Not Allow Users to Add/Delete Sites from a Security Zone.

3. You need to configure the user authentication so that the user logs on automatically only when accessing an Internet-based site. How can you do this?

   A. During Stage 4 of the IEAK Wizard, Customizing the Browser, set the Zone Security settings to High Security.

   B. During Stage 4 of the IEAK Wizard, Customizing the Browser, set the Zone Security settings to Medium Security.

   C. During Stage 4 of the IEAK Wizard, Customizing the Browser, set the Zone Security settings to Low Security.

   D. Add the user to the Domain Admins global group.

4. There is a site on the Internet that your users access to gather current pricing information for products your company buys on a regular basis. The site runs Java applications and ActiveX controls, but you trust that this site will not damage any of your users' software. To which zone would you add this site to allow the site to function properly on your users' computers?

   A. Internet Zone

   B. Local Intranet Zone

   C. Trusted Sites Zone

   D. Restricted Sites Zone

3.2.4 Answers and Explanations: Practice Problems

1. **B** Medium security allows the user to log on automatically in the Local Intranet Zone.
2. **D** You can allow or disallow the user from changing zone security settings in the System Policy settings during Stage 5 of the IEAK Wizard.
3. **C** The low security level setting allows the user to log on using the current user name and password.
4. **C** By default, the security level for the Trusted Sites Zone is low.

3.3 Proxy Server Support

Proxy server support can be configured in all three operational modes of the IEAK Wizard. A proxy server provides some isolation between your users and the Internet. A proxy server can provide several different capabilities:

- Local caching of Internet objects
- Can act as a "gateway" so that local users need not use the TCP/IP protocol to access the Internet
- Can help limit access to your internal network from the Internet
- Can act as a focal point for Internet access (users gain access to the Internet through the proxy server)
- The client can be configured to use multiple proxy servers

When configuring the proxy server settings available with IE 4.0, you can designate which Internet protocols will use which proxy server, or you can use the same proxy server for all Internet access (see Figure 3.3.1).

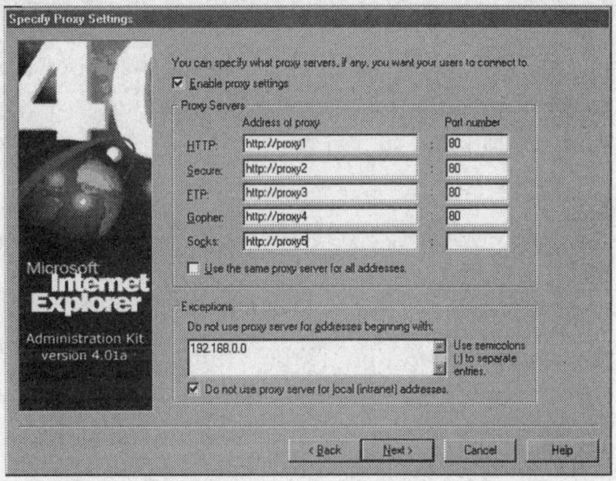

Figure 3.3.1 Configuring proxy server clients.

Following are the Internet protocols that can be directed to various proxy servers:

- HTTP
- Secure (SSL)
- FTP
- Gopher
- Socks

In the Specify Proxy Settings dialog box, under the listed protocols, is a check box. When selected, this option sets all the listed Internet protocols to use the same proxy server. This is one way to achieve load balancing in a multiple proxy server environment. Other ways include creating CNAME resource record entries in DNS, creating multihomed entries in WINS, or configuring a proxy array (if all proxy servers are running Microsoft Proxy Server 2.0).

A Domain Name System (DNS) server resolves host names to IP addresses. DNS entries, also called *resource records*, can be configured with the same host name resolving to multiple IP addresses. When the client requests an IP address for the proxy server host name entered in the Specify Proxy Settings dialog box, the DNS server sends the list of IP addresses that use that host name. The client then attempts to establish communications with the first IP address provided.

DNS uses a round-robin method of providing these IP addresses. When a request is made and a list of IP addresses is provided, the DNS server moves the top entry to the bottom of the list. This approach should balance the distribution of clients evenly across all the proxy servers listed.

A Windows Internet Name Server (WINS) resolves NetBIOS names to IP addresses. To configure load balancing in a multiple proxy server environment with WINS, you would configure a multihomed entry with multiple IP addresses.

The WINS server provides address resolution to the proxy server on the same physical network as the client (if a server is located on the same segment), or on the same network. If a server isn't on the same network, an IP address of one of the listed proxy servers is selected at random.

At the bottom of the Specify Proxy Settings dialog box is a check box that allows you to set exceptions to the proxy server settings. This option allows you to bypass the proxy server for local sites; you can also list specific address ranges the client will bypass the proxy server to access.

3.3.1 Exercise

In this exercise, you will use the IEAK Wizard to configure proxy server settings. This exercise assumes that you have installed the IEAK and received a license number.

To configure the proxy settings through the IEAK Wizard, follow these instructions:

1. From the Start menu, select Programs|Microsoft IEAK and then select IEAK Wizard. This action starts the IEAK Wizard.
2. Enter the Corporate Administrator mode and navigate to Stage 4: Customizing the Browser, accepting the current settings.
3. In the Specify Proxy Settings dialog box, select the Enable Proxy Settings check box. This action activates the Proxy Servers and Exceptions portion of the dialog box.
4. To configure one proxy server for all Internet protocols, select the Use the Same Proxy Server for All Addresses check box. This action grays all protocol entries except the HTTP entry. Enter your proxy server or IP address in the box and accept the default port number.
5. Select the Do Not Use Proxy Server for Local (Intranet) Addresses check box. This action allows the client to access local sites directly.
6. To allow clients to access an address range directly, enter the common portion of the address range in the Exceptions box, using zeros for the octets that include the entire range. For example, if you enter `140.1.0.0`, the client would be able to directly access all hosts that belong on the `140.1` network.
7. Click Cancel to quit the IEAK Wizard without saving your changes.

3.3.2 Practice Problems

1. You have a network with 100 Windows NT 4.0 workstation computers and a proxy server. The proxy server is used to cache Internet sites so that access is quicker. Some of the local NT workstations are running Peer Web Services to provide access to information on their computers. You want the local users to access the local Web sites directly but to access the Internet sites through the proxy server. How would you configure this in the IEAK Wizard? (Select two.)

   A. Place a check in the Enable Proxy Settings box.

   B. Configure a new proxy zone.

   C. Add a second network interface card to each client computer for access to local computers.

   D. Place a check in the Do Not Use Proxy Server for Local (Intranet) Addresses box.

2. You have been using a proxy server with a host name of `proxy` for all Internet traffic, but have decided to route all FTP traffic through a proxy server with a host name of `ftp`. You want all other Internet traffic to use your current proxy server. How would you configure the proxy server settings? (Select all that apply.)

   A. Remove the check in the Use the Same Proxy Server for All Addresses check box.

   B. For the FTP protocol, type **http://FTP**.

   C. For all protocols other than FTP, type **http://proxy**.

   D. For all other protocols, type **http://ftp**.

3.3.3 Answers and Explanations: Practice Problems

1. **A, D** By enabling proxy server settings, clients can access Internet sites through the proxy server. By setting the client to bypass the proxy for local sites, the client can access local sites directly.

2. **A, B, and C** The host name can be used to configure proxy settings, and different proxy servers can be configured for each of the Internet protocols.

3.4 Profile Manager

The Profile Manager is used to modify the files created with the IEAK Wizard. The Profile Manager allows a corporate administrator to reconfigure files so that, if a change must be made to the deployment options, the entire package doesn't have to be reconfigured and deployed.

You can use the IEAK Wizard to configure the user for automatic updates. Doing so allows the corporate administrator to use the IEAK Profile Manager to configure a centrally located `.INS` file; the browser on each client's computer will pick up the changes on a scheduled basis or each time the client's system is restarted. This approach gives the corporate administrator an easy way to update users' browsers as changes are made.

The Profile Manager has a GUI interface for modifying the `.INS` files that contain all the IE 4.0 configuration information. Separate `.INS` files can be created for different groups so that deployment can be customized by the group to which the client belongs.

Another way to automate the process of updating your user's IE 4.0 configuration is to store a master copy of the `.INS` file for a deployment package on a network server; you make any modifications you want to deploy to the master `.INS` file. You can then modify your users' logon scripts to download the updated `.INS` file each time they log on.

3.4.1 Exercise

In this exercise, you will use the Profile Manager to modify the settings selected while running the IEAK Wizard. You will open an existing `.INS` file and modify the settings. This exercise assumes that you have created a custom deployment package.

To run the IEAK Profile Manager, follow these instructions:

1. From the Start menu, select Programs|Microsoft IEAK and then select IEAK Profile Manager. This action starts the IEAK Profile Manager.
2. From the File menu, select Open, then navigate to the custom deployment directory you created using the IEAK Wizard. You should find a file named `Install.INS`. Select the file and click the Open button to load the `Install.INS` file into the Profile Manager GUI. Note that there are two areas you can modify: Wizard Settings and System Policies and Restrictions. Take several moments to look at each option listed in the IEAK Wizard Settings and the System Policies and Restrictions sections.
3. Under Wizard Settings, select Start and Search Page. The right side of the dialog box should display the home page URL and the search page URL.
4. Keeping the IEAK Profile Manager open, run Notepad and open the `Install.INS` file you are viewing with the IEAK Profile Manager. In the `[URL]` section of the file, find the entry for `Home_Page` and verify that the setting in the file matches the setting in the IEAK Profile Manager.
5. In the Profile Manager, configure a new home page. If you are connected to the Internet, click the Test URL button to ensure that you have entered the site name correctly.
6. From the File menu, select Save. You may be prompted to provide the URL path to the `.CAB` files. If so, provide the path and complete the save operation.
7. In Notepad, open the `Install.INS` file again and verify that the `Home_Page` setting has changed.

In this exercise, you used the IEAK Profile Manager to open an existing `.INS` configuration file and modify the settings created with the IEAK Wizard.

3.4.2 Practice Problems

1. Your manager is reviewing the settings you have made with the IEAK Wizard to determine whether the installation will be acceptable. Your manager has determined that the Search button should point to a different search engine. What is the best way to reconfigure this setting and test the site?

   A. Run the IEAK Wizard again and implement the change.

   B. After deploying IE 4.0, send an email to each client explaining how to implement the change.

   C. Edit the `.INS` file manually.

   D. Run the IEAK Profile Manager and make the change to the `.INS` file.

2. You need to quickly view the configuration settings for a custom package you created using the IEAK Wizard. Which file would you view?

   A. `Install.INS`

   B. `Deploy.INS`

   C. `Install.INF`

   D. `Deploy.INF`

3. You are the corporate administrator for a small company with an installed base of 50 Windows 95 computers and 25 Windows NT computers. All your users need Internet access. Your users in the engineering department want to test some of the new features of IE 4.0, but the office management team wants a very stable IE 4.0 environment and has no desire to try the new IE 4.0 features. You want to maintain control of all the IE 4.0 browsers, but you also want to be able to make and implement modifications to the installed browsers for the engineering group while leaving the office management group's deployment the same. You have decided to use the IEAK Wizard to deploy IE 4.0 on all the users' desktops, but don't want to go to each engineering user's desktop and change the configuration every few weeks. How can you automate the update process? (Select two.)

   A. Create an `.INS` file for the engineering group and a second one for the office management group.

   B. Modify all the users' logon scripts to download the new `.INS` file for the group they belong to each time they log on.

   C. Create an `.INF` file for the engineering group and a second one for the office management group.

   D. Add the users to the Power Operators group.

4. At the last minute, you installed a new proxy server you want your users to use for Internet access when you deploy IE 4.0. You have already created the deployment package. What is the best way to reconfigure the proxy server setting in your deployment package?

   A. Run the IEAK Wizard again and change the proxy server settings.

   B. Run the IEAK Profile Manager to make the change to the `.INS` file.

   C. After deploying IE 4.0, send an email to each client explaining how to set proxy server access.

   D. Edit the `.INS` file manually.

3.4.3 Answers and Explanations: Practice Problems

1. **D** You can use the IEAK Profile Manager to make any changes to a custom deployment package. The IEAK Profile Manager can make the necessary modifications to the `.INS` file and allows you to test the URL for the Home Page and Search Page settings.

2. **A** The configuration information is stored in the `Install.INS` file and can be viewed with any text editor.
3. **A, B** You can automate updates by modifying a master copy of the `.INF` file and appending the user's logon script to download the `.INF` file when the user logs on.
4. **B** To modify a deployment package you have already created, use the IEAK Profile Manager.

3.5 Microsoft JScript

Microsoft autoproxy files use JScript as the scripting language. A JScript file can be used to determine which sites will be accessed through the proxy server and which sites will bypass the proxy server. The extensions used on these autoproxy files are `.JS` and `.PAC`. A `.PAC` file is an industry-standard file and extension used for proxy script files.

If you specify a site and file in the autoproxy URL portion of the Automatic Browser Configuration page while running the IEAK Wizard, a JScript (`.JS`) or Proxy Auto-Config (`.PAC`) file can be run against every URL requested by a proxy client. The script determines whether the client will use the proxy server to access the site or bypass the proxy server. The script can also be used to configure proxy server clients to automatically use different proxy servers for different domains.

3.5.1 Exercise

In this exercise, you will configure the browser to use a script file for proxy configuration and set an update interval for autoconfiguration.

To configure the browser for proxy script support, follow these instructions:

1. From the Start menu, select Programs|Microsoft IEAK and then select IEAK Wizard. This action starts the IEAK Wizard.
2. Enter the Corporate Administrator mode and navigate to Stage 4: Customizing the Browser, accepting the current settings.
3. In the Automatic Browser Configuration dialog box, select the Enable Automatic Browser Configuration check box. This action activates the Auto-Configure and Auto-Proxy options for configuration.
4. In the Auto-Proxy URL box, type the URL and filename of the script file you want to use (for example, `http://proxy/proxy.js`). The update interval can be configured in minutes. If you leave the update interval blank or set it to zero, the updates occur when the system is restarted.
5. Click Cancel to abort the IEAK Wizard without saving your changes.

3.5.2 Practice Problems

1. You are preparing to deploy Microsoft Internet Explorer 4.0 on 50 Windows 95 computers that will access the Internet through a proxy server for most sites, but will bypass the proxy server for a list of sites that change daily. The sites are listed in a script file that is updated every night. Your users are forced to log off nightly. How would you configure this arrangement in the IEAK Wizard?

   A. Define the URL and filename under Auto-Proxy URL

   B. Define only the URL under Auto-Proxy URL

   C. Define only the filename of the script

   D. Define the URL and filename under Auto-Configure URL

2. You are preparing to deploy Microsoft Internet Explorer 4.0 on 25 Windows NT Workstation computers that will access the Internet through a proxy server for most sites, but will bypass the proxy server for sites located on the local network. You use a `.PAC` script file to configure the clients' proxy settings. This is a test deployment, and you expect the configuration to change several times a day. How would you configure the settings in the IEAK Wizard to automatically implement updates to the script files hourly?

   A. Configure Auto-Proxy URL with the URL and script filename and have the users restart their computers each hour.

   B. Configure Auto-Proxy URL with the URL and script filename and set Auto-Configure Every to 1.

   C. Configure Auto-Proxy URL with the URL and script filename and set Auto-Configure Every to 60.

   D. Configure Auto-Configure URL with the URL and `.INS` filename and have users restart their computers every hour.

3.5.3 Answers and Explanations: Practice Problems

1. **A** A script file can be used to define domains that will bypass the proxy server. The script file is run each time a user requests a site.

2. **C** By setting the URL and filename for the script file, the client gets the update to the script whenever the system is restarted. By setting the Auto-Configure Every setting to 60, the updates occur every hour (every 60 minutes).

3.6 .*INS* Files

When using the Auto-Configure option, the corporate administrator can create an `.INS` file that contains configuration information for the browser.

The user's browser is configured to obtain the changes made to the `.INS` file on a timed basis or each time the client restarts his or her system. You make these settings in the IEAK Wizard Stage 4: Customizing the Browser, by configuring the information in the Automatic Browser Configuration dialog box.

Custom `.INS` files can be created for different users or groups. To create a custom `.INS` package for a group of users, you use the IEAK Profile Manager to create a new `.INS` file. After configuring the information, save the file and provide an URL site at which you will store the files. When the save is done for the `.INS` file, Cabinet (`.CAB`) files are created for that custom setup. The `.CAB` files contain compressed information (`.INF`) files that are unpacked on the user's system and used by IE 4.0 for configuration purposes.

If an autoproxy file is also specified, that file is incorporated into the `.INS` file and provided to the user. Figure 3.6.1 shows the relationship of the steps in automatic configuration process.

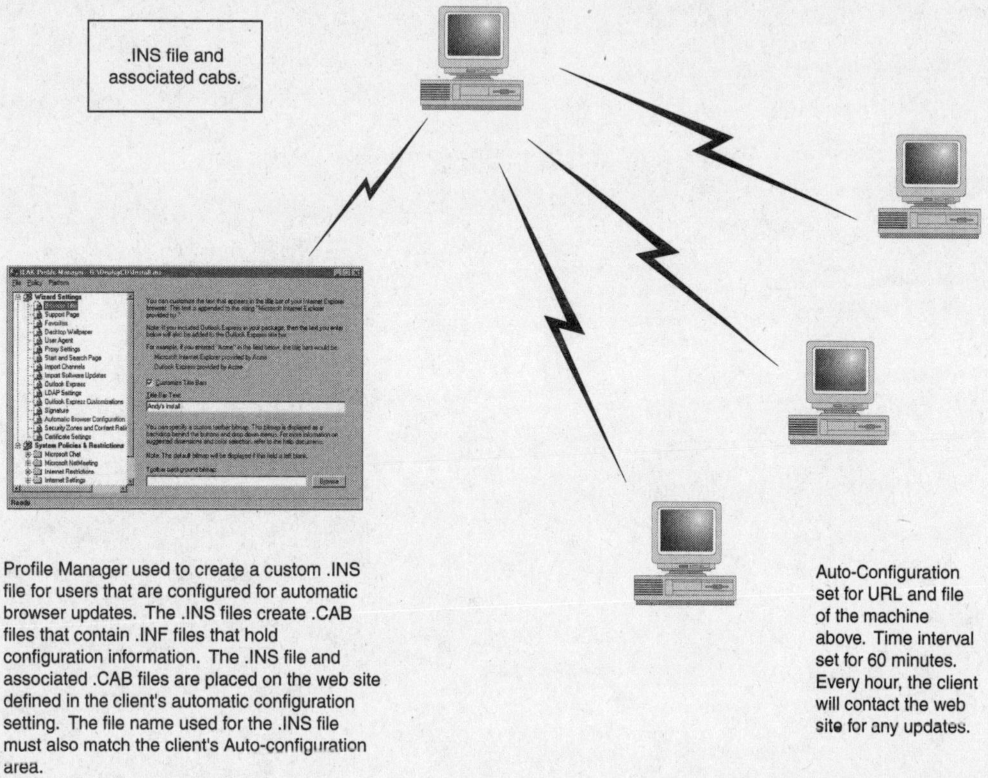

Figure 3.6.1 The automatic browser configuration process.

3.6.1 Exercise

In this exercise, you will use the IEAK Wizard to configure the browser for automatic updates. You will then set the timing for updates at one-hour intervals.

To configure the browser for automatic updates, follow these instructions:

1. From the Start menu, select Programs|Microsoft IEAK and then select IEAK Wizard. This action starts the IEAK Wizard.
2. Enter the Corporate Administrator mode and navigate to Stage 4: Customizing the Browser, accepting the current settings.
3. In the Automatic Browser Configuration dialog box, select the Enable Automatic Browser Configuration check box. This action activates the Auto-Configure and Auto-Proxy options.
4. In the Auto-Configure URL box, type the URL and filename of the `.INS` file you want to use (for example, `http://server1/autoconfig/usersdata.ins`).
5. Specify the update interval the client will use in minutes. If you leave this option blank or set it to zero, the updates occur whenever the system is restarted.
6. Click Cancel to abort the IEAK Wizard without saving your changes.

3.6.2 Practice Problems

1. You are preparing to deploy Microsoft Internet Explorer 4.0 on 50 Windows 95 computers. You want to be able to implement changes to the browser automatically when changes are made. How can you do this?

   A. Enable automatic browser configuration. Provide the filename only for the .INS file.

   B. Enable automatic browser configuration. Provide the URL only for the .INS file.

   C. Enable automatic browser configuration. Provide the URL and filename for the .INF file.

   D. Enable automatic browser configuration. Provide the URL and filename for the .INS file.

2. You are preparing to deploy Microsoft Internet Explorer 4.0 on 100 Windows NT Workstation computers. The deployment is to two different groups. The Engineering group needs a different browser configuration than the Human Resources group. Both configurations will change on a regular basis, and you want to be able to provide automatic updates to each group. How can you do this? (Select two.)

   A. Use the IEAK Profile Manager to create two different .INS files, one for the Engineering group and one for the Human Resources group.

   B. Use the IEAK Wizard to create two custom packages, one for each group, each enabling automatic browser updates. The Engineering group configuration should point to one .INF file, and the Human Resources group configuration should point to a different .INF file.

   C. Use the IEAK Profile Manager to create two different .INF files, one for the Engineering group and one for the Human Resources group.

   D. Use the IEAK Wizard to create two custom packages, one for each group, each enabling automatic browser updates. The Engineering group configuration should point to one .INS file, and the Human Resources group configuration should point to a different .INS file.

3

3.6.3 Answers and Explanations: Practice Problems

1. **D** You would want to enable automatic configuration and then provide the URL and filename for the location of the .INS file.

2. **A, D** You would configure two deployment packages. Both would have automatic browser configuration update enabled. You would configure one group to obtain updates from one .INS file and configure the other group to obtain updates from a different .INS file.

3.7 *.ADM* Files

Policy Template (`.ADM`) files are used to create `.INF` files. The information that can be configured in an `.INF` file is displayed in the IEAK Profile Manager.

You make configuration selections with the IEAK Profile Manager, using the template file as a guide, and then save the configuration in an `.INF` file. The Profile Manager creates nine `.ADM` files when either the IEAK Wizard or the IEAK Profile Manager is run. The files are stored in the IEAK folder in a subfolder named `Profiles`.

Using the IEAK Policy Manager, you can open an `.ADM` template file, create a configuration, and save it. The IEAK Profile Manager creates an `.INF` file and adds it to a `.CAB` file for deployment to the user's browser.

Table 3.7.1 lists the nine `.ADM` files and `.INF` files created by the Profile Manager and gives a brief description of the settings affected by each.

TABLE 3.7.1 `.ADM` and `.INF` Files Created by the Profile Manager

Filenames	Area Affected	Description
`Conf.ADM`	Microsoft NetMeeting	User and computer permissions for the NetMeeting community
`Conf.INF`	Internet Properties	Defines Internet settings for users
`Inetres.ADM`	Internet Code Download	Specifies Internet code download settings
`Inetres.INF`	Channel and Subscriptions	Specifies some of the channel settings
`Oe.ADM` `Oe.INF`	Outlook Express	Specifies policies used to reduce mail and news support costs
`Shell.ADM`	Web Desktop	Limits access to system shell functions
`Shell.INF`	Active Desktop	Limits a user's ability to access, modify, or delete portions of the desktop
`Inetres.ADM` `Inetres.INF`		
`Subs.ADM` `Subs.INF`	Channels and Subscriptions	Specifies policies governing channels and subscriptions
`Chat.ADM` `Chat.INF`	Microsoft Chat	Limits access to Chat features and functions
`Inetset.ADM` `Inetset.INF`	IE Advanced Settings	Specifies and locks settings for IE 4.0 advanced settings

3.7.1 Exercise

When you use the IEAK Profile Manager and set System Policies and Restrictions, the template (.ADM) files are automatically loaded. When you make changes and save the profile, the .INF files are reconfigured and stored in the various .CAB files. Therefore, using the IEAK Profile Manager does not make an effective exercise.

3.7.2 Practice Problems

1. You want to view the IE 4.0 Advanced Settings using a text editor such as Notepad. What file would you view?

    A. `Inetset.INF`

    B. `Inetset.ADM`

    C. `Inetset.INS`

    D. `Inetset.CAB`

2. You want to view the NetMeeting policies for users and computers using a text editor such as Notepad. What file would you view?

    A. `Conf.CAB`

    B. `Conf.INS`

    C. `Conf.INF`

    D. `Conf.ADM`

3. What is the template file used to help define Active Desktop settings and limits?

    A. `Shell.INF`

    B. `Shell.ADM`

    C. `Shell.INS`

    D. `Shell.CAB`

4. Which statement is true of `.CAB` and `.INF` files?

    A. `.CAB` files are stored in `.INF` files for distribution to clients.

    B. `.INF` files are stored in `.CAB` files for distribution to clients.

    C. `.INS` files are stored in `.CAB` files for distribution to clients.

    D. `.INS` files are stored in `.INF` files for distribution to clients.

5. You want to view the Outlook Express settings using a text editor such as Notepad. What file would you view?

    A. `Oe.INS`

    B. `OE.ADM`

    C. `Oe.CAB`

    D. `Oe.INF`

3.7.3 Answers and Explanations: Practice Problems

1. **A** You could use a text editor to view the IE 4.0 Advanced settings, which are stored in the `Inetset.INF` file.

2. **C** NetMeeting configuration information is stored in the `Conf.INF` file.

3. **B** `Shell.ADM` is the template file that stores Active Desktop settings.

4. **B** `.INF` files are organized into `.CAB` files for distribution.

5. **D** Outlook Express settings are stored in the `Oe.INF` file.

Chapter 4

Integration and Distribution

This chapter deals with upgrading clients that already have browsers configured, upgrading clients that already have mail clients configured, configuring and limiting Microsoft NetMeeting, and configuring distribution media.

There are upgrade paths available from Netscape Navigator and previous versions of the Internet Explorer browser. There are also upgrade paths available from most major mail clients. With the IEAK, a number of deployment media are available for distributing your custom packages.

Here are the test objectives covered by this chapter:

- In CA or ISP mode, deploy a preconfigured version of IE 4.0 using floppy disks, CD-ROM, and a download site as the distribution method.
- Replace other browser software, including Microsoft IE 3.x and Netscape Navigator.
- Replace other Internet mail clients, including Internet Mail and News, Netscape Mail, and Eudora.
- Configure NetMeeting for various tasks, including multipoint application sharing, transferring files, and video conferencing.

4.1 Upgrading Browsers

Upgrade paths are available from Internet Explorer 3.x and Netscape Navigator 3.0. Proxy settings, favorites or bookmarks, and cookies will be imported, but plug-ins or add-ins must be reinstalled.

4.1.1 Exercise

This paper-based exercise provides a scenario and then, based on the knowledge you have gained to this point, asks questions that must be answered based on that cumulative knowledge.

Scenario:

You have a network of 100 Windows NT Workstation 4.0 computers running IE 3.01, and 45 Windows 95 computers running Netscape Navigator 3.0. The network has an IIS server that provides company-specific data to the internal network users. A proxy server is also installed, and all users gain Internet access through the proxy server.

It has been decided that your company will standardize on Internet Explorer 4.0 and use Outlook Express for Internet mail and news. You have been tasked with upgrading all users on your network to IE 4.0 and Outlook Express.

Required Result:

- You must upgrade all users to IE 4.0 and Outlook Express.

Desired Optional Results:

- You want to keep all proxy server settings in place.
- You want to import all favorites and bookmarks.
- You want to import all cookies.
- You want to keep all plug-in and add-on capabilities in place.

Proposed Solution:

Create a custom deployment package using the IEAK Wizard and upgrade from the previous version of the browser on the client's desktop.

Questions About the Proposed Solution:

1. Will the proposed solution achieve the desired result of upgrading from previous versions of the browsers your clients are currently using?
2. Will the proposed solution provide the desired result of importing proxy server settings?
3. Will the proposed solution provide the desired result of importing favorites and bookmarks?
4. Will cookies be imported or lost?
5. Will plug-ins and add-ons be imported?

Some kind of scenario-based question always appears on Microsoft certification tests. The purpose of this exercise is to help familiarize you with the wording used with this type of question and to highlight some of the topics that are covered in this chapter. The answer for all the questions is *yes*, with the exception of question 5. Plug-ins and add-ons must be reinstalled or added to the custom optional components that can be installed through the custom deployment package.

4.1.2 Questions

1. You have a network of 100 Windows NT Workstation 4.0 computers running IE 3.01, accessing the Internet through a proxy server. You are configuring a custom deployment package to upgrade all your users to IE 4.0. Can you import current proxy settings?

   A. Yes, proxy settings can be imported from IE 3.01.

   B. No, proxy server settings cannot be imported.

   C. No, proxy server settings can be imported only from IE 2.x browsers.

   D. No, proxy server settings can be imported only from Netscape Navigator 3.0.

2. You have a network of 100 Windows NT Workstation 4.0 computers running IE 3.01, accessing the Internet through a proxy server. You are configuring a custom deployment package to upgrade all your users to IE 4.0. Will current plug-ins that your users have be imported?

   A. Yes, plug-ins will be imported from IE 3.01.

   B. No, plug-ins are not imported.

   C. No, plug-ins can be imported only from IE 2.x browsers.

   D. No, add-ons can be imported only from Netscape Navigator 3.01.

3. You have a network of 100 Windows NT Workstation 4.0 computers running IE 3.01, accessing the Internet through a proxy server. You are configuring a custom deployment package to upgrade all your users to IE 4.0. You want your user's favorites to be imported in to IE 4.0. Will your user's favorites be preserved?

   A. No, favorites settings cannot be imported from IE 3.01.

   B. No, favorites settings can be imported only from IE 2.x browsers.

   C. No, bookmark settings can be imported only from Netscape Navigator 3.0.

   D. Yes, favorites will be preserved from IE 3.01.

4.1.3 Answers

1. **A** Proxy server settings are preserved when upgrading from IE 3.x and Netscape Navigator 3.0.
2. **B** No, plug-ins have to be reinstalled.
3. **D** Yes, favorites from IE 3.x and bookmarks from Netscape Navigator are imported into the new IE 4.0 favorites area.

4

4.1.4 Internet Explorer 3.x

An upgrade path is available from Internet Explorer 3.x to Internet Explorer 4.x. The items that are imported into the new version of IE 4.0 are as follows:

- Cookies
- Favorites
- Proxy server settings

The only items that are not imported into IE 4.0 are plug-ins. These must be reinstalled and configured for installation in the custom deployment package you create, or the plug-ins will not work. Before installing a plug-in, make sure that it is compatible with Internet Explorer 4.0.

Internet Explorer 3.x and Internet Explorer 4.x cannot both be installed when running Windows 95 or Windows NT. Only IE 3.x or IE 4.x can be installed. If you need both Internet Explorer 3.x and Internet Explorer 4.x installed on the same computer, the computer must be configured for dual-boot—where one copy of the operating system is running IE 3.x, and the other copy of the operating system is running IE 4.x.

4.1.5 Exercise

This exercise assumes that you have a computer running Internet Explorer 3.x (Computer1 for this exercise), configured to access the Internet through a proxy server, and a download server (Computer2 for this exercise) for deploying Internet Explorer 4.0 custom packages.

1. From Computer1, verify that Internet Explorer 3.x is running and is configured to access the Internet through a proxy server.
2. From Computer2, run the IEAK Wizard and create a custom package. Do not configure proxy server settings in the custom package.
3. From Computer1, connect to the download site created on Computer2. Start the IE 4.0 installation process. When the installation is complete, you are prompted to reboot. Reboot Computer1.
4. From Computer1, right-click the Internet Explorer icon located on the desktop. Select Properties from the menu. Verify that the proxy server configuration was migrated from IE 3.x.

This exercise shows the end result when a user upgrades from Internet Explorer 3.x to Internet Explorer 4.0, and that the proxy server configuration is imported from IE 3.x.

4.1.6 Questions

1. You have a network of 100 Windows NT Workstation 4.0 computers running IE 3.01, accessing the Internet through a proxy server. You are configuring a custom deployment package to upgrade all your users to IE 4.0. Can you import current proxy settings as part of the upgrade process?

   A. Yes, proxy settings can be imported from IE 3.01.

   B. No, proxy server settings cannot be imported.

   C. No, proxy server settings can be imported only from IE 2.x browsers and earlier.

   D. No, proxy server settings can be imported only from Netscape Navigator 3.0.

2. You have a network of 100 Windows NT Workstation 4.0 computers running IE 3.01, accessing the Internet through a proxy server. You are configuring a custom deployment package to upgrade all your users to IE 4.0. Can you import a user's Favorites folder?

   A. No, favorites information cannot be imported.

   B. No, favorites information can be imported only from IE 2.x browsers.

   C. Yes, favorites information can be imported from IE 3.01.

   D. No, favorites information (Bookmarks in Netscape Navigator) can be imported only from Netscape Navigator 3.0.

3. You have a network of 100 Windows NT Workstation 4.0 computers running IE 3.01, accessing the Internet through a proxy server. There is also an IIS server on your intranet that users connect to for company confidential information. A cookie is used to help keep track of how often users are connecting to the site. You are configuring a custom deployment package to upgrade all your users to IE 4.0. Will the user's cookies be imported when the user upgrades to IE 4.0?

   A. No, cookies cannot be imported.

   B. No, cookies are imported only from IE 2.x browsers.

   C. No, cookies are imported only from Netscape Navigator 3.0.

   D. Yes, cookies are imported from the IE 3.x configuration.

4. You have a network of 100 Windows NT Workstation 4.0 computers running IE 3.01, accessing the Internet through a proxy server. You are configuring a custom deployment package to upgrade all your users to IE 4.0. You want to configure all new plug-ins for use with the new deployment and don't want any other plug-ins from the previous version of Internet Explorer imported. What must be done?

   A. A script file must be run by each user before the upgrade is run to uninstall the plug-ins.

   B. Nothing. Plug-ins are not imported when an upgrade is performed.

   C. Select the Do Not Import Plug-ins option when creating the custom package.

   D. Nothing. Plug-ins are imported. You then have to go to each user and uninstall the plug-ins after the upgrade is complete.

4.1.7 Answers

1. **A** Proxy server settings can be imported from Internet Explorer 3.x browsers.

2. **C** Favorites information is imported when IE 3.x browsers are upgraded to IE 4.0.

4

3. **D** Cookies are imported when an upgrade from IE 3.x to IE 4.0 occurs.

4. **B** Plug-ins are not imported from IE 3.x browsers. You must reinstall the plug-ins after the upgrade is performed.

4.1.8 Netscape Navigator

Users running Netscape Navigator can be upgraded to Windows Internet Explorer 4.0. The information imported includes the following:

- Bookmarks (similar to favorites in Internet Explorer)
- Cookies
- Proxy server settings

As with upgrading from Internet Explorer 3.x, plug-ins must be reinstalled to work. Not all plug-ins are compatible with IE 4.0. Before installing plug-ins, always make sure that the plug-ins are compatible with IE 4.0.

Unlike Internet Explorer 3.x, Netscape Navigator can coexist with Microsoft Internet Explorer 4.0. When Internet Explorer 4.0 is installed, it is configured as the default Web browser, but it does not uninstall Netscape Navigator 3.0.

4.1.9 Exercise

In this exercise, you will import bookmarks from Netscape Navigator to Internet Explorer 4.0 when performing a deployment.

This exercise assumes that you have a computer running Netscape Navigator 3.0 (Computer1 for this exercise), configured to access the Internet through a proxy server, and a download server (Computer2 for this exercise) for deploying Internet Explorer 4.0 custom packages.

1. From Computer1, verify that Netscape Navigator 3.0 is installed and operational. Create several bookmarks and at least one new folder, placing several bookmarks in the new folder.
2. From Computer2, verify that you have a valid custom package ready for use. Use the Profile Manager to modify the ActiveX installation title to reflect the Netscape upgrade.
3. From Computer1, connect to the download site created on Computer2. Start the IE 4.0 installation process. When the installation is complete, you are prompted to reboot. Reboot Computer1.
4. From Computer1, open the new installation of Internet Explorer 4.0. View the Favorites folders and verify that the bookmarks from Netscape Navigator were imported into the new version of Internet Explorer 4.0.

In this exercise, you verified that when upgrading from Netscape Navigator to Internet Explorer 4.0, favorites information was preserved.

4.1.10 Questions

1. You have a network of 40 Windows NT Workstation 4.0 computers running Netscape Navigator 3.0, and want only the plug-ins configured with your custom deployment to be used. What must be done?

   A. A script file must be run by each user before the upgrade is run to uninstall the plug-ins.

   B. Nothing. Plug-ins are not imported when an upgrade is performed.

   C. Select the Do Not Import Plug-ins option when creating the custom package.

   D. Nothing. Plug-ins are imported. You then have to go to each user and uninstall the plug-ins after the upgrade is complete.

2. You have a network of 35 Windows 95 computers running Netscape Navigator 3.0, accessing the Internet through a proxy server. You are configuring a custom deployment package to upgrade all your users to IE 4.0. How would you save a user's bookmarks?

   A. Save all the bookmark information before deploying Internet Explorer 4.0 and then import the bookmarks after the deployment is complete.

   B. Upgrade from Netscape Navigator 3.0 to Internet Explorer 3.01, then upgrade from IE 3.01 to IE 4.0.

   C. Nothing. Bookmarks are incompatible with IE 4.0 favorites.

   D. Nothing. The upgrade imports the bookmarks from Netscape Navigator 3.0.

3. You have a network of 60 Windows 95 computers running Netscape Navigator 3.0, accessing the Internet through a proxy server. You are configuring a custom deployment package to upgrade all your users to IE 4.0. Can you import current proxy settings as part of the upgrade process?

   A. No, proxy server settings can be imported only from IE 2.x browsers and earlier.

   B. No, proxy server settings can be imported only from IE 3.x and newer browsers.

   C. Yes, proxy settings can be imported from Netscape Navigator 3.0.

   D. No, proxy server settings cannot be imported from any browser.

4. You have a network of 40 Windows 95 computers running Netscape Navigator 3.0, and 25 computers running Windows NT Workstation 4.0. All the computers use a proxy server to access the Internet. There is also an IIS server on your intranet that users connect to for company confidential information. Cookies are used to help keep track of how often users are connecting to the site, and what Web pages are being accessed. You are configuring a custom deployment package to upgrade all your users to IE 4.0. Will the user's cookies be imported when the user upgrades to IE 4.0?

   A. No, cookies cannot be imported.

   B. No, cookies are imported only from IE 2.x browsers.

   C. Yes, cookies are imported from Netscape Navigator 3.0 browser when an upgrade is performed.

   D. No, cookies are imported from the IE 3.x configuration only.

4.1.11 Answers

1. **B** Plug-ins are not imported from IE 3.x or Netscape Navigator.

2. **D** Netscape Navigator bookmarks are imported into the IE 4.0 Favorites folders.

3. **C** Proxy server settings are imported when an upgrade is performed from IE 3.x or Netscape Navigator browsers to IE 4.0.

4. **C** Cookies are imported from Netscape Navigator 3.0 and IE 3.x browsers when an upgrade to IE 4.0 is performed.

4.2 Upgrading Mail Support

Internet mail support configuration through the IEAK Wizard is flexible. Internet Explorer 4.0 can be configured to work with existing Internet email and news applications. Alternatively, during deployment, an upgrade to Outlook Express can be performed. Information that can be imported for Outlook Express includes the following:

- Messages from any folder
- Address book entries
- Mail account settings

During the upgrade process to IE 4.0, the custom deployment package can update the user to Outlook Express as the default Internet mail and news client. In addition, upgrade paths are available from these industry-standard mail and news readers:

- Eudora Light (up to version 3.0)
- Eudora Pro (up to version 3.0)
- Netscape Mail (version 2.0 or 3.0)
- Netscape Communicator
- Microsoft Exchange Client
- Microsoft Mail and News
- Microsoft Windows Messaging
- Microsoft Outlook

During the build of the IEAK custom deployment package, you can specify Outlook Express settings and can set Outlook Express as the default mail and news client. The information you can configure when building a custom deployment package with the IEAK Wizard includes the following:

- Internet mail servers, domain servers, and news servers
- Configure Outlook Express as the default Internet mail and news client
- Specify Secure Password Authentication (SPA) to authenticate users as they log on
- Configure Lightweight Directory Access Protocol (LDAP) settings
- Specify infopane and welcome message for Outlook Express
- Configure default signature files for email and news messages

The infopane is a one-inch window located at the bottom of the Outlook Express window that can be customized to display an HTML file. When configuring the mail server, the POP3 mail server (shown in Figure 4.2.1) should be configured using a Fully Qualified Domain Name (FQDN)—for example, `mail.server.com`.

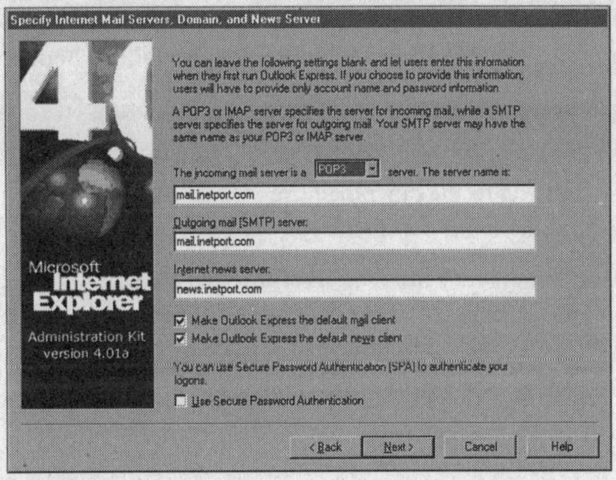

Figure 4.2.1 Outlook Express POP3 configuration.

4

4.2.1 Internet Mail and News

An upgrade path is available from Microsoft Internet Mail and News. The information imported into Outlook Express includes mail account settings, address book entries, and messages contained in folders. This information can also be imported to Outlook Express after the installation is complete. The user can also do this manually.

4.2.2 Netscape Mail

Netscape Mail messages, address book entries, and account configuration information can be imported into Outlook Express. Information can be imported from Netscape Mail (versions 2.0 and 3.0) and from Netscape Communicator.

Netscape Mail and Outlook Express can both be configured on the same computer, but only one can be used as the default news and mail client.

4.2.3 Eudora

Outlook Express can import mail messages, user configuration information, and address books from Eudora Light (up through version 3.0) and Eudora Pro (up through version 3.0).

If Eudora Light or Pro is configured as the default mail and news reader, the IEAK custom deployment package can be configured to set Outlook Express as the default Internet mail and news client, just as it can for the other listed mail and news clients.

4.2.4 Exercise

In this exercise, you will configure Outlook Express to be the default Internet mail and news client. You will import the address book, email messages, and user account configuration information from Netscape Communicator.

This exercise assumes that you have a computer running Netscape Communicator (Computer1 for this exercise), configured to use the Netscape Communicator as the default mail and news client, and a download server (Computer2 for this exercise) for deploying Internet Explorer 4.0 custom packages.

1. From Computer1, verify that Netscape Communicator is installed and operational. Verify that some mail messages are present. Add a test address to the address book for the mail client.
2. From Computer2, create a custom deployment package. During Stage 5 of the installation, Customizing Components, configure Outlook Express as the default mail and news client.
3. From Computer1, connect to the download site created on Computer2. Start the IE 4.0 installation process. When the installation is complete, you are prompted to reboot. Reboot Computer1.
4. From Computer1, open the new installation of Internet Explorer 4.0. Open Outlook Express and verify that the mail messages and address book were imported into Outlook Express.
5. From the Tools menu, select Accounts. Select the News tab and then click Properties. Review the information and ensure that the settings from Netscape Communicator were imported correctly. Verify that the mail server configuration imported correctly.

In this exercise, you deployed Internet Explorer 4.0 and Outlook Express. You imported address book and mail messages from Netscape Communicator and set up Outlook Express as the default mail and news server.

4.2.5 Questions

1. Your company has a network of 40 Windows NT Workstation 4.0 computers running Netscape Navigator 3.0. You will be using the IEAK Wizard to create a custom deployment package and want all your users to use Outlook Express for email. The company wants a signature appended to the end of each email message your users send. How do you configure this in the IEAK Wizard?

   A. A script file must be run by each user to configure the signature portion of Outlook Express.

   B. Nothing. The signature cannot be configured using the IEAK Wizard.

   C. In the Include a Signature dialog box, select the Append the Following Signature to Every Mail Message option and enter the text to append to the end of each mail message.

   D. In the Include a Signature dialog box, select the Use Mail Signature Also as News Signature option.

2. You have a network of 40 Windows NT Workstation 4.0 computers running IE 3.x and using Internet Mail and News as the email program. What information can be imported into Outlook Express? (Select all that apply.)

   A. Mail account settings

   B. Any deleted messages that have been purged

   C. Address book entries

   D. Email messages

3. You are upgrading from Eudora Pro to Outlook Express, and want to create a custom welcome and help message that provides the help desk's extension number to appear in the bottom of the Outlook Express window. How would you do this?

   A. Use the infopane feature to display a one-inch pane at the bottom of the Outlook Express window with the help desk's phone number.

   B. Create a custom toolbar bitmap with the help desk's phone number.

   C. Turn on the Tip of the Day feature and create a custom tip with the help desk's phone number.

   D. Nothing. This cannot be done.

4. You want to configure your users to use Secure Password Authentication to log on to your local mail server. How can you do this? (Select the best answer.)

   A. Enter each user's user name and password during the installation of Outlook Express.

   B. Select Use Secure Password Authentication when configuring the Internet Mail Services in your custom deployment package.

   C. Select Encrypted User Authentication. Have the user provide his or her user name and password when prompted.

   D. After the custom package is deployed, go to each user's computer and configure it for Secure Password Authentication.

5. You are configuring Outlook Express using the IEAK Wizard. All your users will use a computer named `Mail`, which is part of the `Company.com` domain. When configuring the POP3 entry, what would you put for the mail server name?

   A. `Company.com.Mail`

   B. `Company.com`

   C. `Mail`

   D. `Mail.Company.com`

4

6. You have a network of 40 Windows NT Workstation 4.0 computers running Netscape Communicator and want to configure Outlook Express to be the default mail and news client. How can you do this? (Select two.)

   A. While creating the custom deployment package, select Make Outlook Express the Default Mail and News Client.

   B. Do nothing. Outlook Express automatically becomes the default mail and news client.

   C. While creating the custom deployment package, select Make Outlook Express the Default Mail Client.

   D. While creating the custom deployment package, select Make Outlook Express the Default News Client.

7. You are upgrading from Internet Mail and News to Outlook Express and want to add a custom welcome and help message that provides the help desk's extension number to the bottom of the Outlook Express window. How could you do this?

   A. Create a custom toolbar bitmap with the help desk's phone number.

   B. Turn on the Tip of the Day feature and create a custom tip with the help desk's phone number.

   C. Use the infopane feature to display a one-inch pane at the bottom of the Outlook Express window with the help desk's phone number.

   D. Do nothing. This is done automatically. You will be prompted to provide the phone number for the help desk as part of the configuration process.

8. You have a network of 40 Windows NT Workstation 4.0 computers running IE 3.x and using Eudora Light as the email program. You are preparing to deploy IE 4.0 and want to make Outlook Express the default mail and news client. Your users are concerned that they will lose all their mail messages and address entries. What information will be imported into Outlook Express? (Select all that apply.)

   A. Address book entries

   B. Email messages

   C. Mail account settings

   D. Any unread email messages

9. A user calls, wanting to configure his or her POP3 mail server information. Your mail server is named `Mail`, which is part of the `Company.com` domain. What would you tell the user to put for the mail server name?

   A. `Mail.Company.com`

   B. `Company.com.Mail`

   C. `Company.com`

   D. `Mail`

10. Your company has a network of 40 Windows NT Workstation 4.0 computers running Internet Explorer 3.01. You will be using the IEAK Wizard to create a custom deployment package and want all your users to use Outlook Express as the email and news client. The company wants a signature that has the company name and slogan appended to the end of each email and news message your users send. How do you configure this in the IEAK Wizard? (Select two.)

    A. In the Include a Signature dialog box, select the Append the Following Signature to Every Mail Message option, and enter the text to append to the end of each mail message.

    B. In the Include a Signature dialog box, select the Use Mail Signature Also as News Signature option.

C. A script file must be run by each user to configure the signature portion of Outlook Express.

D. Do nothing. The signature information is automatically configured for you.

4.2.6 Answers

1. **C** You can configure a signature file to append to every mail message sent.
2. **A, C, and D** The information that can be imported to Outlook Express includes mail settings, address book entries, and all mail messages.
3. **A** The infopane option provides the ability to create a one-inch pane at the bottom of the Outlook Express window.
4. **B** Selecting SPA forces users to provide a valid user name and password.
5. **D** The POP3 setting uses the FQDN to define the mail server.
6. **C, D** Options are available to make Outlook Express the default mail client and the default news client.
7. **C** The infopane option provides the ability to create a one-inch pane at the bottom of the Outlook Express window.
8. **A, B, C, and D** The information that can be imported to Outlook Express includes mail settings, address book entries, and all mail messages.
9. **A** The POP3 setting uses the FQDN to define the mail server.
10. **A, B** Options are available to customize the look of Outlook Express through the IEAK.

4.3 Configuring NetMeeting

The Microsoft NetMeeting application can be used to help support the corporate communications environment by providing audio, video, and data conferencing and collaboration utilities.

If the necessary hardware is available (sound cards and video cameras), audio and video conferences can take place across the network or Internet.

The text-based chat and whiteboard utilities that are an integral part of NetMeeting allow collaborative communications to take place and data files to be transferred among different users. By enabling the Collaborate option, users can share applications such as Microsoft Word and Excel.

The Profile Manager can be used to limit the bandwidth that NetMeeting is allowed to use.

With NetMeeting settings, you can do the following:

- Prevent the user from sending files
- Prevent the user from receiving files
- Disable all application sharing features
- Prevent the user from sharing the Clipboard
- Prevent the user from sharing MS-DOS windows
- Prevent the user from sharing Explorer windows
- Prevent the user from collaborating
- Disable the General, My Information, Calling, Audio, Video, and Protocols option pages
- Prevent the user from answering calls
- Prevent the user from using audio features
- Prevent the user from sending video
- Prevent the user from receiving video
- Prevent the user from using directory services
- Set the default Directory Server
- Set the Exchange Server properties for NetMeeting
- Set the NetMeeting home page
- Limit the audio and video throughput (bps)
- Enable the TCP/IP protocol for NetMeeting
- Preset user information

As you can see, you can use a lot of configuration options to limit user functionality and to limit network resource usage.

4.3.1 Exercise

In this exercise, you will use the IEAK Profile Manager to configure NetMeeting settings. This exercise assumes that you have already run the IEAK Wizard and have a valid custom deployment package created.

1. From the computer on which the IEAK is installed, open the IEAK Profile Manager. From the File menu, select Open, and provide the path to your custom deployment package. The file you will be modifying is named `Install.INS`.
2. When the file opens, click System Policies and Restrictions, located halfway down the left pane of the Profile Manager window. The right pane of the window provides a brief explanation of how to set System Policies and Restrictions.
3. In the left pane, expand the hierarchical structure and select Microsoft NetMeeting. The right pane of the window provides a brief explanation of NetMeeting configuration options.
4. In the left pane, expand the hierarchical structure and select NetMeeting Settings. The right pane displays a list of configuration settings. Review the various settings available.
5. When you are comfortable with the information that can be configured, close the IEAK Profile Manager by selecting Exit from the File menu.

In this exercise, you used the IEAK Profile Manager to view and configure NetMeeting settings. The knowledge you should have gained from this exercise includes the filename you edited using the IEAK Profile Manager and the NetMeeting settings that can be configured.

4.3.2 Multipoint Application Sharing

Multipoint application sharing encompasses using the text-based Chat and Whiteboard utilities, sharing the Clipboard, transferring files, and sharing Microsoft Windows-based applications that support collaboration. Some of these utilities can pose security risks—as well as use large amounts of bandwidth—and should therefore be monitored carefully for estimated resource use. To access the Chat and Whiteboard utilities shown in Figure 4.3.1, follow these steps:

1. Open Internet Explorer 4.0.
2. From the Go menu, select the Internet Call option. This action opens NetMeeting.
3. From the Tools menu, select Chat, Whiteboard, Share or File Transfer.

The Microsoft certification test for IEAK does not cover the actual use of these programs. However, it does cover the configuration of these utilities, and the effects these utilities can have on available resource usage. If you have not made yourself familiar with these utilities and configuration options, it is well worth your time to do so. Note that the sharing option must be enabled before these options can be used.

4.3.3 Transferring Files

Transferring files can be accomplished through the NetMeeting utilities. Files can be transferred in the background during a conference.

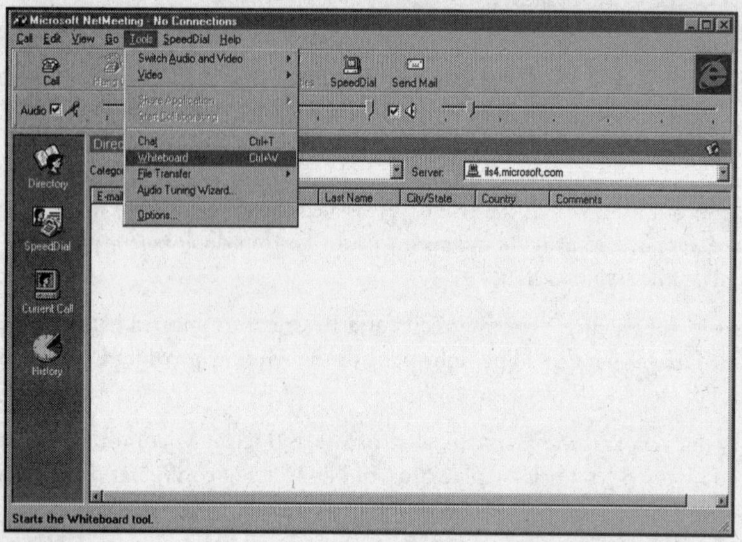

Figure 4.3.1 Accessing the Chat and Whiteboard utilities in NetMeeting.

The ability of users to transfer files can be limited during Stage 5 of the IEAK Wizard, Configuring Components, or by using the IEAK Profile Manager.

By configuring the users' ability to transfer files with the NetMeeting utility, you can limit the use of available network bandwidth and help secure your network by limiting the users that can transfer files using NetMeeting.

4.3.4 Exercise

In this exercise, you will start NetMeeting on two computers and use the Chat and Whiteboard utilities, and collaboration and file transfer features to manipulate data.

This exercise assumes that you have two computers (Computer1 and Computer2) running IE 4.0 with the NetMeeting optional components installed, both located on the same network and using TCP/IP for communications.

1. After verifying simple TCP/IP communications by using the IP configuration utilities (`IPCONFIG` for Windows NT, `WINIPCFG` for Windows 95, and `IPCONFIG` for Windows 98) and the Ping utility, start Internet Explorer 4.0 on both computers.
2. From the Go menu, select Internet Call. This should start NetMeeting (assuming that NetMeeting is installed) on both computers.
3. In the toolbar on Computer1, click the Call icon. A New Call dialog box appears. Under Address, type the IP address of Computer2 and then click the Call button. You should see the call being placed and Computer2 should receive a notice of a call pending. Accept the call on Computer2.
4. On Computer1, click the Current Call icon. Computer2 should be listed. In the toolbar, click the Chat icon. A Chat dialog box opens. Note that the Chat utility also opened on Computer2. On Computer1, type a message and press Enter. The message should appear on the shared windows on both computers.

5. In the toolbar on Computer1, click the Whiteboard icon. This action opens the Whiteboard utility on both computers. Draw a line first on Computer1, then on Computer2. Note that the graphic information is displayed on both computers.

6. If available, start the WordPad editor applet on Computer1. In the toolbar on Computer1, click the Share icon. WordPad should be listed. Select WordPad from the listing. A dialog box may appear informing you that you are about to share an application but that the other members of the conference will not be able to use your application. Click OK. The Call dialog box should indicate that you are sharing, but not collaborating.

7. In the toolbar on Computer1, click the Collaborate icon. You should see a dialog box stating that you are about to allow others to use your application. Click OK. From Computer1, type anything into WordPad. Note that the data appears on Computer2's WordPad window. On Computer2, type something in the shared WordPad dialog box. Note that it appears in Computer1's WordPad window.

8. On Computer1, from the NetMeeting dialog box, select Tools|File Transfer|Send File. This action opens a browse dialog box. Select any text file and click the Send button. You should receive confirmation that the file was sent.

9. On Computer2, you should see a dialog box stating that one file was received. You have the option to close the window, open the file, or delete the file.

10. On both computers, close all open NetMeeting utilities.

In this exercise, you learned to use the NetMeeting conference utilities to transfer files, chat, draw a picture using the whiteboard, and enable the collaboration feature to share the WordPad applet.

4.3.5 Video Conferencing

Video conferencing can be accomplished between two computers with some form of video capture equipment—be it an 8mm camcorder and video capture card, or a video conference camera. If only one of the computers has a video camera, the other computer can still receive the video feed but (as expected) cannot send video.

The bandwidth required for video conferencing might be prohibitive for your network, so it is advisable to test the bandwidth used in a lab environment before attempting a full-scale deployment.

The IEAK Profile Manager can be used to limit a user's ability to send or receive video. A setting is also available to limit the total bandwidth (in bps) a computer can use for audio and video communication in the NetMeeting utilities. Settings are available to balance video update performance with quality of picture.

4.3.6 Questions

1. You are configuring NetMeeting on your local network and want to limit the user's ability to send and receive files. Is this possible? (Select the best answer.)
   A. Yes, you can limit a user's collaboration ability.
   B. Yes, you can limit the user's ability to send files or receive files.
   C. No, you can only limit the user's ability to receive files.
   D. No, you can only limit the user's ability to send files.

2. You are configuring NetMeeting on your local network and want to limit the amount of bandwidth that will be used for audio and video communications. How could you do this?
   A. Configure the Set Limit for Audio/Video Throughput setting.
   B. Configure the Preset User Information Category.
   C. Configure the Restrict the Use of Video/Bandwidth setting.
   D. Configure the Restrict the Use of Audio/Bandwidth setting.

3. You want to disable the user's ability to share applications. How can you do this? (Select the best answer.)
   A. Disable NetMeeting on the user's computer.
   B. In User Manager for Domains, remove the user from the Collaborative local group.
   C. Under Restrict the Use of File Transfer, select Prevent User from Receiving Files.
   D. Under Restrict the Use of Application Sharing, select Disable All Application Sharing Features.

4. You want to review the setting you used when creating a custom deployment package. How can you do this? (Select the best answer.)
   A. Use the System Policy Editor to view the `Install.INS` file for the custom deployment package.
   B. Run a test deployment and view the settings.
   C. Use the IEAK Profile Manager to view the `Install.INS` file for the custom deployment package.
   D. Use the IEAK Profile Manager to view the `Install.INF` file for the custom deployment package.

5. You want to disable the user's ability to change the My Information options you configured before deploying IE 4.0 with the NetMeeting components. How would you do this?
   A. Under Restrict the Use of the Options Dialog, select Disable the 'My Information' Options Page.
   B. Under Restrict the Use of the Options Dialog, select Disable the 'General' Options Page.
   C. Set the default directory server to a domain controller and remove the user from the Collaborative local group.
   D. Set the directory server and member server, then remove the user from the Power Users group.

6. You want to allow the user to share applications but want to disable the user's ability to collaborate. How can you do this? (Select the best answer.)
   A. Disable NetMeeting on the user's computer.
   B. In User Manager for Domains, remove the user from the Collaborative local group.

C. Under Restrict the Use of Application Sharing, select Prevent the User from Collaborating.

D. Under Restrict the Use of File Transfer, select Prevent User from Receiving Files.

7. You are configuring NetMeeting on your local network and want to limit the user's ability to send files. Is this possible? (Select the best answer.)

   A. No, you can only limit a user's ability to both send and receive files.

   B. Yes, by configuring the application sharing feature.

   C. No, you can only limit the user's ability to receive files.

   D. Yes, you can only limit the user's ability to send files.

8. You want to review the settings used when creating a custom deployment package. How can you do this? (Select the best answer.)

   A. Use the IEAK Profile Manager to view the `Install.INS` file for the custom deployment package.

   B. Use the IEAK Profile Manager to view the `Install.INF` file for the custom deployment package.

   C. Use the System Policy Editor to view the `Install.INS` file for the custom deployment package.

   D. Run a test deployment and view the settings.

9. You want to disable the user's ability to change the General options you configured before deploying IE 4.0 with the NetMeeting components. How would you do this?

   A. Set the default directory server to a domain controller and remove the user from the Collaborative local group.

   B. Set the directory server and member server and then remove the user from the Power Users group.

   C. Under Restrict the Use of the Options Dialog, select Disable the 'My Information' Options Page.

   D. Under Restrict the Use of the Options Dialog, select Disable the 'General' Options Page.

10. You are configuring NetMeeting on your local network and want to prevent the user from using the audio features. How would you do this?

   A. Configure Set Limit for Audio/Video Throughput.

   B. Select the Prevent the User from Using Audio Features setting.

   C. Configure the Restrict the Use of Video/Bandwidth setting.

   D. Configure the Restrict the Use of Audio/Bandwidth setting.

4

4.3.7 Answers

1. **B** There are two file transfer options for NetMeeting, one for sending files and one for receiving files.

2. **A** You can limit the average bandwidth usage for audio/video measured in bps.

3. **D** You can restrict the user's ability to share applications.

4. **C** You can use the IEAK Profile Manager to view the `Install.INS` file for a custom deployment package.

5. **A** You can restrict the user from modifying the General and My Information options pages by using the IEAK Profile Manager.

6. **C** You can allow a user to share an application, but disallow collaboration.

7. **D** There are two file transfer options for NetMeeting, one for sending files and one for receiving files.

8. **A** You can use the IEAK Profile Manager to view the `Install.INS` file for a custom deployment package.
9. **D** You can restrict the user from modifying the General and My Information options pages by using the IEAK Profile Manager.
10. **B** You can prevent the user from using the audio features under the Restrict the Use of the Options Dialog setting in the IEAK Profile Manager.

4.4 Selecting Distribution Media

Distribution media has been discussed in earlier chapters. As stated elsewhere in this book, there are three types of distribution media available for deployment:

- Floppy disk
- CD-ROM
- `Download` directory

The `Download` directory is always created, regardless of the other deployment methods selected.

4.4.1 Exercise

In this exercise, you will start the IEAK Wizard and review the deployment methods available for selection from the Corporate Administrator mode, the Content Provider mode, and the ISP mode.

4

This exercise assumes that you have installed the IEAK Wizard on the computer on which you are performing this exercise.

1. Start the IEAK Wizard and begin the configuration process. When prompted, provide the customization code. Select the Content Provider mode of operation. Deselect the AVS option. Click Next.
2. Continue the configuration process until you reach the media selection dialog box. Note that the CD-ROM and multiple floppy disks options are available. Click Cancel.
3. Start the IEAK Wizard and begin the configuration process. When prompted, provide the customization code. Select the Service Provider mode of operation. Deselect the AVS option. Click Next.
4. Continue the configuration process until you reach the media selection dialog box. Note that the CD-ROM and multiple floppy disks options are still available, but there is also a single floppy option available. Click Cancel.
5. Start the IEAK Wizard and begin the configuration process. When prompted, provide the customization code. Select the Corporate Administrator mode of operation. Deselect the AVS option. Click Next.
6. Continue the configuration process until you reach the media selection dialog box. Note that the CD-ROM and multiple floppy disks options are available, but the single floppy option is no longer available. Click Cancel.

This exercise was meant to show the different deployment methods available while running under each of the three operation modes. Note that the download site option is never available. The download site is always created, no matter what operational mode is selected.

4.4.2 Download Site

The download site is not an option you can select or deselect as a deployment method, but is created every time a custom deployment package is created.

In the folder you specify when selecting the deployment method is the `Install.INS` file that stores your custom deployment package selections, along with the `Download`, `IE4site`, and `Ins` folders:

- **`\Dir\Download\En`**: Stores an English language custom package's `Ie4setup.EXE` executable file.
- **`\Dir\Ie4site\En`**: Stores an English language custom package's `.CAB` files. The `.CAB` files are expanded and contain `.INF` files.
- **`\Dir\Ins\En`**: Stores an English language custom package's `Install.INS` file.

Under each of the three folders is the language folder for the language specified during configuration. The `EN` folder is used to specify an English language deployment package. If using a newer version of the IEAK, an additional layer of folders is created, specifying Windows 95/NT, UNIX, or Windows 3.1 deployment packages.

4.4.3 Exercise

In this exercise, you will configure a custom deployment package. The only deployment media you will configure is the download site method.

1. Start the IEAK Wizard and begin the configuration process. When prompted, provide the customization code. Select the Corporate Administrator mode of operation. Deselect the AVS option. Click Next.
2. Continue the configuration process until you reach the media selection dialog box. Note that the CD-ROM and multiple floppy disks options are available. Do not select either deployment media check box. For the deployment directory, select the drive as folder. The folder you want to use will be named `Deploy` (for example, `X:\Deploy`).
3. Complete the custom deployment configuration. Select Finish to allow the custom package to be created.
4. From Explorer, find the `Deploy` directory that stores the custom package. Note that the folder stores the `Install.INS` file and three folders: `Download`, `IE4site`, and `Ins`. Verify the folders each contain an `EN` folder that stores the `.EXE` files, `.CAB` files, and `.INS` files, respectively.

In this lab, you created a custom deployment package and elected to use only the download site as a deployment media. You verified that the hierarchical structure defined in the text portion of this topic was created.

4.4.4 Questions

1. While running the IEAK Wizard, you selected the multiple floppy deployment method. What deployment packages were created? (Select all that apply.)

   A. Single floppy

   B. Multiple Floppy

   C. CD-ROM

   D. `Download` directory

2. Because you are expecting to create a deployment package for your Asian office, you want to view the `.CAB` files created in your `Download` directory to get an idea of how big the files are. The directory you stored the deployment package in is `C:\Deploy`. What directory stores the `.CAB` files for a custom deployment?

   A. `C:\Deploy\IE4site\En`

   B. `C:\Deploy\IE4Site`

   C. `C:\Deploy\Download`

   D. `C:\Deploy\Download\En`

3. You created a deployment package and selected the single floppy option for deployment media. What deployment methods were created? (Select all that apply.)

   A. Single floppy

   B. Multiple floppy

   C. CD-ROM

   D. `Download` directory

4.4.5 Answers

1. **B, D** The `Download` directory is created every time a custom deployment package is created.

2. **A** The `.CAB` files for the deployment are stored in the `\IE4site\`*language* directory, where *language* is the language selected for the custom deployment package.

3. **A, D** The `Download` directory is created every time a custom deployment package is created.

4.4.6 Single Floppy

The single floppy method of deployment is available only when running in the Service Provider mode of the IEAK Wizard. This method allows the creation of a single floppy deployment package.

The single floppy stores the information needed to get to the download site and perform the custom setup of Internet Explorer 4.0. The directory structure used to store the information is the same as it is for the `Download` site deployment media, with the exception that an additional folder is created in the deployment directory:

- **`Dir\Floppy\En:`** This directory contains the information that can be placed on a single floppy to support the single floppy deployment method.

To use this method, dial-up networking must be installed on the client computer. The Internet connection can be configured as part of the deployment package, but dial-up networking must be installed.

4.4.7 Exercise

In this exercise, you will configure a custom deployment package. The deployment media you will configure will be the single floppy method.

1. Start the IEAK Wizard and begin the configuration process. When prompted, provide the customization code. Select the Service Provider mode of operation. Deselect the AVS option. Click Next.
2. Continue the configuration process until you reach the media selection dialog box. Note that the CD-ROM, multiple floppy disks, and single floppy disk options are available. Select only the single floppy deployment method. For the deployment directory, select the drive as folder. The folder you want to use will be named `DeploySF` (for example, `X:\DeploySF`).
3. Complete the custom deployment configuration. Select Finish to allow the custom package to be created.
4. From Explorer, find the `DeploySF` directory that stores the custom package. Note that the folder stores the `Install.INS` file and four folders: `Download`, `IE4site`, `Ins`, and `Floppy`. Verify that each folder contains an `EN` folder that stores the `.EXE` files, `.CAB` files, and `.INS` files, respectively.
5. View the information stored in the `Floppy` folder. The files in this directory will fit on a single floppy and contain all the data needed to use dial-up networking to connect to a deployment site and complete the installation of IE 4.0.

In this lab, you created a custom deployment package and elected to use only the single floppy method of deployment. You verified that the hierarchical structure defined in the text portion of this topic was created. Note that the `Download` site was also created.

4.4.8 Questions

1. You want to be able to specify the single floppy, multiple floppy, and CD-ROM deployment methods. What role must you select to have all of these options available to you?

   A. Content Provider/Developer.

   B. Service Provider

   C. Corporate Administrator

   D. None of these will provide you with that ability. You must have the IEAK Extra to have all options available.

2. You have created a single floppy deployment package for use in the United States and stored the package in `D:\SFDeploy`. What directory stores the information that is placed on the floppy for distribution?

   A. `D:\SFDeploy\En\Floppy`

   B. `D:\SFDeploy\Floppy`

   C. `D:\SFDeploy\Floppy\En`

   D. `D:\SFDeploy\En`

3. You have just installed Windows 95 on a client computer and want to use the single floppy method to install IE 4.0. The deployment package you have configured has a custom ICM profile included. You do have a modem, but haven't configured dial-up networking. What must you do to configure the connection? (Select two.)

   A. Run the single floppy deployment.

   B. Run the Dial-Up Networking Wizard.

   C. Run the Internet Connection Wizard.

   D. Run the Windows 95 installation. When it asks for custom programs, insert the floppy disk.

4.4.9 Answers

1. **B** The only role that provides the single floppy deployment method is the Service Provider role.

2. **B** The information to be placed on the single floppy is stored in the `\Floppy\En` directory (if the build is configured for the English language).

3. **A, B** You must install dial-up networking before the single floppy installation can take place.

4

4.4.10 Multiple Floppy

The multiple floppy method of deployment creates a set of floppy disks that stores all the information needed to do a complete installation of IE 4.0.

In the hierarchical structure of the deployment package, an `Mfloppy` folder is created, which holds a Windows 95, Windows 95 and Windows NT, and Windows NT floppy set. The information under these three folders is separated and stored in folders labeled `Disk1` through `DiskX`.

4.4.11 Exercise

In this exercise, you will create a custom deployment, specify the multiple floppy deployment method, and then verify that the directory structure is as expected.

1. Start the IEAK Wizard and begin the configuration process. When prompted, provide the customization code. Select the Corporate Administrator mode of operation. Deselect the AVS option. Click Next.
2. Continue the configuration process until you reach the media selection dialog box. Note that the CD-ROM and multiple floppy disks options are available. Select only the multiple floppy deployment method. For the deployment directory, select the drive as folder. The folder you want to use will be named `DeployMF` (for example, `X:\DeployMF`).
3. Complete the custom deployment configuration. Select Finish to allow the custom package to be created.
4. From Explorer, find the `DeployMF` directory that stores the custom package. Note that the folder stores the `Install.INS` file and four folders: `Download`, `IE4site`, `Ins`, and `MFloppy`. Verify the folders each contain an `EN` folder that stores the `.EXE` files, `.CAB` files, and `.INS` files, respectively.
5. Verify that the `MFloppy` directory has a `Win95`, `Win95_NT`, and `WinNT` directory, each containing an `EN` folder that stores separate floppy folders for each floppy that must be created to deploy IE 4.0.

In this lab, you created a custom deployment package and elected to use only the multiple floppy method of deployment. You verified that the hierarchical structure defined in the text portion of this topic was created.

4.4.12 Questions

1. You have created a multiple floppy disk set to use for deployment of IE 4.0. What statement best describes the information stored on the floppy set?

   A. The information stored on the floppy set is all the information needed to deploy IE 4.0, with the exception of the `.INS` files.

   B. The information stored on the floppy set is all the information needed to deploy IE 4.0, with the exception of the `.CAB` files.

   C. The information stored on the floppy set is all the information needed to deploy IE 4.0, with the exception of the `.INF` files.

   D. The information stored on the floppy set can completely install IE 4.0 without connecting to a download.

2. What folder is the floppy set stored in when the multiple floppy deployment method is selected, the download folder is `C:\MFDeploy`, and the deployment language is English? (Select all correct answers.)

   A. `C:\MFDeploy\Mfloppy\Win95\En`

   B. `C:\MFDeploy\Mfloppy\Win95_NT\En`

   C. `C:\MFDeploy\Mfloppy\WinNT\En`

   D. `C:\MFDeploy\Mfloppy\En`

3. You created a deployment package and selected multiple floppy as the deployment media. What deployment methods were created?

   A. Single floppy

   B. Multiple floppy

   C. CD-ROM

   D. `Download` directory

4.4.13 Answers

1. **D** The information stored on the floppy set allows a user to do a complete installation of IE 4.0.

2. **A, B, and C** Floppy disk sets are created under `Win95`, `Win95_NT`, and `WinNT` directories in the `EN` folder if the deployment language is English.

3. **B, D** The download media is always created. The other deployment media is the multiple floppy media.

4

4.4.14 CD-ROM

The CD-ROM method of deployment works in the same way as the multiple floppy method of deployment, but includes an optional configuration page for the CD-ROM autorun features (see Figure 4.4.1). The items that can be configured for autorun include the following:

- Autorun screen title bar
- Custom background bitmap
- Text colors
- Button style (including custom button bitmaps)

To configure custom button bitmaps, you must provide the directory path and filename for the custom bitmap.

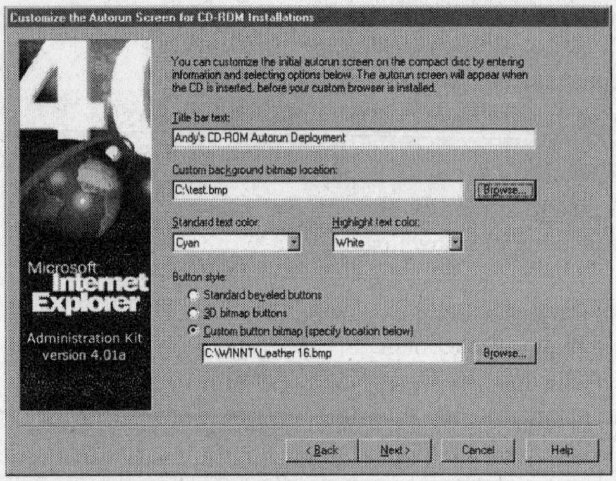

Figure 4.4.1 Autorun screen configuration.

The directory structure for the CD-ROM is the same as it is for the other deployment methods in that the `Download`, `IE4site`, and `Ins` folders are created along with a folder named `CD`, which stores the CD-ROM deployment files.

In the `CD` folder is the `Autorun.INF` file and the `Iesetup.EXE` file. The folders created in the `EN` directory are listed here:

- **`\Dir\CD\En\Demobin`:** This folder contains support software needed for the installation.
- **`\Dir\Cd\En\packages`:** This folder contains all the `.CAB` files needed for the installation.

The `EN` folder also contains the files `Ie3inst.EXE` and `Iecd.EXE`.

4.4.15 Exercise

In this exercise, you will create a custom deployment package, specify the CD-ROM deployment method, and then verify that the directory structure is as expected.

1. Start the IEAK Wizard and begin the configuration process. When prompted, provide the customization code. Select the Corporate Administrator mode of operation. Deselect the AVS option. Click Next.
2. Continue the configuration process until you reach the media selection dialog box. Note that the CD-ROM and multiple floppy disks options are available. Select only the CD-ROM deployment method. For the deployment directory, select the drive as folder. The folder you want to use will be named `DeployCD` (for example, `X:\DeployCD`).
3. Complete the custom deployment configuration. Select Finish to allow the custom package to be created.
4. From Explorer, find the `DeployCD` directory that stores the custom package. Note that the folder stores the `Install.INS` file and four folders: `Download`, `IE4site`, `Ins`, and `CD`. Verify that the folders each contain an `EN` folder that stores the `.EXE` files, `.CAB` files, and `.INS` files, respectively.
5. Verify that the `CD` directory has a `Win95` directory that contains an `EN` folder. The `EN` folder should contain the `Demobin` and `Packages` folders.

In this lab, you created a custom deployment package and elected to use only the CD-ROM method of deployment. You verified that the hierarchical structure defined in the text portion of this topic was created.

4.4.16 Questions

1. You have created a custom deployment package and selected CD-ROM as a deployment media. You want to change the title bar for the autorun dialog box. What file would you edit?

   A. `Iecd.INI`

   B. `Autorun.INF`

   C. `Install.INI`

   D. `Title.INI`

2. You are creating a custom deployment package and selected CD-ROM as a deployment media. Your boss has asked whether you can add a custom background with your company's logo. How could you accomplish this?

   A. In the Custom Background Bitmap Location, provide the path and filename to the `.BMP` file.

   B. In the Custom Background Bitmap Location, provide the path and filename to the `.JPG` file.

   C. In the Custom Background Bitmap Location, provide the path and filename to the `.GIF` file.

   D. In the Custom Background Bitmap Location, provide the filename only to the bitmap file.

3. You are creating a custom deployment package and have selected CD-ROM as the deployment media. The package is for the Spanish language, and the directory specified to create the package in was `D:\Cdeploy`. What directory will contain the `Autorun.INF` file?

   A. `D:\Cdeploy\Cd\Win95\EN`

   B. `D:\Cdeploy\Cd\Win95\SP`

   C. `D:\Cdeploy\CD`

   D. `D:\Cdeploy\Cd\SP`

4.4.17 Answers

1. **A** The file that stores the custom bitmap and title bar information is the `Iecd.INI` file.

2. **A** Provide the path and filename to the custom bitmap file. The bitmap will be included in the deployment package that is created.

3. **C** The `Autorun.INF` file is always created in the `\CD` folder, regardless of the language selected.

CHAPTER 5

Monitoring and Optimization

Chapter 1 covered what is typically the most often neglected and least appreciated aspect of any installation: effective planning. But even the most thorough project plan includes some degree of guesswork because the use of new products and features and the resulting impact on system and network resources is impossible to accurately predict before implementation. Some users will jump on everything new just because it is new, while other users avoid change at all cost. The time required for usage levels to approach a "norm" obviously varies from product to product.

Microsoft considers the following four resources in a computing environment:

- CPU subsystem
- Memory subsystem
- Disk subsystem
- Network subsystem

It has been said that one measurement of a well-tuned installation is how often the phone at the help desk rings. Minimizing the number of complaint calls can be accomplished only if a proactive approach to system monitoring and optimization is taken. Also, it can be pretty tough to determine what is causing system or network problems if you do not have a baseline picture of things when the system is running well.

Numerous tools are available for monitoring system and network resource utilization. Windows NT provides the Event Viewer, Task Manager, Windows NT Diagnostics, Performance Monitor, and Network Monitor (to name a few). This chapter covers the options available to you during and after the deployment of Internet Explorer 4.0 to help ensure effective use of available system and network resources.

5.1 Customizing

The IEAK Profile Manager enables you to create and (of particular interest in this chapter) maintain customized autoconfiguration files containing a wide range of browser, user, desktop, and system settings and restrictions. As you are already aware from previous chapters, there is no shortage of options that can be customized using the IEAK. In this chapter, we look at the options relating to optimizing system performance.

5.1.1 Exercise

Many of the configuration options that can affect system performance probably went unnoticed when you used the IEAK Wizard. One good way to become more familiar with the options available from the wizard is to use the IEAK Profile Manager to take an in-depth look at an `.INS` configuration file. This exercise does just that.

1. Open the IEAK Profile Manager (from the Start menu, select Programs|Microsoft IEAK and then select IEAK Profile Manager).
2. Open a configuration file you previously created (probably by using the wizard) by selecting File|Open, and then double-clicking the desired .INS file.
3. If the option is not already expanded, click the plus (+) sign on the left side of the screen for Wizard Settings and the plus sign for System Policies and Restrictions. Then click the plus signs for each of the items listed under System Policies and Restrictions. Figure 5.1.1 shows the IEAK Profile Manager with the System Policies and Restrictions expanded.

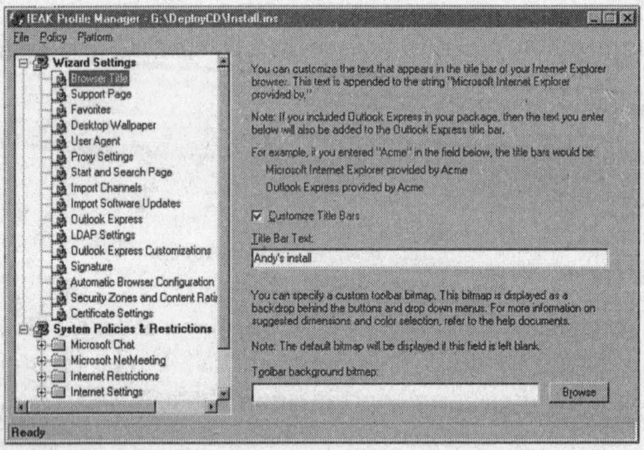

Figure 5.1.1 IEAK Profile Manager with System Policies and Restrictions expanded.

4. Work your way down the list of available topics by clicking on each. Take a few minutes to familiarize yourself with the options at your disposal and read the supporting text for each.

5.1.2 Active Desktop

There are several purposes behind the Active Desktop in Internet Explorer 4.0:

- To establish a consistent environment for the user, regardless of whether the information he or she is working with resides on the local computer, the Internet, or the company's intranet.

- To provide current information to the user from a specified location—usually from the Internet or the company's intranet.
- To be able to provide information in various formats to the user's desktop.

The information displayed on the user's desktop can arrive in one of two ways. The information can be "pushed" onto the desktop or "pulled" onto the desktop:

- **Push:** Data is made available to users with little or no intervention on their part. A network-based server provides the information to the desktop without the user requesting the data.
- **Pull:** Users must take the initiative to go find the information they are looking for—which, as we are all becoming painfully aware, can require a great deal of skill, time, and resources (such as network bandwidth) that are not necessarily in abundance. In this case, the user must request or "pull" the data to the desktop.

The rest of this chapter details ways that you, as an administrator, can customize the process of pushing real-time (a.k.a. *active*) information to the users' desktops and can help users customize their information-pulling techniques. The end result is to optimize the availability of information as well as system resources.

5.1.3 Exercise

You are in the final planning stages of deploying IE 4.0 to all members of your organization when you discover that a group of individuals in the Accounting department has a reputation for changing other individuals' desktop environments when PCs are left unattended.

Because you have plans to use the IE 4.0 Active Desktop functionality to distribute information to employees, keeping desktops standardized is a concern. This exercise will walk you through steps you can take to ensure standardization yet provide a customized Active Desktop environment.

This exercise assumes that you have already run through the IEAK Wizard and have created an `.INS` file that meets almost all your needs. (Be forewarned that this exercise details quite a number of steps because this may well be your first exposure to customizing the Active Desktop.)

1. Open the IEAK Profile Manager (from the Start menu, select Programs|Microsoft IEAK and then select IEAK Profile Manager).
2. Open the configuration file you previously created by selecting File|Open and then double-clicking the desired .INS file.
3. If the option is not already expanded, click the plus (+) sign on the left side of the screen for Wizard Settings and the plus sign for System Policies and Restrictions.
4. From the left pane of the display window, select Desktop Wallpaper under Wizard Settings. The right side of the display now contains some text briefly explaining what your Desktop Wallpaper options are. You opt to leave this setting at the default for the time being.
5. Navigate down to Specify Active Desktop Components.
6. Click the Import the Current Active Desktop Components radio button. The Modify Settings button becomes active.

7. Click Modify Settings. The Display Properties window opens.
8. Click the Web tab at the top of the Display Settings window. You will probably see that the View My Active Desktop as a Web Page option is selected and Internet Explorer Channel Bar is the only active component by default.
9. Click New. The New Active Desktop Item pop-up window displays. What's the Active Desktop Gallery you've heard about? Well, Microsoft and other providers have made Active Desktop Components (ADCs) available on the Internet at sites referred to as galleries. From this point on, things should be pretty self-explanatory about how to add ADCs. Once you get things configured the way you want, click OK or close until you get back to the IEAK Profile Manager Specify Active Desktop Components screen.
10. Scroll down to the Desktop option under Web Desktop. On the right side of the display, click the box to activate the Do Not Allow Changes to Active Desktop restriction. This option prevents users from changing their Active Desktop environment.
11. Select File|Exit and save your changes.

5.1.4 Practice Problems

1. What steps could you take to add new items to your Active Desktop? (Select all that apply.)

   A. Right-click an open part of your desktop, go to Active Desktop, and click Customize My Desktop.

   B. Select Start|Settings|Active Desktop|Customize My Desktop.

   C. Select Start|Settings|Control Panel|Display and then click the Web tab.

   D. Select Start|Settings|Control Panel|Display|Settings|Customize My Desktop.

2. You want to keep users from changing the custom desktop wallpaper on which your organization has standardized. How could you do this?

   A. Clear the Users May Specify Wallpaper check box under the Desktop Wallpaper option of the Wizard Settings.

   B. Clear the Users May Specify Wallpaper check box under the User Agent option of the Wizard Settings.

   C. Check the Disable Changing Wallpaper box under the System option under System Policies and Restrictions.

   D. Check the Disable Changing Wallpaper box under the Desktop option under System Policies and Restrictions.

3. A Windows 3.11 user who recently upgraded to IE 4.0 can't get Active Desktop to work and calls you for help. What do you have the user check first?

   A. How much memory is in the computer.

   B. What speed CPU is in the computer.

   C. The user's Active Desktop settings to see whether View as Web Page is checked.

   D. Nothing. Windows 3.11 does not support Active Desktop.

4. With the IEAK, can you (1) permanently disable your users' Active Desktop and (2) do you have the option of leaving it up to them whether or not they run an Active Desktop but prohibiting them from making any changes to it if they do enable it?

   A. No to both questions.

   B. No to 1 and Yes to 2.

   C. Yes to 1 and No to 2.

   D. Yes to both questions.

5.1.5 Answers and Explanations: Practice Problems

1. **A, B, and C** There are numerous ways to get to the Customize My Desktop menu.

2. **D** Restricting desktop wallpaper settings are just two of the options available to you under System Policies and Restrictions, Web Desktop, Desktop.

3. **D** Active Desktop applies only to 32-bit Windows platforms (Windows 95 and Windows NT).

4. **D** With the IEAK, you can restrict just about any component of the users' desktops.

5.1.6 Active Channels

Active Channels are Web sites made available by publishers to users of Internet Explorer 4.0 for the purpose of customizing what is available for downloading from the Web site.

Users subscribe to channels as they subscribe to any other site (site subscriptions are covered later in this book)—the difference being that the author of the site creates and adds a Channel Definition Format (CDF) file to the site. Figure 5.1.2 shows an example of a CDF file. The CDF file contains the following elements:

- An index of URLs for site content
- A schedule for content updates (optional)
- Information about subchannels used to organize content structure (optional)

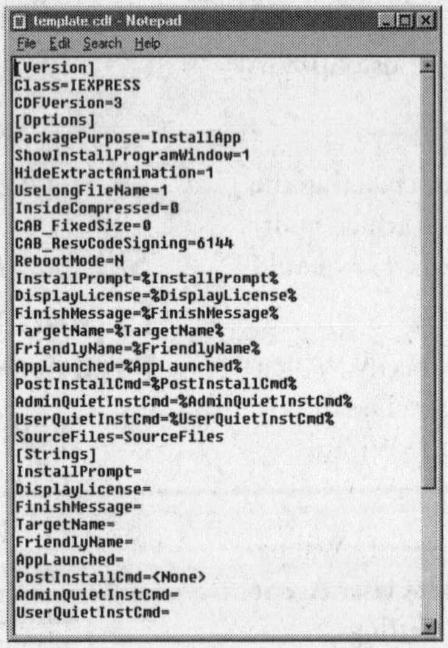


```
[Version]
Class=IEXPRESS
CDFVersion=3
[Options]
PackagePurpose=InstallApp
ShowInstallProgramWindow=1
HideExtractAnimation=1
UseLongFileName=1
InsideCompressed=0
CAB_FixedSize=0
CAB_ResvCodeSigning=6144
RebootMode=N
InstallPrompt=%InstallPrompt%
DisplayLicense=%DisplayLicense%
FinishMessage=%FinishMessage%
TargetName=%TargetName%
FriendlyName=%FriendlyName%
AppLaunched=%AppLaunched%
PostInstallCmd=%PostInstallCmd%
AdminQuietInstCmd=%AdminQuietInstCmd%
UserQuietInstCmd=%UserQuietInstCmd%
SourceFiles=SourceFiles
[Strings]
InstallPrompt=
DisplayLicense=
FinishMessage=
TargetName=
FriendlyName=
AppLaunched=
PostInstallCmd=<None>
AdminQuietInstCmd=
UserQuietInstCmd=
```

Figure 5.1.2 An example of a Channel Definition Format (CDF) file.

Subscribers receive updated information from Active Channels on demand or at scheduled intervals.

Channel subscriptions provide the following benefits to the end user, the site author, and the administrator:

- **User:** The ability to perform what has been referred to as "smart pulls."
- **Author:** The ability to provide what has been referred to as "smart pushes."
- **Administrator:** More customization and optimization flexibility resulting in more efficient use of available resources.

5.1.7 Exercise

With the IEAK, you can completely customize the channels displayed in the channel bar. This exercise will walk you through the process of customizing Active Channels.

1. Open an existing .INS file with the IEAK Profile Manager and highlight the Import Channels option under Wizard Settings. (See steps 1 through 3 of the previous exercise if you need details on how to do this.)
2. Note that the right side of the display contains text explaining the three steps for customizing the channel bar: Delete Channels, Add Channels, and Import the Current Channel and Subscription Information. (Although Optimizing Performance is also mentioned on this screen, it is covered later in this chapter, when channels and optimization are detailed.)
3. Click the Launch Channel Guide button. (Because everything to do with channels relates to the Internet, you will see an error message if you are not currently connected to the Internet or cannot open the site `http://www/iechannelguide.com` for any reason.)
4. From this point on, things should be pretty self-explanatory about adding channels to and customizing the channel bar. Once you get things configured the way you want, click OK or close until you get back to the IEAK Profile Manager Import Channels screen.
5. Scroll down to the Channels Settings option under Internet Restrictions. The right side of the display lists the numerous options available to you for determining how much flexibility users will have in doing their own channel customization.
6. Click File|Exit and save your changes.

5.1.8 Practice Problems

1. Any Web site can be converted into a channel by the site author by:

   A. Adding a Channel Definition Format (CDF) file to the site and registering the site with Microsoft for entry into the Active Channel Guide.

   B. Simply adding a `.CDF` file to the site.

   C. Adding a `.CDF` file to the site and registering the site to get a content rating.

   D. Not all Web sites can be converted into channels.

2. Select the correct answer regarding the display of a channel as a screen saver.

   A. The screen saver must be configured in the `.CDF` file for the channel to be used as a screen saver.

   B. Any channel can be used as a screen saver.

   C. Any channel content can be used as a screen saver.

   D. Channels cannot be used as screen savers.

3. Select the answer most applicable to channels.

   A. You have to subscribe to a channel to view it from your channel bar.

   B. All channels are listed in the Microsoft Active Channel Guide.

   C. Channels typically require a subscription fee.

   D. Most Web sites that are channels can be identified by a special Add Active Channel icon.

4. How can you add a channel to your channel bar? (Select two.)

   A. By adding it to your list of Favorites and clicking the Add to Channel bar option.

   B. By clicking the Add Active Channel icon on the Web page (channel).

   C. By clicking the Channels button on the toolbar, clicking Channel Guide in the Explorer bar, and then following the instructions on Microsoft's Web page.

   D. By selecting File|Add to Channel Bar when viewing the desired Web page (channel).

5.1.9 Answers and Explanations: Practice Problems

1. **B** A `.CDF` file is all that is necessary to convert a standard Web site into a channel.

2. **A** Channels and channel content can typically be used as screen savers, but not all can be so used.

3. **D** The Add Active Channel icon is the best way to identify a Web site as a channel.

4. **B, C** You can add channels to your channel bar by clicking the Add Active channel bar or by clicking the Channel Guide in Explorer.

5.2 Monitoring and Updating

You should realize that monitoring and updating are ongoing, never-ending processes. The intent of these processes is to improve system performance or, at a minimum, keep system performance from degrading as new applications and functionality are added over time.

There are no monitoring tools provided with IE 4.0 or the IEAK; these tools should already exist in your arsenal and you should be familiar with their use. Some of these tools are covered briefly in Chapter 6, "Troubleshooting."

With IE 4.0, a whole new world of possibilities opens up regarding the updating of information provided to users (pushed) or searched for by users (pulled). The previous section briefly explained Active Channels and how they have led to two relatively new terms: smart pull and smart push.

You and some of your users may already be familiar with the process of subscribing to a Web site. With the release of IE 4.0, this process has taken on much greater meaning and functionality. As an administrator, you now have control over how much of your network bandwidth users are allowed to consume with site subscriptions.

5

A term you may not be familiar with is *Webcasting*. One Microsoft White Paper, available on TechNet as well as on the Internet, states that "Webcasting is the automated delivery of personalized and up-to-date information." There are three delivery methods available in IE 4.0 for receiving such information:

- Site subscriptions
- Channels
- Active Desktop (including channel screen savers)

For more information on Webcasting and push-updating in general, search the Internet for `what is Webcasting` to find several articles of interest. It should be noted that the terms *Webcasting* and *netcasting* are synonymous.

5.2.1 Site Subscriptions

Site subscriptions are new with Internet Explorer 4.0, although third-party products have been available for some time, containing the basic functionality IE now contains.

The following features are now available with IE 4.0:

- Users can configure IE 4.0 to check any or all of the Web sites in their Favorites folder for new content on a daily, weekly, or monthly basis. Figure 5.2.1 shows the screen from which this is accomplished.
- Users can choose to be notified if site content has changed and how the notification is to take place. (If users choose to be notified by email, they must supply an address to which the notification should be sent.)
- Users can choose to download all or some of the site's content.

- Users can choose when downloads will take place. Preferably, this is done during off-hours when network activity is at a minimum.
- Users can choose how much of a site they want to have IE 4.0 monitor by either subscribing to a higher level (or home) page or by subscribing to an individual page.
- Optionally, users can specify a "crawl depth," which tells IE 4.0 how many layers below the page subscribed to should be monitored for updates.

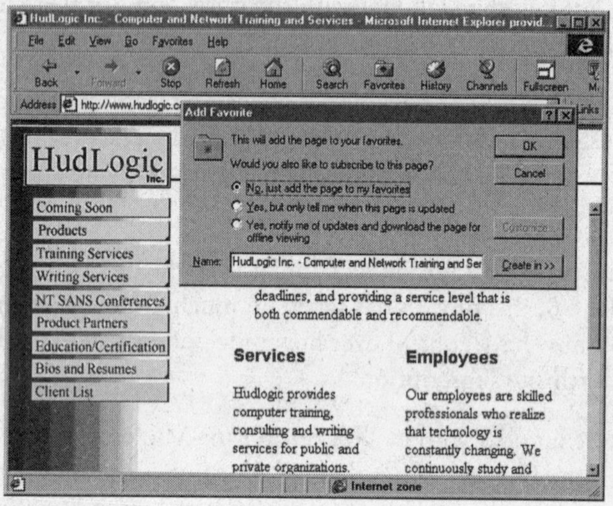

Figure 5.2.1 While adding a Web site to your Favorites folder, you can subscribe to the site.

Figure 5.2.2 shows the various settings you can configure.

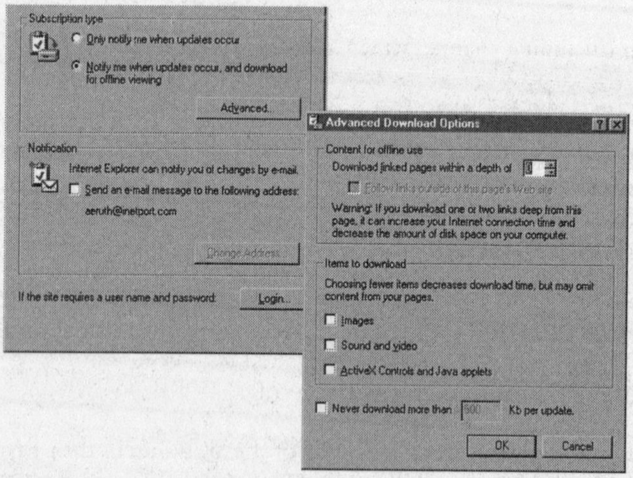

Figure 5.2.2 Configuring subscription type, notification options, download depth, and the item to download. You can also limit the size of the update.

Allowing channel subscriptions and the downloading of Web pages for viewing at a later date can be extremely taxing for network resources. Make sure that you evaluate your available bandwidth before enabling these features.

The IEAK offers these options to administrators:

- Limit the maximum size of site subscription updates
- Limit the maximum number of sites to which users can subscribe
- Limit the number of minutes between scheduled subscription updates
- Specify a range of time during which subscription updates will not be allowed to occur
- Specify a maximum site subscription crawl depth

5.2.2 Exercise

Online help just keeps getting better and better. IE 4.0 is a very good example of this truth. This exercise will familiarize you with the extensive help available in IE 4.0.

1. In Internet Explorer 4.0, select Help|Contents and Index. (If you are new to IE 4.0, you probably should read through the Introducing the Web Browser section, at a minimum.)
2. Click the Index tab (located between the Contents and Search tabs).
3. Begin typing the word *subscriptions* in the box at the top of the menu frame. Notice that when you have entered the letters su, the topics you are interested in learning more about are at the top of the list (subscribing to Web sites, subscribing to channels, and general information on maintaining your subscriptions).
4. Close the Help window. The integrated online help in IE 4.0 will prove to be an excellent resource, regardless of whether you are an administrator or a user. For help on any item, click the question mark icon (?) in the title bar of the window and then click the item about which you want help. Click anywhere to close the Help pop-up window. Close IE 4.0.
5. Select Start|Programs|IEAK and then select IEAK Help. The IEAK Help utility opens.
6. In the left pane of the Help window, click the Index button. An alphabetical list of defined topics appears.
7. Close the IEAK Help utility.

In the next exercise, you will follow the steps involved in subscribing to a site and take note of the differences between a partial subscription and a full subscription.

1. Using IE 4.0, open the Web page to which you want to subscribe.
2. From the Favorites menu, select Add to Favorites. The Add Favorite window that appears presents the following options:
    - Not subscribing to the page (just adding it to your Favorites folder).

- Partially subscribing to the page (tell me only when this page has been updated).
- Fully subscribing to the page (notify me of updates and download the page for offline viewing).

3. If you choose a full subscription, the Customize button becomes active. Click Customize to specify your schedule, delivery, and notification options. To change subscription settings at some later time, select Manage Subscriptions from the Favorites menu, right-click the subscription you want to change, and then click Properties. Scheduling can be configured from the Scheduling tab.

5.2.3 Practice Problems

1. A user wants to subscribe to a Web site but is interested in getting the updates for only part of the site. Select the answer that best describes the options available to the user.

   A. If the user does not subscribe to the site, partial updates are possible.

   B. If the user subscribes to the site, partial updates are possible.

   C. If the user subscribes to the site, only complete site updates are available.

   D. If the user does not subscribe to the site, only complete site updates are possible.

2. You have a network with 50 percent of available bandwidth being used, with peaks of up to 70 percent utilization during the day. You are afraid that if your users subscribe to sites, bandwidth will become a bottleneck. Can you configure times when site subscription updates occur? (Select the best answer.)

   A. No, Web site subscriptions occur on a timed basis that cannot be modified.

   B. No, Web sites subscriptions can only be stopped permanently.

   C. Yes, Web site subscriptions can be set to occur only during particular times of the day.

   D. Yes, Web site subscriptions can be set to occur only during a particular time of the day, but the time is defined by the Web site author.

3. You are the administrator for a network with 400 users, and you want to place limits on user subscriptions. What limits can you place on user subscriptions? (Select all that apply.)

   A. You can limit the size of bitmaps that are updated.

   B. You can limit the size of site subscription updates.

   C. You can limit the minimum number of minutes between updates.

   D. You can limit the number of users that can subscribe to a site.

4. You are the administrator for a network with 400 users, and you want to place limits on user subscriptions. What limits can you place on user subscriptions? (Select all that apply.)

   A. You can limit the crawl depth for site updates.

   B. You can limit the number of sites to which a user can subscribe.

   C. You can limit the length of time a user can stay subscribed to a site.

   D. You can specify the range of time during which subscription updates can occur.

5. You are preparing to deploy IE 4.0, and users are asking which Web site subscription options are available. Of the options listed, which are valid? (Select all that apply.)

   A. Users can configure IE 4.0 to check any and all of the Web sites in their Favorites folders for new content.

   B. Users can configure IE 4.0 to push changes on to other computers.

   C. Users can choose to download all or some of the site's content.

   D. Users can choose how much of a site to monitor.

6. You are preparing to deploy IE 4.0, and users are asking which Web site subscription options are available. Of the options listed, which are valid? (Select all that apply.)

5

A. Users can choose to obtain updates only if network utilization drops below 40 percent.

B. Users can choose to be notified if the site content has changed on a site to which they have subscribed.

C. Users can choose when downloads will take place.

D. Users can choose the crawl depth of a site.

5.2.4 Answers and Explanations: Practice Problems

1. **B** If a user subscribes to a site, the user can receive partial site updates.
2. **C** You can configure a Web site subscription to perform site updates only during particular times of the day.
3. **B, C** You can limit the number of sites a user can subscribe to and the size of the site updates, but you cannot configure the number of users that can subscribe to a site.
4. **A, B, and D** The only invalid answer mentioned in this question is C, the length of time a user can stay subscribed to a site.
5. **A, C, and D** The user can receive partial site updates, monitor only certain portions of a site, and choose some or all of the sites in their Favorites folder to subscribe to.
6. **B, C, and D** The user can choose the site crawl depth, when downloads will take place, and how they want to be notified of changes.

5.2.5 Active Channels

An *Active Channel* and a *channel* are the same thing. You will find both terms used in documentation on the product. As defined earlier, a channel is a Web site to which you can subscribe and from which you receive a portion of the site based on your preferences. Channels were designed for dial-up Internet users who required a specialized form of site subscription because of the following factors:

- They were not permanently connected
- Severe bandwidth limitations (how fast does that new 56K modem really run?)

Subscribing to a channel for the purpose of receiving automatic updates is similar to subscribing to a normal Web site. What makes channels so special was touched on in "Active Channels," earlier in this chapter. To review, the author of the site creates and adds a Channel Definition Format (CDF) file to the site. The `.CDF` file contains the following elements:

- An index of URLs for site content
- A schedule for content updates (optional)
- Information about subchannels used to organize content structure (optional)

The `.CDF` file allows users to subscribe to portions of the site. For example, you might tell a sports channel to send you just football and basketball updates, while other users might tell the same sports channel to send them nothing but golf updates.

When you use IE 4.0 to connect to a channel you have previously configured, only the selected pages are transferred. Another thing that differs between channels and standard site subscriptions is that if you have a permanent connection to the Internet, the channel's author can configure the site's `.CDF` file to tell IE 4.0 when to download new information if you so choose. Talk about timely information—you can receive updates the minute they take place.

The functionality available for site subscriptions is available to administrators in the IEAK for the purpose of restricting network bandwidth use by users scheduling channel updates.

5.2.6 Exercise

The reasons for subscribing to a channel are similar to the reasons for subscribing to a Web site. Technically, a channel is nothing more than a special site. The steps you go through to subscribe to a channel are slightly different than those you use to subscribe to a site. Although you can begin this exercise while offline, you must be connected to the Internet to complete it.

1. Click the Channels button on the IE 4.0 toolbar. The channels you are currently subscribed to are listed in the left pane of the IE 4.0 window. This pane is known as the Explorer bar. The contents of the Explorer bar depend on which toolbar button (Search, Favorites, History, or Channels) you click to open it.

Left to right, the toolbar buttons are Back, Forward, Stop, Refresh, Home, Search, Favorites, History, Channels, Fullscreen, and Mail. By default, the buttons to the right of Favorites or History may not be visible. If they are not, either maximize the window or widen it by dragging the right edge of the window to the right until the Channels button becomes visible.

2. In the Explorer bar, click the top entry, Microsoft Channel Guide. Additional instructions appear on your screen.

5.2.7 Practice Problems

1. You subscribe to a Web site that has technical information you want to review on your notebook computer from home tonight, but you don't have Internet access at home. How would you configure IE 4.0 to store the information on your computer so that you could read it offline? (Select all that apply.)

   A. Bring up the Web site. From the toolbar, select Favorites and Manage Subscriptions.

   B. Bring up the Properties for the site. On the Schedule tab, click the Update Now button. This action downloads the site for viewing offline.

   C. Bring up your home page and review the Properties for that page. Select the Make My Home Page Store Requested Web Site Information option.

   D. Bring up the Properties page for the site. From the Subscription tab, select Update Now. This action downloads the site for viewing offline.

2. You are subscribed to a Web site and want to limit the amount of information you receive with each update to 0.5M. How would you do this?

   A. In the Web site's Property page, select the Schedule tab and set the maximum size for updates to 500K.

   B. In the Web site's Property page, select the Subscription tab and set the maximum size for updates to 500K.

   C. In the Web site's Property page, select the Receiving tab, display the Advanced Settings dialog box, and then set the maximum size for updates to 500K.

   D. In the Web site's Property page, select the Receiving tab and set the maximum size for updates to 500K.

5.2.8 Answers and Explanations: Practice Problems

1. **A, B** You manage subscriptions and can modify or update subscription information for each site to which you subscribe.

2. **C** You set the maximum download size per update from the Advanced Settings dialog box, accessed from the Receiving tab of the Properties page.

5.2.9 Active Desktop

Dictionaries generally define the word *active* as follows:

- Capable of exerting influence
- Constantly engaged; lively
- The opposite of passive
- Does something

The Active Desktop included in Internet Explorer 4.0 can host any HTML item (a.k.a. *Active Desktop Component*, or *ADC*). For example, users can have images, ActiveX controls, Java applets, and even Web pages right on their desktops, resulting in highly customized, automatically updated environments. Active Desktop items are defined by content providers using a specialized form of `.CDF` file.

The simplest way to enable or disable the Active Desktop option in IE 4.0 is to right-click an open area of the desktop, move the mouse pointer over the Active Desktop menu option, and then click View as Web Page. This option is not available unless the Windows Desktop Update has been installed. A check mark next to the View as Web Page option means that Active Desktop is enabled; no check mark means that the option is disabled.

Disabling the Active Desktop does not disable all the Windows Desktop Update features, such as the updated Explorer and My Computer.

There are several ways to configure the Active Desktop:

- Right-click an open area of the desktop and then click the Customize My Desktop option. This action displays the Display Properties window with the Web tab selected.
- Go to one of the sites on the Internet containing Active Desktop components, choose one you like, and then click the Put It On My Desktop link.
- Launch the Channel Viewer and look through the list of available channels, many of which now offer one or more Active Desktop components.

To resize or move any of your Active Desktop components, simply move the mouse pointer over the top title bar of the component to make the frame visible. You can then drag or resize the frame in the conventional manner.

You can close an individual Active Desktop component by clicking the × in the top-right corner in the component's frame or by clicking the down arrow in the top left-corner and selecting Close.

By now, you should realize that there are numerous ways to get to the Customize My Desktop menu item, which allows you to view your complete list of currently available Active Desktop components.

As an administrator, you have numerous options available to you from the IEAK Profile Manager that you can use to dictate system policies and enforce corporate restrictions about desktop restrictions and Active Desktop items.

5.2.10 Exercise

When you ran the IEAK Wizard, many of the options available to you probably went unnoticed. One good way to become more familiar with the available options in the wizard is to use the IEAK Profile Manager to take an in-depth look at an `.INS` configuration file. This exercise will do just that, paying particular attention to the options relating to the desktop.

1. Open the IEAK Profile Manager (from the Start menu, select Programs|Microsoft IEAK|IEAK Profile Manager).
2. Open a configuration file you previously created (probably by using the wizard): From the File menu, select Open and then double-click the desired `.INS` file.
3. If the option is not already expanded, click the plus (+) sign on the left side of the screen for System Policies and Restrictions and then click the plus sign for Web Desktop.
4. Finally, click Desktop and scroll down through the list of available options on the right side of the window. In particular, notice that you can disable the adding, deleting, editing, and closing of *any* desktop item.

5.2.11 Practice Problems

1. You want to keep users from changing the custom desktop wallpaper on which your organization has standardized. How could you do this?

   A. Clear the Users May Specify Wallpaper check box under the Desktop Wallpaper option of the Wizard Settings.

   B. Clear the Users May Specify Wallpaper check box under the User Agent option of the Wizard Settings.

   C. Check the Disable Changing Wallpaper box under the System option under System Policies and Restrictions.

   D. Check the Disable Changing Wallpaper box under the Desktop option under System Policies and Restrictions.

5.2.12 Answers and Explanations: Practice Problems

1. **D** Restricting desktop wallpaper settings by selecting No HTML Wallpaper and Disable Changing Wallpaper are just two of the options available to you with the IEAK Profile Manager under System Policies and Restrictions, Web Desktop, Desktop.

5.3 Optimizing

A great deal of the responsibility for optimizing what we have spoken about so far lies with the individuals who author Web sites and create `.CDF` files.

Some Web site authors create huge, inefficient Web pages that require complete downloading before users discover that there is nothing of value on the pages. If users insist on subscribing to these sites—and therefore consume more than their share of resources (disk space and network bandwidth)— you, as the administrator, can do something about it.

Here are some additional optimization techniques available to the administrator:

- Enabling smooth scrolling
- Enabling page transitions
- Limiting audio and video capabilities
- Optimizing Java VM settings

5.3.1 Caching

In IE 4.0, there are two aspects of caching of which you should be aware:

- The Temporary Internet Files folder
- The History folder

All Web pages (including all the sites and channels to which the user has subscribed) are downloaded to the user's local system before they are displayed. The place in which these files are stored as well as the amount of disk space allocated to the storage of these pages are defined by the Temporary Internet Files settings.

You can view these settings in IE 4.0 by selecting View|Internet Options and then clicking the Settings button in the Temporary Internet Files section of the General page. Also on the General page, you will find a History section directly below the Temporary Internet Files section. Use the History settings to tell IE 4.0 how long to keep pointers to pages on your system.

Caching (storing locally) of previously accessed pages allows the pages to be displayed without having to download them again. There are pros and cons to caching.

Here are some of the pros to caching:

- Decreased access time
- Decreased network traffic (reduced I/O)
- Offline access

Here are some of the cons of caching:

- The possibility of viewing stale data
- Increased disk storage requirements
- Security risks caused by sensitive information residing in numerous locations

5.3.2 Exercise

In this exercise, you will use the IEAK Profile Manager to access an existing `.INS` configuration file and modify the available options that affect caching.

1. Open the IEAK Profile Manager (from the Start menu, select Programs|Microsoft IEAK|IEAK Profile Manager).
2. Open a configuration file you previously created (probably by using the Wizard): From the File menu, select Open and then double-click on the desired `.INS` file.
3. Expand the System Policies and Restrictions settings.

Note that although the IEAK Profile Manager allows you to prevent users from changing the default cache and history settings, it does ***not*** provide a way to customize the settings.

5.3.3 Practice Problems

1. The History folder has undergone several changes for IE 4.0. What new functionality is now available to users? (Select all that apply.)

   A. The user can set the History folder size based on kilobytes of disk space.

   B. The user can set the History folder size based on the number of days the items are stored in the folder.

   C. The user can set the History folder size based on the number of entries in the folder.

   D. The user can review entries for a specific day.

2. You have just installed a 4-gigabyte hard disk on your system. You want to move the folder you use to receive site and channel updates to which you subscribe. How do you do this?

   A. From IE 4.0, select Favorites|Manage Subscriptions and then click Settings under Temporary Internet Files.

   B. From IE 4.0, select View|Internet Options and then click Settings on Temporary Internet Files under the General tab.

   C. From IE 4.0, go to Advanced, then enable the Let Me Specify Cache Setting option.

   D. This can be done only by the corporate administrator, using the IEAK Profile Manager.

5.3.4 Answers and Explanations: Practice Problems

1. **D** Selecting the History button from the toolbar brings up the History dialog box. Answer B is not a new feature of IE 4.0.

2. **B** The Temporary Internet Files dialog box has not changed from IE 3.x, but the steps to get to the settings dialog box are slightly different in IE 4.0. For answer D, the IEAK allows administrators to restrict access to the History folder, but access is granted by default.

5.3.5 Performance

As mentioned at the beginning of this chapter, there are four resources in a computing environment:

- CPU subsystem
- Memory subsystem
- Disk subsystem
- Network subsystem

Maximizing system performance is a matter of balancing the use of these four resources so that a shortage of any one resource does not become a system bottleneck. You should remember that changing any one of the parameters that control these subsystems can affect one or all of the remaining subsystems. For example, insufficient system memory results in increased paging and swapping (disk I/O), which eats up more CPU cycles.

You must also understand and take into consideration the users' requirements when you are striving to optimize system performance. For example, a user who needs relatively real-time video for NetMeeting requires a system with a higher-end video card with maximum memory and processing capability and increased network bandwidth than does the system of a user who has no or minimal video requirements.

An efficient strategy for the distribution to end users of custom packages of Internet Explorer 4.0 is another area of performance optimization that is often overlooked. Chapter 1 of the *Microsoft Internet Explorer 4.0 Deployment Guide* (available on TechNet, or on the Internet at `http://www.microsoft.com/ie/corp/?/ie/corp/deployguide.htm`) contains a section on specifying distribution strategies and covers network performance and bandwidth issues in some detail.

5.3.6 Exercise

CPU speed has increased, the cost of memory (RAM) has decreased, and disk drive capacity and disk controller performance have increased. Network I/O has emerged as the typical bottleneck of today. Add to this the ever-increasing size of some of today's Internet pages, and it is not hard to understand why a proactive approach to managing how and what users can download must be taken. This exercise will familiarize you with some of the steps you can take to control the amount of information downloaded by users and when scheduled downloads take place.

1. Open the IEAK Profile Manager (from the Start menu, select Programs|Microsoft IEAK|IEAK Profile Manager).
2. Open a configuration file you previously created (probably by using the Wizard): From the File menu, select Open and then double-click on the desired `.INS` file.
3. If the option is not already expanded, click the plus (+) sign on the left side of the screen for System Policies and Restrictions and then click the plus sign for Internet Restrictions. Click the General tab to display the available options:

- Click the Disable Changing Cache Settings check box to prohibit users from changing the cache settings (available in Internet Explorer by selecting View|Internet Options|Temporary Internet Files|Settings). Specifically, this option keeps users from consuming great quantities of disk space as Internet cache.
- Click the Disable Changing History Settings check box to prohibit users from changing the cache settings (available in Internet Explorer by selecting View|Internet Options|History). Specifically, this option keeps users from worsening stale data issues.

4. Open an existing configuration file using IEAK Profile Manager as outlined in previous exercises.
5. Under System Policies and Restrictions, expand the Subscriptions folder and then click the Subscriptions option.
6. Make note of the various parameters available that you can use to restrict bandwidth utilization. In particular, notice that you can restrict the hours during which updates are performed.

Although restricting updates to the middle of the night has the most impact on the overall improvement of network performance, do not change the bandwidth settings unless you have a complete understanding of the following issues:

- What each parameter does.
- The overall network utilization (accidentally restricting subscription updates to the same time frame during which network backups take place would not be a good thing).

One of the capabilities of Microsoft's NetMeeting is video conferencing. Video conferencing requires a tremendous amount of network bandwidth. And just because a user does not have video hardware (a camera) on his or her desktop doesn't mean that he or she cannot receive video. Restricting the use of video to only those users who have a need for it can help to ensure efficient use of available network resources.

In this exercise, you will disable the Video Options page for certain users.

1. Open an existing configuration file using IEAK Profile Manager as outlined in previous exercises. For example, if you created one configuration file for upper management called `UPRMGMT.INS` and another file for everyone else called `EVRYONE.INS`, open `EVRYONE.INS` for this exercise.
2. Under System Policies and Restrictions, expand the Microsoft NetMeeting folder and then click the NetMeeting Settings option.
3. Notice the various options available on the right side of the display.
4. Scroll about halfway down the right side of the display until you see a box labeled Disable the Video Options Page. Check this box to prohibit users from modifying the NetMeeting video options you have predefined for them.
5. Scroll a little further down the right side of the display until you see a section titled Restrict the Use of Video. The options available here allow you to prevent the user from sending video and/or prevent the user from receiving video.

5.3.7 Practice Problems

1. You are performing a demonstration highlighting NetMeeting capabilities between two of your company's sites. Everyone is relatively happy with the way NetMeeting performs until you enable video, at which time total response no longer meets expectations. What could be done to improve performance with video enabled? (Select all that apply)

   A. Purchase higher quality video hardware (cameras)

   B. Use faster PCs for the demonstration

   C. Upgrade the video cards

   D. Change the refresh rate on the monitors

2. Most of the systems on your network are older 486/66 PCs. Your users think that the Pipes and Maze screen savers "are really cool." Some users are complaining that they need faster CPUs to ensure that the batch jobs they run at night complete in time. What is one thing you can do to most improve things immediately?

   A. Install more memory.

   B. Disable all screen savers.

   C. Delete all 3D screen savers.

   D. Order CPU upgrade chips.

3. What is one of the first steps you take in IE 4.0 to view files offline that have been loaded from a subscription?

   A. On the toolbar, click File|Work Offline.

   B. On the toolbar, click View|Offline Files.

   C. On the Explorer bar, click View|Offline Folder.

   D. On the Explorer bar, click Files|Offline.

4. How many download sites can you specify for each installation package you build with IEAK 4.0?

   A. 1

   B. 5

   C. 10

   D. An unlimited number

5. What IEAK Profile Manager menu option allows you to prevent users from changing the settings for the space allocated for channel downloading?

   A. Internet Restrictions, General

   B. Internet Restrictions, Code Download

   C. Internet Restrictions, Channel Settings

   D. Subscriptions, Subscriptions

5.3.8 Answers and Explanations: Practice Problems

1. **B, C** Better video cards or faster PCs would enhance performance. Although altering the refresh rate on the monitor and improving the quality of the video equipment will provide better quality video, it will not enhance performance.

2. **C** The 3D screen savers take up a great deal of available CPU resources. Deleting all screen savers isn't the best choice because the screen savers are probably password protected and, hence, are in place as a security measure.

3. **A** Selecting File|Work Offline from the toolbar places you into Working Offline mode.

4. **C** You can specify up to 10 download sites. On large networks, you would want to make download sites available on multiple segments to minimize network traffic.

5. **A** Internet Restrictions, General, Disable changing cache settings.

CHAPTER 6

Troubleshooting

A perspective voiced by many individuals is that there are no such things as problems, there are only opportunities. In this chapter, we will cover the tools available to you when these "opportunities" arise and detail some of the more common problem indications, troubleshooting techniques, and problem resolutions associated with IE 4.0 and the IEAK.

The Microsoft certification exam objectives covered in this chapter are listed here:

- Diagnose and resolve the deployment failure of a preconfigured version of Internet Explorer 4.0.
- Diagnose and resolve problems related to the IEAK Wizard.
- Diagnose and resolve connection failures of Outlook Express.
- Diagnose and resolve connection failures of NetMeeting.
- Diagnose and resolve failures of Webcasting, including site subscriptions, channels, and Active Desktop items.
- Diagnose and resolve failure of caching.
- Choose the appropriate tool for troubleshooting network connection failures, including IP configuration, Ping, Trace Route, Network Monitor, and NSLOOKUP.

Internet Explorer 4.0 has more configuration options than either Windows 3.1 or Windows for Workgroups 3.11. Considering the following, the potential for configuration issues to arise is pretty good:

- Users have far more options available to configure (customize) their desktops than they have ever had in the past.
- Corporate administrators, content providers, and Internet Service Providers (ISPs) have more flexibility in deciding what to allow users to do and what to restrict them from doing than they have ever had in the past (and with far greater ease).
- Webmasters now have Channel Definition Format files available to them through which they may have certain control over what happens to the desktops of users who have subscribed to channels. (The amount of "may have" can be restricted with the IEAK.)

- Do *not* reinstall IE 3.x after installing IE 4.x without completely uninstalling/removing IE 4.x first. Even if you install IE 3.x in a different folder or on a different drive, weird problems could be encountered. You can uninstall IE 4.0 and its associated components with the Add/Remove Programs icon in the Control Panel.

> **If you wind up with problems caused by something like an install or uninstall not completing properly, a tool worth researching is** `ieremove.exe`**.**

Divide and conquer is a saying you have probably heard in the past. If you are asked to define the word *troubleshoot* in as few words as possible, *divide and conquer* would be hard to beat. What this means is to segment the problem (oops, I mean *opportunity*) into smaller pieces. Although you can move the steps around from time to time, there are certain given components of any successful troubleshooting procedure:

- Above all else, don't panic.
- Maintain a positive attitude. This can be more important than how quickly you resolve things.
- Document, document, document. Keeping a written record of what you did to resolve things—or to attempt to resolve things—can be invaluable at a later date.
- Believe none of what you hear and only half of what you see. Just kidding (kind of), but don't run off half-cocked based on the first thing or two you are told or see. And, yes, documentation has been known to be in error.
- Don't overlook the obvious. User-applied configuration changes aren't as simple to spot as they used to be, but this is still one obvious place to start. Ask the user what he or she last changed, even though you already know the answer is going to be, "Nothing."
- Don't assume anything.
- Have fun. Keep things in perspective.

Okay, now that we have covered the *how* of troubleshooting, let's move on to *what with*.

6.1 Tools

In the beginning, the tools required to repair computers consisted of a hammer and a bigger hammer. (Again, just kidding—at least partially. In the days of vacuum tubes, tapping on the tubes to check for noise was done all the time. In the days of thousands of printed circuit cards, vibrating them slightly was the accepted approach when looking for intermittent failures.) The hammers of today are bundled into most operating systems or are available as add-on tools and utilities.

The troubleshooting tools you need to be familiar with for the IEAK exam are listed here:

- IP configuration tools (IPCONFIG and WINIPCFG)
- Ping

- Trace Route
- NSLOOKUP
- Network Monitor

You should have a good understanding of TCP/IP and the utilities just listed, which are TCP/IP utilities.

6.1.1 IP Configuration

The IP (Internet Protocol) configuration of your computer determines what other computers, if any, you can communicate with. The tool used to display IP settings varies based on the platform.

- For Windows 95, from the Start menu, select Run, enter **`WINIPCFG`** in the box in the Run window, and click OK. Then click the More Info button. Alternatively, you can enter **`WINIPCFG/all`** to get the same results (see Figure 6.1.1).

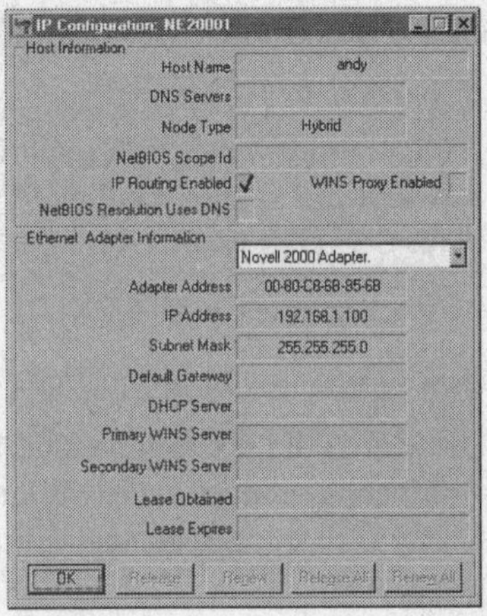

Figure 6.1.1 IP configuration in Windows 95

- For Windows NT, type **`IPCONFIG/all`** at the command prompt. Windows 98 will offer the IPCONFIG utility as well.

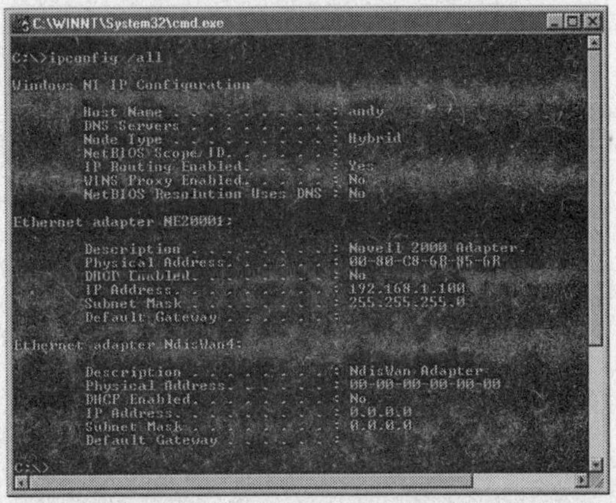

Figure 6.1.2 IP configuration in Windows NT

IP settings vary depending on whether your computer is on a network or is a standalone system used for dialing in to an ISP or corporate network. Settings also vary depending on whether or not you are connected to a network at the time. The following exercise walks you through the use of WINIPCFG (or IPCONFIG if you are on a Windows NT system).

6.1.2 Exercise

To include multiple scenarios, this exercise covers dialing in to an ISP and bringing up a tunneling product to access a private network. Point-to-Point Tunneling Protocol (PPTP) provides a way to create a virtual private network by encapsulating encrypted packets in PPP packets across an asynchronous communications link.

1. From a Windows 95 computer that is not connected to any other computers, click Start, select Run, enter **`WINIPCFG`** in the box in the Run window, and click OK. Then click the More Info button. (On a Windows NT system, go to a DOS command prompt and enter **`IPCONFIG/all`**.)
2. Note the IP configuration information displayed on the screen. In particular, the settings for IP Address, Subnet Mask, Default Gateway, and DNS Servers are of interest.
3. Dial in to your ISP and establish a connection. Note that the display is *not* dynamic. You must exit the tool and invoke it again to get current information.
4. Note the changes to the IP configuration, which are a result of the PPP handshaking that took place between your client system and your ISP. (Understanding PPP is beyond the scope of what you will be required to know about IP for the IEAK exam.)
5. Tunnel into your corporate network (if one is available).
6. Exit the tool and invoke it again to get current information.
7. Note that the IP configuration settings did not change. This is because your client system is really talking to your ISP and your tunneling product (which assigns you IP information based on your corporate network's address range) is running as an application on top of PPP.

6.1.3 Questions

1. You are having trouble accessing some channels as well as some of your favorite Web sites. You want to check the IP settings on your Windows NT system. What utility would you use?

   A. IPCONFIG

   B. WINIPCFG

   C. Help

   D. Network Monitor

2. You are running a Windows 95 client system and you cannot access any Web pages. What tool would you use and how would you access it?

   A. IPCONFIG from a DOS prompt.

   B. IPCONFIG from the Start, Run window.

   C. WINIPCFG from a DOS prompt.

   D. WINIPCFG from the Start, Run window.

3. A user can access a certain Web site by using its IP address, but can't get to it using its name. You suspect DNS problems. What tool would you use to view the DNS setting?

   A. IPCONFIG.

   B. WINIPCFG.

   C. IPCONFIG on an NT system and WINIPCFG on a Windows 95 system.

   D. You can't view this; it is dynamic and is continually changing.

4. What do you type at the command prompt on a Windows NT 4.0 system to view IP configuration information?

   A. `IPCONFIG`

   B. `IPCONFIG /all`

   C. `show ip configuration`

   D. `show ip /configuration`

6.1.4 Answers

1. **A** IPCONFIG is the Windows NT utility you would use to view your IP configuration settings.

2. **D** WINIPCFG is the Windows 95 utility you would use. Because it is a Windows utility, it is better to run it from the Start, Run window instead of running it from a DOS prompt.

3. **C** An easy way to remember this is that the *win* part of WINIPCFG goes with Win95. (Most people refer to Windows NT simply as NT.)

4. **B** Don't forget the `/all` switch.

6.1.5 Ping

Ping is one of the most useful IP protocol tools available for checking primitive TCP/IP communications. If you are not already familiar with Ping and its use, you soon will be. It is the quickest, easiest, and most widely available tool for determining connectivity status and resolving issues.

Computers talk to each other on the Internet by using TCP/IP (Transmission Control Program/Internet Protocol) and by referencing each other by their IP addresses. IP addresses currently consist of four sets of numbers separated by periods. When a user attempts to contact a site on the Internet, the user attempts to establish the connection by providing the computer's name rather than the IP address. DNS is used to translate computer names into their IP addresses.

Ping sends a packet of information from the system you are currently on to the specified destination and listens for a reply. If you do get a reply, you are also given some additional information such as how long it took to receive the reply. An experienced pinger can use this information to determine how well the network is running (to some degree) as well as whether it is working at all.

To use Ping, you issue a `Ping` command at the command prompt. Depending on the platform you are using, there are several ways to get to a command prompt. On a Windows 95 system, you have the following options:

- You can click the MS-DOS icon available on the Microsoft Office shortcut bar (if you are running Office and have the shortcut bar configured to display the MS-DOS icon).
- You can click the Start button, select Programs, and select the MS-DOS Prompt option.
- You can click the Start button, select Run, and enter **`command.com`** in the Run window. (This approach yields slightly different results than the preceding two options. This command brings up a DOS window; the preceding two options turn your whole terminal into a DOS screen.)

After you are at a command prompt, you simply enter the `Ping` command followed either by a Fully Qualified Domain Name (FQDN) or an IP address, depending on where you are in the troubleshooting process.

Entering the `Ping` command by itself, with no destination, returns the equivalent of help on Ping: a list of usage instructions and options.

Here is a brief overview of the steps you might take when using Ping to troubleshoot a suspected network problem (see Figure 6.1.3):

1. `Ping 127.0.0.1`. This is the built-in IP loopback address provided for testing purposes. If this fails, you have a major TCP/IP problem on your local client node. There is absolutely no reason to go any further until you get this working.
2. Ping your own IP address. If step 1 worked, this step better work as well, because pinging yourself also uses the loopback feature. If this step fails and step 1 worked, verify the IP address of your local system.

3. Ping your gateway. Gateways (also known as routers) connect sections (segments) of a network. If this step doesn't work, you can either try the ping from another system or check this system for cable problems.
4. Ping a node on the other side of the gateway.

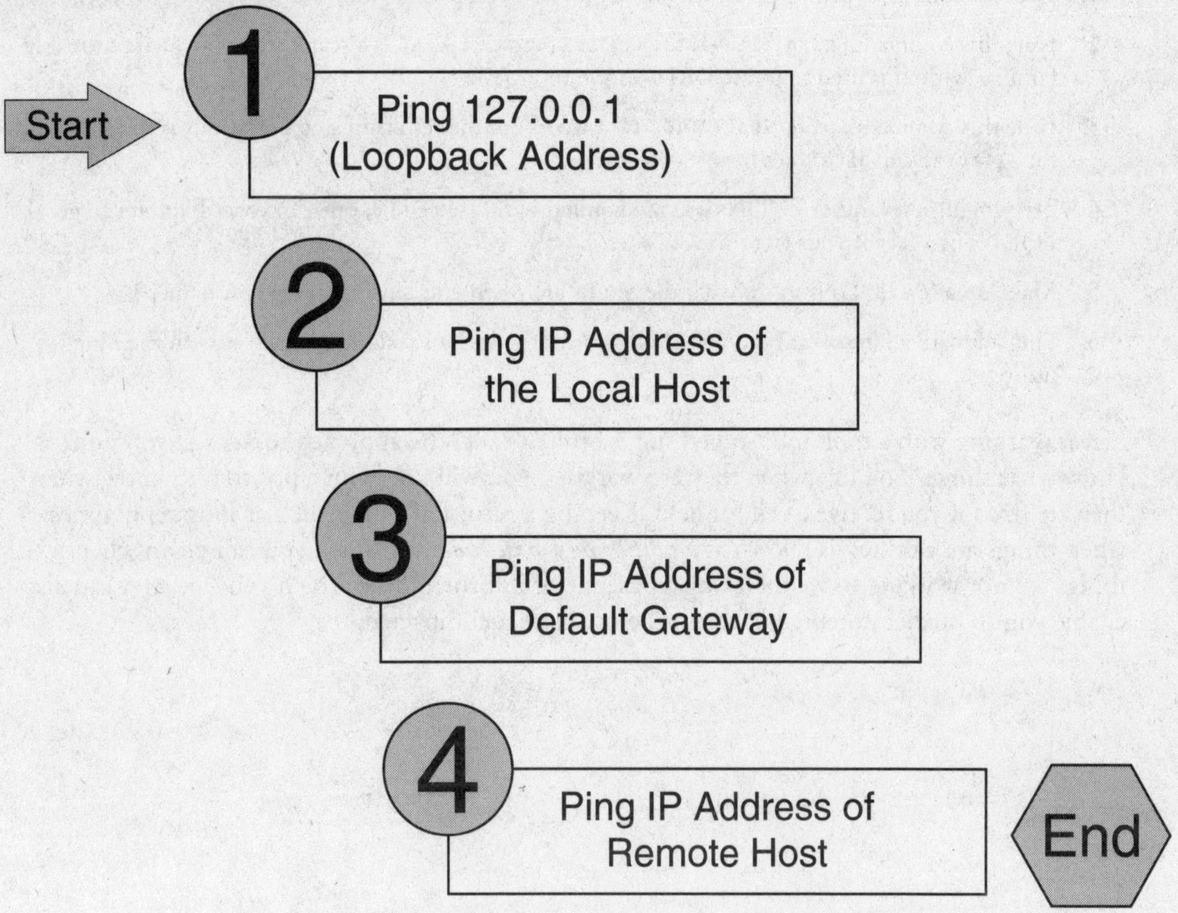

Figure 6.1.3 Troubleshooting network problems with Ping

If steps 1 through 4 worked, your network hardware is working and it is time to test DNS.

5. Ping your system by its name.
6. Ping several other systems by name.

If step 6 works and your application (for example, IE 4.0) still doesn't work, begin looking at setup and the options for the application. Try some other application to see whether *it* can talk to other systems.

6.1.6 Exercise

This exercise will show you the results of pinging a Fully Qualified Domain Name as well as pinging an IP address. You then ping a nonexistent name and a nonexistent IP address.

1. Get to a command prompt with whichever method you prefer.
2. Issue this command: **`ping altavista.digital.com`** (AltaVista is a search engine you are probably familiar with; it is used to locate URLs on the Internet).
3. Issue this command: **`ping 204.74.103.37`** (note from the results of step 2 that this is the IP address for `altavista.digital.com`).
4. Try pinging a few other FQDNs you are familiar with. If need be, open Internet Explorer to get the FQDNs of a few of your favorite Web sites.
5. Make up a few FQDNs to see what the results are when you ping a nonexistent name.
6. Ping a few IP addresses at random. Make note of the various results you can see with the Ping utility.

Never working with a tool until something is broken is *not* the approach to take. If you don't know what things look like when they are working, you will not be in a position to know when they are fixed if you receive a call for help. Keeping a record of things such as Ping reply times when things are working is known as *establishing a baseline* from which you can begin when things are not working so well. Having a baseline of information to which you can refer can also enable you to predict potential problems before users are impacted.

6.1.7 Questions

1. One of your users has called stating that she cannot access your company's Web site on the Internet, but others in her department can. She has been using an IE 4.0 deployment kit you created two weeks ago. What are some things you would have her try? (Select all correct answers.)

   A. See whether she can access any other sites. If so, have her click the IE 4.0 Refresh button to ensure that she is not displaying data from cache.

   B. Have her go to a command prompt and issue a few `Ping` commands.

   C. Have her try reinstalling IE 4.0.

   D. Have her try rebooting her system.

2. You issue the command `ping 127.0.0.1` and the request times out. What can cause this? (Select two answers.)

   A. You forgot to install a loopback connector.

   B. The NIC card could be bad.

   C. The cable from your system to the network hub could be defective.

   D. TCP/IP is not installed properly.

3. You can ping your company's IP address on the Internet, but you get a `Bad IP Address` message when you ping its FQDN. What can cause this?

   A. Stale cache data.

   B. Running an out-of-rev version of Internet Explorer.

   C. A DNS problem.

   D. You typed in the IP address wrong when you issued the `Ping` command.

4. You can ping yourself and some of the nodes in your office, but you receive a `Request Timed Out` message when you ping other nodes in your office. Results are consistent regardless of whether you use FQDNs or IP addresses. What could be wrong? (Select all correct answers.)

   A. A gateway or router could be down.

   B. The nodes you can't ping could be misconfigured.

   C. There could be a cable problem.

   D. The nodes you can't ping could be powered off.

5. Your company rolled out IE 4.0 about a month ago and now most of the information you need to do your job is made available to you over Web pages on an intranet. You can reach most sites, but some of the data seems to be old, and there are some sites you cannot reach. What could be wrong?

   A. There is an intermittent cable between your system and the hub.

   B. A router is down.

   C. The IE 4.0 deployment kit had several restrictions imposed in it.

   D. The wrong version of IEAK was used to build the IE 4.0 deployment kit you installed.

6.1.8 Answers

1. **A, B** Answers A and B are the only correct answers. Although C and D are things you may have to resort to, they are not things you would have her try initially. Answer C is incorrect because the question states that the user has been using IE 4.0, so you can assume that it worked at one time. Answer D is incorrect because it is advisable to take a minute to find out some details about what doesn't work before doing something like rebooting.

2. **B, D** `127.0.0.1` is an internal loopback, and therefore does not require any special test connectors or external cables, ruling out answers A and C.

6

3. **C** The generic term for being able to ping an IP address and not being able to ping an FQDN is *a DNS problem* (at least from the perspective of the IEAK exam). Arguably, answer D could also be correct in this case, but to use that line of thinking is beyond the scope of the IEAK exam.

4. **A, B, C, and D** All answers are correct. We aren't told enough about the configuration or history of the problem. A gateway or router problem would be the obvious answer, but there may not even be a gateway or router in the configuration. If this is a thinwire installation with all nodes running on a single hub, one cable segment could be bad. If this is a new installation, several nodes could be misconfigured. Nodes must be powered on, connected to the network, and properly configured to respond to a `Ping` command.

5. **B** A router (or gateway) being down is the correct answer. If the problem was caused by restrictions in the IE 4.0 deployment kit, you would have noticed it immediately.

6.1.9 Trace Route

You can think of Trace Route (`tracert`) as a `Ping` command that also gives you information about interim stops along the way to your destination. Ping tells you whether or not a site is accessible; `tracert` helps answer the question of why a site is not accessible. If Ping tells you there's a problem, you should next use `tracert` to find out where the problem is (see figure 6.1.4).

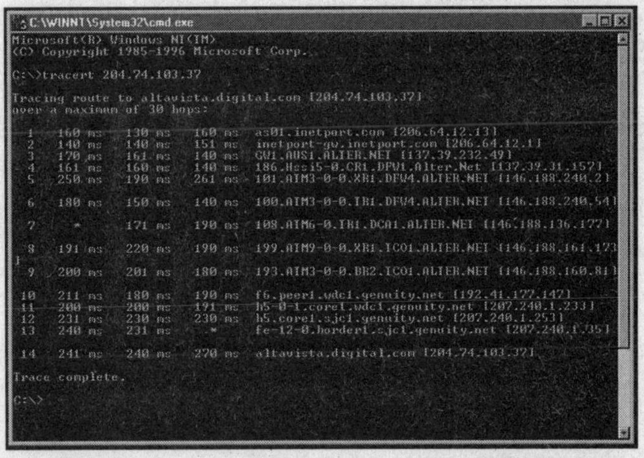

Figure 6.1.4 Locating network problems with `tracert`

One interesting item of note regarding `tracert` is that several Web sites on the Internet have implemented a sort of reverse Trace Route functionality: you can plug in your IP address or FQDN and see what the route *to* you looks like from that node.

6

6.1.10 Exercise

This exercise will show you the results of `tracert` commands issued to the same Fully Qualified Domain Name and IP address you used for the Ping command in the preceding exercise.

1. Get to a command prompt with whichever method you prefer.
2. Issue this command: `tracert altavista.digital.com`.
3. Issue this command: `ping 204.74.103.37` (note from the results of step 2 that this is the IP address for `altavista.digital.com`).
4. If you want, issue a `tracert` command for a few of the other FQDNs you experimented with in the previous exercise.

6.1.11 Questions

1. You issue a `Ping` command to a FQDN and receive a `Request Timed Out` message. What could you try next?

   A. Issue the same Ping command except use the `-v` (verbose) switch.

   B. Issue the same Ping command except use the `-r` (route) switch.

   C. Issue a `tracert` command to the same FQDN.

   D. Issue a Ping command from the original destination node and see whether you can ping yourself (the original source node).

2. Under what circumstances would you issue the command `tracert 127.0.0.1`?

   A. When troubleshooting a local loopback problem.

   B. When troubleshooting a problem on a thinwire segment.

   C. When troubleshooting a 10BaseT cable problem between your system and the hub.

   D. Probably never.

3. Why would you ever want to run a `tracert` command from a distant node to your node?

   A. Never. No value can be gained from this because you have no idea how the remote node is configured.

   B. Running `tracert` commands from one or more remote systems back to your system can help give you a better picture of what the network looks like and possibly shed some light on where the bottlenecks are.

   C. Trace Route information from point A to point B is useless without knowing the information from point B to point A.

   D. Ping information without `tracert` information is of little or no value.

6.1.12 Answers

1. **C** A `tracert` command will give you some detail about where the Ping command failed.

2. **D** `127.0.0.1` is the local loopback IP address. If the `ping 127.0.0.1` command fails, no additional information can be gained by issuing a `tracert 127.0.0.1` command.

3. **C** C is the only correct answer.

6.1.13 NSLOOKUP

NSLOOKUP (see Figure 6.1.5) is a Windows NT TCP/IP diagnostic utility you can run from an MS-DOS command prompt to display information from DNS name servers. There is no equivalent tool for Windows 95.

Here is the syntax for NSLOOKUP:

```
nslookup [-option] hostname
```

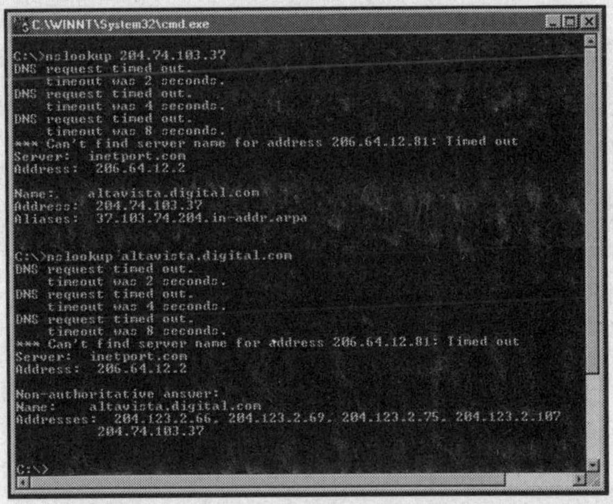

Figure 6.1.5 Viewing information from DNS servers

Entering `nslookup` without a *hostname* gets you to a > prompt from which you can type **`help`** to display the NSLOOKUP help file. Additional information about how to use `NSLOOKUP` (as well as other TCP/IP utilities) is available under Control Panel Help in the topic TCP/IP Procedures Help.

6.1.14 Exercise

> **This exercise can be performed only on a Windows NT system. NSLOOKUP does not exist on Windows 95.**

1. From the Start menu, select Programs and then select Command Prompt. This action opens a command prompt window and gets you to a `C:\>` prompt.
2. Type **`nslookup`** and press Enter. The name and IP address of your default server is displayed, and the prompt changes to >.
3. Type **`help`** and press Enter to display the NSLOOKUP help information.
4. Type **`exit`** and press Enter to return to the `C:\>` prompt.
5. Type **`exit`** and press return to close the command prompt window.

6

6.1.15 Questions

1. You suspect DNS problems with your Windows NT system. How do you run the DNS Name Server utility NSLOOKUP?

   A. Click Start, Run, NSLOOKUP.

   B. From an MS-DOS command prompt. The utility is bundled into Windows NT.

   C. From TechNet.

   D. From Microsoft's Active Channel Web page on the Internet.

2. When you run NSLOOKUP, you receive an error message after the DNS times out stating, `Can't find server name for address 127.0.0.1: Timed out, Default servers are not available, Default Server: Unknown, Address 127.0.0.1`. What is wrong?

   A. You have specified the IP address of your DNS server as `127.0.0.1`, which is an illegal address.

   B. You have specified the IP address of your system as `127.0.0.1`, which is an illegal address.

   C. You have not specified a DNS server in your TCP/IP properties.

   D. You have specified multiple DNS servers in your TCP/IP properties, which is illegal.

3. You suspect DNS problems with your Windows 95 system. How do you run the DNS Name Server utility NSLOOKUP?

   A. Click Start, Run, NSLOOKUP.

   B. From an MS-DOS command prompt. The utility is bundled into Windows 95.

   C. From TechNet.

   D. NSLOOKUP is not available on Windows 95.

6.1.16 Answers

1. **B** The NSLOOKUP utility comes with Windows NT Workstation and Windows NT Server.

2. **C** There is a KnowledgeBase article on this subject (numbered Q172060). If you have no DNS server configured on your client, NSLOOKUP defaults to the local loopback address (`127.0.0.1`). Other utilities may react similarly.

3. **D** NSLOOKUP is a Windows NT-only tool.

6.1.17 Network Monitor

The basic Network Monitor tool is included with Windows NT Server 4.0. This version allows you to monitor network traffic to and from the server on which you are running Network Monitor and to display and analyze the captured information.

The full version of Network Monitor is available only with Systems Management Server (SMS). This version allows you to monitor all traffic on the network and also provides additional features and functionality over the version supplied with Windows NT Server 4.0 (see Figure 6.1.6).

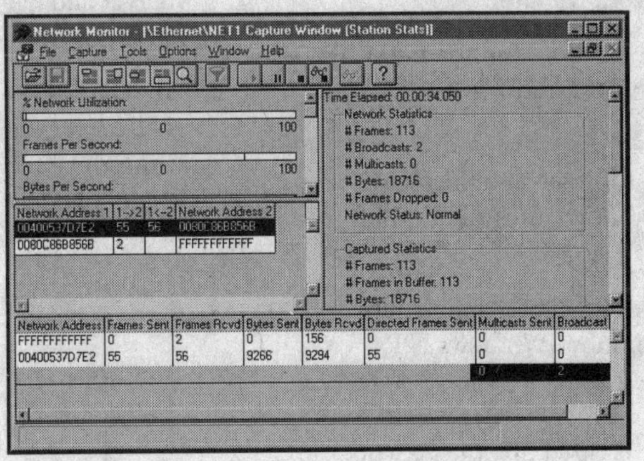

Figure 6.1.6 Monitoring network traffic

6.1.18 Exercise

This exercise assumes that you have a system available running Windows NT Server.

To install Network Monitor, follow these steps:

1. Right-click the Network Neighborhood icon on your desktop and then click Properties.
2. Click the Services tab to display Network Services.
3. Scroll down through the list of installed services to see whether Network Monitor Tools and Agent is present. If it is, skip steps 4 and 5.
4. Click Add, scroll through the list, click Network Monitor Tools and Agent, and click OK.
5. You are prompted to reboot the system to complete the installation.

To run Network Monitor, follow these steps:

1. Click Start|Programs|Administrative Tools (Common)|Network Monitor.
2. See the built-in online help for specifics on configuring and running Network Monitor.

6

6.1.19 Questions

1. Your system is running Windows NT Workstation 4.0. You want to monitor all network traffic in and out of your computer. How do you do this?

   A. You have to be running Windows NT Server to monitor network traffic to and from your local computer with Network Monitor.

   B. Bring up Network Monitor and select Monitor Entire Network under Options.

   C. Install the full version of Network Monitor from your distribution of SMS.

   D. Click Start|Programs|Administrative Tools (Common)|Windows NT Diagnostics.

2. Your users have reported that the network is slow. How would you monitor network traffic?

   A. With a Time Domain Reflectometer (TDR).

   B. With Windows NT Network Performance Monitor.

   C. On a Windows NT Server, run the SMS version of Network Monitor.

   D. With Windows NT Server Event Manager.

3. Your system is running Windows NT Server 4.0. You have to monitor traffic between two other systems on the network. How do you do this?

   A. You bring up Network Monitor and select the Monitor Remote Nodes option.

   B. You must be running the Network Monitor included with SMS.

   C. The systems you want to monitor must be on the same network segment as your system.

   D. You have to enter the IP addresses of the systems you want to monitor into the Network Monitor database.

6.1.20 Answers

1. **A** Network Monitor only comes with (and only runs on) Windows NT Server.

2. **C** You must be running Windows NT Server and have installed the Network Monitor from the SMS kit.

3. **B** The Network Monitor that comes with NT Server only monitors traffic to and from the node you run it on. To monitor remote nodes, you must install the Network Monitor from the SMS kit.

6.2 Find and Fix

When troubleshooting any problem, the procedure to follow is given here:

1. Gather the indications.
2. Diagnose the problem.
3. Form a method for resolution.
4. Implement the method until resolution occurs.
5. Document the process.

The same troubleshooting technique can be used with the IEAK Wizard, IEAK Profile Manager, and IE 4.0. For the certification exam, you are expected to take a set of indications and various methods for resolving a problem, and to select the answer that will most likely aid in diagnosing a problem or implementing a resolution.

6.2.1 IEAK Wizard

The IEAK Wizard is the tool used to create custom deployment packages for IE 4.0. There are minimum hardware and software requirements for the computer on which the IEAK Wizard will be running, and you are expected to know these requirements.

The wizard can run in one of three different modes: CP, ISP, and CA. You must know the differences between these modes, and what functionality each provides.

Microsoft states that if you are not connected to the Internet, the IEAK Wizard may appear to run correctly but may not create a valid deployment package. You must know the indications if you are not connected to the Internet while running the IEAK Wizard, along with the effect this will have on the AVS functionality. The AVS feature verifies that you have the most current version of a component available locally (see Figure 6.2.1).

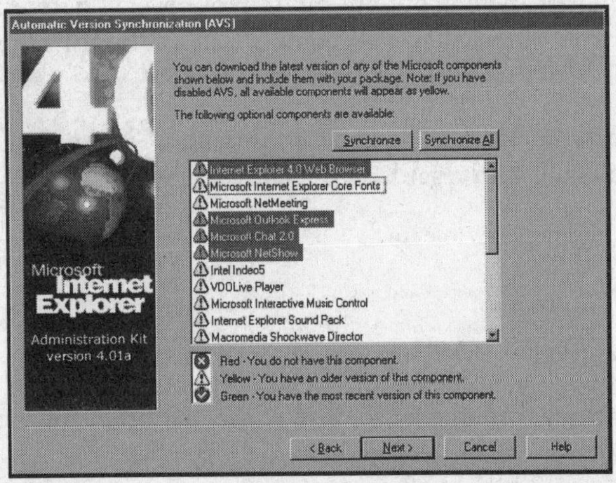

Figure 6.2.1 Automatic Version Synchronization with the IEAK Wizard

6

If you are not connected to the Internet or if AVS is not selected, all components that are available locally are displayed with a yellow icon. If you are connected to the Internet, the icons available are red, green, and yellow:

- **Red icon:** Indicates that you do not have a component available locally that is available from a download server on the Internet.
- **Yellow icon:** Indicates that you have a version of the component available locally, but that it is not as current as the version available from the download server on the Internet.
- **Green icon:** Indicates that you are connected to the Internet and you have the most current version of the component available locally.

When running the IEAK Wizard, you must realize what functionality is available in each of the modes. Here are some key points:

- Creation of single floppy deployment media is only available in ISP mode.
- The CMAK profile can be added only if you are running in CMAK mode.
- Automatic update is available only in CA mode.
- CA mode provides the ability for the administrator to control and limit more settings and functionality than ISP or CP mode.

6.2.2 Exercise

The first exercise in Chapter 3, "Configuring and Managing Resource Access," had you run the IEAK Wizard in ISP mode, making note of the configuration screens available. Then you ran the IEAK Wizard in Corporate Administrator mode, comparing and contrasting the differences between the two modes. If you have not performed that exercise, do so at this time.

6.2.3 Caching

Caching is a key concept to understanding the new capabilities available with IE 4.0 and the IEAK. Properly configured, caching options can improve overall system and network performance; if improperly configured, they will certainly lead to dissatisfied users, resulting in trouble calls.

As explained in Chapter 5, "Monitoring and Optimization," in the section "Optimizing," the two components of caching with regards to IE4 are as follows:

- The Temporary Internet Files folder
- The History folder

The area of primary concern is the Temporary Internet Files folder.

This section covers caching from the perspective of the user problems that can be encountered. The three most common problem areas relate to the following:

- Stale data
- Increased network I/O
- Reduced user disk space

The term *stale data* can refer to any data that is not current to the point of causing concern. Obviously, this is not a problem with static Web sites because the information never changes. But with active content, all data stored in a user's local cache could be stale to some extent. Subscribing to sites and channels is a way in which users can minimize the risk of dealing with stale data.

One downside to site subscriptions and channels is the increased network I/O they generate. Minimizing this risk potential requires users and authors alike to maintain awareness when scheduling download times and configuring subscription parameters.

Another potentially negative aspect of subscribing to sites and channels is the disk space requirements on local users' systems. Again, this requires vigilance, primarily on the part of users.

When a user subscribes to a Web site or channel, one or more of the following variables is available for customizing:

- Whether or not automatic downloading of the site will take place.
- Whether or not email notification of pages that have changed will take place.
- To what crawl depth will followed links be checked for updates.
- Which items from the updated page will be downloaded.
- Whether or not a limit will be imposed on how much content can be downloaded per update and, if so, what the limit will be.
- For channels, whether or not the subscription should allow updating based on the publisher's recommended schedule or the user's schedule.

6.2.4 Exercises

The first exercise will walk you through the process of subscribing to a site so that you can see what options are available to you regarding the downloading of updated information from the site. The second exercise will familiarize you with the options available for maintaining the cache and minimizing the potential problems caused by its misuse. As you go through these exercises, think of what user problems could be caused by a misuse of each of the variables.

1. While viewing a Web page with IE 4.0, click Favorites, Add to Favorites. This action brings up the Add Favorite window.
2. You are given three options:
   - Add the page to your Favorites folder, but do *not* subscribe to the page.
   - Add the page to your Favorites folder, subscribe to the page to receive notification of updates, but do *not* automatically download updates. (This option is called a *partial subscription.*)
   - Add the page to your Favorites folder, subscribe to the page to receive notification of updates, and automatically download updates for offline viewing. (This option is called a *full subscription.*)
3. Select the full subscription option and click the Customize button. You are walked through a subscription wizard, one function of which is to give you the opportunity to change your email address for notifications. (Note that when a page to which you have subscribed is updated, a red "gleam" is added to its icon in the Favorites menu.)

4. On the Advanced Download Page, you can choose a crawl depth (the Download Linked Pages Within a Depth Of option) and whether or not you want to follow links to pages outside the Web site to which you are subscribing. This is also where you choose which optional items you want to download from the page:
   - Images
   - Sound and video
   - ActiveX controls and Java applets
5. Last, but certainly not the least of the available options when it comes to affecting caching, you can limit the size of updates.

You can always modify subscription specifics at a later time by selecting Manage Subscriptions from the Favorites menu. As a final note, you should be familiar with the restrictions available with the IEAK that can affect each of the subscription items.

Now that you have established a site subscription, this second exercise will address how to customize, manage, and troubleshoot caching (see Figure 6.2.2).

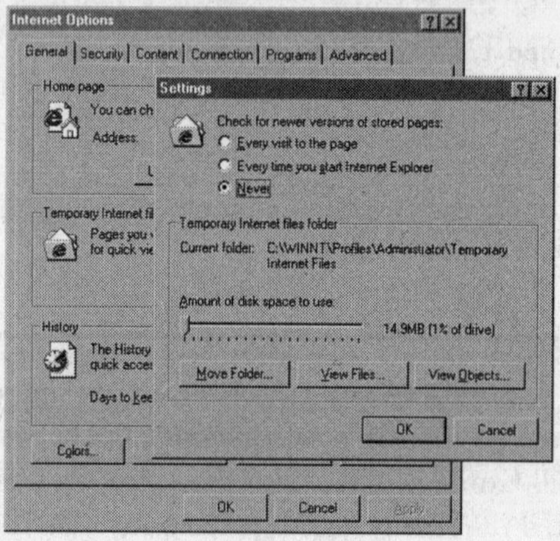

Figure 6.2.2 Caching options for temporary Internet files

1. With IE 4.0 open, select View|Internet Options.
2. Under Temporary Internet Files, click Settings. Note that you have the option of checking for newer versions of stored pages:
   - Every Visit to the Page. This option addresses the problem of stale data, but can create a network traffic issue.
   - Every Time you Start Internet Explorer.
   - Never. Although this option presents no network traffic issues, it creates a real potential for stale data.
3. By moving the sliding bar, you can limit the amount of disk space to be used for the Temporary Internet Files folder.

4. You can move the Temporary Internet Files folder to a different disk drive or partition. (Moving it off your system disk may be something you want to do depending on the space available.)
5. Click the View Files or the View Objects button to go to the Temporary Internet Files folder and display the available files or objects. (Although the View Objects button looks as though it has taken you to a different folder, you are, indeed, in the same folder as View Files.)
6. Selectively deleting files from the Temporary Internet Files folder is one sure way of resolving a suspected stale data problem. (The other is to click the IE Refresh button.)

6.2.5 Questions

1. Three users share one system. The system is running Windows NT 4.0 with IE 4.0 and has four large-capacity SCSI disk drives, three of which are allocated to the users. Two of the three users have requested much larger cache settings for IE because of some development work they are doing. What is the best way to meet their needs?

   A. Move the Temporary Internet Files folder to each user's respective disk drive and increase the amount of disk space the folder is allowed to grow to.

   B. Simply increase the IE setting of Amount of Disk Space to Use for the two users who need more space.

   C. Give the one user an IE deployment kit restricting his or her IE cache settings; give the other two users IE deployment kits with fewer cache restrictions.

   D. Extend the C partition.

2. What does it mean when an icon in your Favorites folder has a red gleam on it?

   A. The site contains adult material.

   B. The site is offline at the moment.

   C. The site content has changed since you last viewed it.

   D. You have password-protected the site.

3. A user says that he is sure that a site has been updated, but all he sees when he accesses the site is old information. What is the quickest thing you can have him do to ensure that he is not viewing stale data with IE?

   A. Have him contact the site author.

   B. Have him click the Refresh button.

   C. Have him click the Update Now button.

   D. Have him delete all entries from his Temporary Internet Files folder.

4. A user has called to say that she can't increase the size of her Temporary Internet Files folder to meet her needs. What could be wrong? (Select all correct answers.)

   A. She has been restricted from changing her cache settings.

   B. She is out of disk space.

   C. She has to delete all files from her Temporary Internet Files folder.

   D. She has to delete all objects from her Temporary Internet Files folder.

5. What is the minimum size the Temporary Internet Files folder can be set to?

   A. You can delete the folder.

   B. 5M

   C. 10M

   D. 1 percent of the size of the drive on which the folder resides.

6. How do you delete all files from your IE 4.0 Temporary Internet Files folder?

   A. Select View|Options|Folders|Settings and click the Empty Folder button.

   B. Select View|Internet Options, select the General tab, and delete the files under the Temporary Internet Files section.

   C. Select View|Internet Options|Settings and click the Empty Folder button.

   D. You have to do this from Windows Explorer.

6.2.6 Answers

1. **A** With profiles on NT, each user can have his or her own IE settings. One setting defines the location of the Temporary Internet Files folder. Assigning the

three users' cache folders to their respective disk drives is the best approach in this situation.

2. **C** The red gleam is one way to know that site content has been updated.

3. **B** Clicking on Refresh will initiate a new download of the site currently being viewed.

4. **A** A is the only correct answer.

5. **D** The size of the Temporary Internet Files folder is set as a percentage of the size of the drive on which the folder resides; 1 percent is the minimum value.

6. **B** Answer A is how this task was accomplished with IE 3.0.

6.2.7 Preconfigured IE 4.0 Deployment

There are two primary benefits to preconfiguring an IE 4.0 deployment package with the IEAK:

- Ease of deployment
- Manageability

The IEAK allows an administrator to automate the browser deployment and configuration process, thereby minimizing the time and effort required by users.

All the IE 4.0 options available to users can prove to be pretty overwhelming for them. By preconfiguring a deployment package, an administrator can simplify the installation for users.

In addition to simplifying things for users, an administrator can make his or her own life run much more smoothly: The administrator can improve the manageability of IE 4.0 by creating a preconfigured deployment package.

6.2.8 Outlook Express

The Internet Explorer 4.0 suite of products includes Microsoft's "full, Internet standards-based email client," Outlook Express. Outlook Express gives users the ability to send and receive items such as entire Web pages right from their browsers. Some of the features of Outlook Express include the following:

- A step-by-step Internet Connection Wizard.
- Automatic detection of, and the opportunity to import from, previous installations of Outlook, Exchange, Netscape, and Eudora email applications (including address books and messages).
- Users can personalize their mail by using stationary from Microsoft Greetings Workshop or customized backgrounds.
- Support for Internet standards as well as Internet protocols beyond SMTP, POP3, and NNTP.

6.2.9 Exercise

In this exercise, you will remove the name of your POP3 mail server and verify you cannot communicate with your mail server.

This exercise assumes that you are running Internet Explorer 4.0 with Outlook Express and have a valid POP3 mail server user account.

1. Open Outlook Express and establish communications with your mail server.
2. From the Tools menu, select Accounts. This action opens the Internet Accounts dialog box.
3. Click the Mail tab, click your mail account, and then click the Properties button. The Properties dialog box for that mail account appears. Select the Servers tab.
4. Record the setting for the Incoming POP3 Mail Server. (Note that this is a Fully Qualified Domain Name.)
5. Change the name of the incoming mail server to `Test`.

6. Click the Apply button and then click the OK button. This action closes the Properties dialog box for that mail account. Click Close to accept the settings.
7. From the main window of Outlook Express, click the Send and Receive button. You should receive a message stating that the mail server could not be found.
8. From the Tools menu, select Accounts. This action opens the Internet Accounts dialog box.
9. Click the Mail tab, click your mail account, and then click the Properties button. The Properties dialog box for that mail account appears. Select the Servers tab.
10. Change the name of the incoming mail server back to the FQDN you recorded in step 4.

In this exercise, you modified the incoming mail server FQDN and viewed the error message you receive when Outlook Express cannot communicate with the incoming mail server.

6.2.10 Questions

1. When configuring the POP3 mail server, how can you identify the mail server?

    A. NetBIOS name

    B. MAC address

    C. Email address

    D. FQDN

2. What is LDAP?

    A. Logically Dynamic Applied Programming; used for generating active components.

    B. Lightweight Directory Access Protocol; used to locate individuals on the Internet.

    C. Local Directory Application Protocol; replaces the Windows Explorer.

    D. Long Distance Access Program; allows you to send mail to far-off places.

6.2.11 Answers

1. **D** You specify the POP3 mail server by its FQDN.

2. **B** LDAP stands for Lightweight Directory Access Protocol. It is an Internet protocol that enables email programs to look up names and addresses from a server.

6.2.12 NetMeeting

NetMeeting is another product included in the Internet Explorer 4.0 suite. It provides desktop functionality to the user well beyond that of the typical browser. This functionality includes the following features:

- Real-time two-way audio communication across the Internet—even over 14.4 kbps modems.
- A text-based chat function.
- A basic whiteboard.
- Data conferencing—the sharing of applications such as presentations, word processing documents, and spreadsheets.
- Video communications and conferencing.

Obviously, this functionality depends on the hardware configuration. For example, cameras are required for video conferencing; a microphone, sound card, and speakers are required for audio communication. For near real-time video, high-end video processors are required, as is sufficient network I/O bandwidth capability.

6.2.13 Exercise

This exercise assumes that you are running IE4, have the IEAK CD-ROM available, and have not previously installed NetMeeting.

1. Insert the IEAK CD-ROM into your CD-ROM drive. If autorun is enabled, the Microsoft Internet Explorer Administration Kit Setup screen will be displayed.
2. Click Install Internet Explorer 4.01 Add-On Components.
3. The IE4 Component Download screen displays. A message box is then displayed, asking whether it is okay for Active Setup to examine your system. Press Enter or click Yes to continue.
4. Under Communication Components, you will see a box labeled Microsoft NetMeeting. (You will probably have to scroll down a little to see this option.) Click the box to select it. Note the Status column on the right side of the display. This column tells you which components are already installed and which ones are not.
5. Click Next in the bottom-right corner of the IE 4.0 Component display to continue.
6. Click Install Now.
7. Continue to follow the instructions.
8. When the installation completes, start NetMeeting for the first time.
9. On the second screen you come to, take note of the message regarding the sharing of applications.
10. Continue to follow the instructions through the remainder of the installation process.

6.2.14 Questions

1. Using NetMeeting, you are working on your PowerPoint presentation with several co-workers who are located in other sites. What must you do to enable all participants to make changes to the presentation?

   A. Everyone must have a copy of the presentation running on their local systems.

   B. You must create user accounts for everyone else on your local system.

   C. Only up to three people can have write access to a file or application at a time.

   D. You must grant permission to other conference participants to edit the content or control the application.

2. You are performing a demo between two of your company's sites to highlight NetMeeting's capabilities. Everyone is relatively happy with the way NetMeeting performs until you enable video, at which time total response no longer meets expectations. What things could be done to improve performance with video enabled? (Select two answers.)

   A. Purchase higher quality video hardware (cameras).

   B. Use faster CPUs with MMX for the demo.

   C. Upgrade the video cards.

   D. Change the refresh rate on the monitors.

3. You have scheduled weekly NetMeeting conferences with your parents who live 3000 miles away. They really appreciate being able to see their grandchildren on a regular basis and watch them grow up. What strategy could you implement to best use the available system resources, network I/O in particular?

   A. Freeze the video after you capture the picture you want on both ends.

   B. Shrink the video frame to the size of a postage stamp.

   C. Schedule the meetings for the middle of the night when traffic is the lowest.

   D. Tell everyone to move as little as possible.

6.2.15 Answers

1. **D** The person sharing the application must grant permission for others to edit or control the application.

2. **B, C** Using high-end video processing cards with maximum available memory to offload the CPU is the one place to start when attempting to improve the response of video conferencing. Using a faster CPU with MMX also helps (possibly considerably).

3. **A** Freezing the video will free up that portion of network I/O. Your parents, your spouse, and your kids will not put up with any of the other three proposals.

6.2.16 Webcasting

Webcasting is a relatively new term that encompasses push updating of selected information on a user's desktop through inconspicuous distribution over the Internet or an intranet at prearranged times. The push updates are a result of the user's request in the form of a site or channel subscription.

Site Subscriptions

Webcasting of existing Web sites is made available through IE 4.0 with no action on the part of site authors or changes to the sites. Users initiate the process by using their Favorites folder to subscribe to a site. IE 4.0 then periodically checks the site for updated content; if any updated content is discovered, IE 4.0 notifies the user of the update and, optionally, downloads the site content for offline viewing.

Although Webcasting is new to IE 4.0, third-party products that provide basic site subscription functionality have been available for some time. Users and administrators who have experienced some of the unfavorable aspects of earlier subscription products will be pleased with many of the options available to them with IE 4.0 and the IEAK.

6.2.17 Questions

1. You have placed some new entries in your Favorites folder, and you told IE 4.0 that you wanted to subscribe to the sites. When you come to work the next day, you open your Favorites folder to discover a red gleam on all the new entries. What does this mean?

   A. The site content has changed since the last time you viewed those sites.

   B. Something is wrong with the URLs for these entries.

   C. The sites are over 30 hops away, which will result in extremely long download times.

   D. You told IE 4.0 that you did not want to receive notification of updates to the sites.

2. You receive email notifying you of an update to a site to which you have a partial subscription. You go to your Favorites folder and click the site's icon. The page is displayed, but you can tell from the date that the page has not been updated. What could cause this to happen?

   A. Only full subscriptions are automatically downloaded.

   B. You didn't provide a download location when you subscribed to the site.

   C. You haven't paid for your subscription in a while.

   D. You checked the Never option under IE 4.0 Internet Options, Settings.

3. What are the ramifications of setting the Days to Keep Pages in History value to 0 on the IE 4.0 Internet Options screen? (Select all that are correct.)

   A. Partial site subscriptions will be disabled.

   B. Full site subscriptions will be disabled.

   C. None of the information will be stored.

   D. All present channel settings will be cleared.

4. What is the cost differential between a partial site subscription and a full site subscription? (Select the best answer.)

   A. Partial site subscriptions are free; full site subscriptions require the user to pay a monthly fee.

   B. Full site subscriptions are free; partial site subscriptions (also known as *channels*) require the user to pay a monthly fee.

   C. Full site subscriptions are less efficient than partial site subscriptions.

   D. Full site subscriptions are more efficient than partial site subscriptions.

5. How do you delete all subscription content from your Temporary Internet Files folder?

   A. In IE 4.0, select View|Internet Options|Settings and then select Delete All Subscription Content.

   B. In IE 4.0, select View|Internet Options|Delete Files, select the Delete All Subscription Content check box, and click OK.

   C. This has to be done with the IEAK Profile Manager.

   D. You don't have this option with IE 4.0.

6.2.18 Answers

1. **A** A red gleam on the site's icon in the Favorites folder is one way IE 4.0 can notify you of site updates.

2. **D** By definition, a partial subscription only notifies you of updates to a site. A full subscription is required if you want to automatically download the updated content. Answer A is a true statement, but doesn't explain what could have caused the problem in this case. Because automatic downloads do not occur with partial subscriptions, updates are performed based on the option you have selected on the Settings screen under IE 4.0 Internet Settings. Selecting Never causes updates to never take place for partial site subscriptions. This falls into the "operator error" category.
3. **C** Setting this value to 0 only disables the History bar; it has no impact on site subscriptions or channels.
4. **D** Because full site subscriptions can schedule downloads for off-hours and also enable offline viewing, they are more efficient than partial site subscriptions, which require the updated site content to be downloaded either the next time you start IE or the next time you access the page. There is no monetary charge for site subscriptions or channels (at least not yet).
5. **B** Note that the Delete All Subscription Content check box clears itself when you click OK.

Channels

Two TechNet articles sum up the difference between site subscriptions and channels:

- "Basic Webcasting with Subscriptions"
- "Managed Webcasting with Channels"

Channels are managed (or are at least manageable); site subscriptions are not managed.

The only thing required for a Web site author to convert an existing site into a channel is the addition of a Channel Definition Format (CDF) file to the site. The simplest of CDF files contains nothing but a list of URLs pointing to site content. More sophisticated CDF files contain the following items:

- URLs pointing to content.
- A schedule for content updates.
- A hierarchical organization of the URLs describing the Web site structure.
- A title or abstract information describing individual content items.

All this information enables a far more efficient way of distributing information to those who require it than that provided by site subscriptions. In particular, by providing a schedule for content updates, the site author can provide more timely updates, server-side load balancing, and the power to decide what content should be Webcast and how often it should be updated.

With IE 4.0, there are four ways Active Channels can be delivered to a user:

- In full-screen mode
- As a screen saver
- On the desktop
- Through email

A good nine-page article on channels, titled "CDF 101: Creating a Simple Channel with Active Channel Technology," (authored by Microsoft) is available from the Microsoft Web site. Microsoft's CDF specification is available on the Internet at `http://www.microsoft.com/standards/cdf.htm`. Note that neither of these CDF articles are available on TechNet.

Additional and quite useful information can be found at `http://www.microsoft.com/sbnmember/channels/channels.asp`.

6.2.19 Exercise

Active channels can be located in two ways:

- By seeing the Add Active Channel icon on a Web page
- By visiting Microsoft's Active Channel Guide

One of the new features of IE 4.0 is the channel bar. To view the channel bar, click the Channels button on the IE 4.0 toolbar. By default, the top entry on the channel bar is Microsoft's Active Channel Guide.

Assuming that you are connected to the Internet, follow these steps to use the channel bar:

1. Display the channel bar.
2. Click one of the channel bar buttons (other than the Microsoft Channel Guide button) to expand the drop-down menu.
3. Click one of the expanded channel bar buttons to go to the selected Web site.

To add a channel from Microsoft's Active Channel Guide to the channel bar, click the Microsoft Active Channel Guide button on the channel bar to go to Microsoft's Active Channel Guide Web site and follow the instructions.

6.2.20 Questions

1. On a user's system, how are the CDF files for all the channels to which the user has subscribed updated?

   A. CDF files don't reside on the user's system.

   B. Once a user subscribes to a channel, the CDF file is pull-updated according to the schedule the user has defined.

   C. The CDF files are push-updated to the user's system according to the schedule established by the channel's author.

   D. Every time the IEAK Profile Manager is run.

2. What are some benefits of channels over site subscriptions? (Select all correct answers.)

   A. More timely updates. (In some cases, in real-time on the user's desktop.)

   B. Less content has to be moved because subscriptions don't have to push or pull the entire page.

   C. Less network traffic and disk storage requirements because there is no site crawling.

   D. With channels, site content can be logically grouped.

3. How do you identify a Web site as a channel?

   A. There is no way to identify a channel from a typical Web site.

   B. By the Microsoft Active Channel icon.

   C. By the Active Channel disclaimer.

   D. By the Add Active Channel icon.

4. What does it cost to subscribe to a channel?

   A. Nothing

   B. $1 per month

   C. $10 per year

   D. It varies from channel to channel.

6.2.21 Answers

1. **A** CDF files reside on the server and are not pushed to users.

2. **A, B, C, and D** All answers are correct. A good understanding of channels and of partial and full updates is required for the IEAK exam.

3. **D** The Add Active Channel icon is the way to identify a Web site as a channel.

4. **A** Just as for site subscriptions, it doesn't cost anything to subscribe to a channel.

Active Desktop Items

Until now, the desktop has been somewhat underwhelming: A necessary evil users always went back to before going somewhere else. With IE 4.0 and the advent of "active," the desktop has been defined as a sort of Web browser. Web pages and other Web elements can be displayed right on the user's desktop.

As explained in the previous chapter, dictionaries generally define the word *active* as follows:

- Capable of exerting influence
- Constantly engaged; lively
- The opposite of passive
- Does something

The IE 4.0 active desktop is all these descriptives and more.

6.2.22 Exercise

Each installation of IE4 creates a log file that can be quite helpful for troubleshooting purposes. Becoming familiar with the log file and its contents is another one of those things it behooves you to do *before* problems arise.

1. From the Start menu, select Find|Files or Folders.
2. Enter **`active*`** in the Named box and click Find Now.
3. Open the text file named `Active Setup Log` in the `C:\WINDOWS` folder. (You may also have a file named `Active Setup Log.BAK`. If Active Setup finds the `.TXT` file when an installation is started, it renames the `.TXT` file to `.BAK` and creates a new `.TXT` file.)
4. Take a few minutes to scroll through the file. If you see anything completely new to you, go back and review it before taking the IEAK exam. Note that the log file can be quite large.

6.2.23 Questions

1. You have dialed in to your ISP and are unable to view or contact any Web site with IE, but you are able to ping the sites. What would you do?

   A. Select View|Internet Options|Connection and verify that proxies are disabled.

   B. Select View|Internet Options|Security and verify that Internet access has not been disabled.

   C. Select View|Internet Options|General and empty the Temporary Internet Files folder.

   D. Select View|Internet Options|Advanced and empty the Temporary Internet Files folder.

2. Although every indication was that the installation of IE 4.0 completed okay, a user believes that certain components did not install properly. Where would you start with this situation?

   A. Install IE 3.0 over top of IE 4.0 and then reinstall IE 4.0 as an upgrade.

   B. Reboot the system.

   C. Log in with administrator privileges and see whether the user now thinks things are working okay.

   D. Look through the Active Setup log file to see whether you find any indication of installation problems.

3. When you enable Active Desktop with IE 4.0, your display flashes. The flashing is most noticeable on the channel bar when the desktop is refreshed or redrawn. What could be causing this?

   A. Too little system memory.

   B. Too much network traffic.

   C. Your display settings.

   D. Your Temporary Internet Files folder is full.

4. Where would you find the Active Desktop Gallery Web page if you had to locate it manually?

   A. `http://www.activedesktop.com`

   B. `http://www.microsoft.com/ie/ie40/gallery/`

   C. `http://www.microsoft.com/activedesktop`

   D. On the IEAK CD-ROM.

5. You log on to Windows NT, and the only visible object on the screen is the mouse pointer. (The desktop, taskbar, and Start button are all missing.) What could have caused this?

   A. You just added more memory to your system.

   B. You installed IE 4.0 with the Windows Desktop Update component and at some later date you restored the System and Software registry keys from an Emergency Repair Disk (ERD) created before you installed IE 4.0.

   C. You have subscribed to an Active Channel that contains nothing but IE 3.0 desktop content.

   D. Your Temporary Internet Files folder is full.

6.2.24 Answers

1. **A** Proxies are only used to access the Internet from an intranet.

2. **D** The log file is a good place to start in this case. Installing IE 3.0 over IE 4.0 is *not* something you want to do. In fact, installing an older version of anything over a newer version without completely uninstalling or removing the newer version is bad practice.

3. **C** A Microsoft KnowledgeBase article describes this problem (Q176233). KnowledgeBase articles are available on

TechNet or on the Internet. To get to Microsoft's online support search site (which, by the way, is an Active Channel), go to `www.microsoft.com` and select Technical Support from the menu.

4. **B** The location of the Active Desktop Gallery Web page is `http://www.microsoft.com/ie/ie40/gallery/`.

5. **B** This answer is from another Microsoft KnowledgeBase article (Q174659). Troubleshooting IE 4.0 and IEAK problems is much simpler if you get to know your resources and how to use them. Chances are that someone else (or several someone elses) has already worked through any problem you will come up against. Spend a few minutes searching resources such as TechNet and the Internet and you can save hours in the long run. (If you picked answer C, you are not quite ready for the IEAK exam.)

Practice Exam 1: Implementing and Supporting Microsoft Internet Explorer 4.0 by Using the IEAK

You will have 105 minutes to complete 75 questions. The passing score is 703 out of 1000. There will be two types of questions:

- Multiple choice: Select the correct answer
- Multiple multiple choice: Select all answers that are correct

At the end of an actual exam, you will be notified immediately whether you passed or failed. You will also receive a printed Score Report that states your score and your results by section. Do not lose this Score Report.

1. You are connected to the Internet through your ISP and are unable to open any Web pages. You want to check the DNS configuration in NT. What command would you use?

   A. `IPCONFIG`

   B. `WINIPCFG`

   C. `IPCONFIG /all`

   D. `WINIPCFG /all`

2. You cannot ping any host using FQDN or IP addresses. You use `ping 127.0.0.1` and get a return message of `Bad IP address`. What is the most likely cause?

   A. There are no other hosts available.

   B. TCP/IP is not "bound" to your NIC.

   C. Your default gateway address is incorrect.

   D. Your network cable is not connected.

3. Why would you use the `tracert` command? (Select all correct answers.)

   A. To retrieve information about why a ping to a remote site host failed.

   B. To retrieve information on why pinging the loopback address failed.

C. To see where a router fails or is slow.

D. To map a route to a destination NetBIOS node.

4. The IEAK Wizard (version 4.0) can build customized IE 4.0 packages for which operating systems?

A. Macintosh

B. NT 4.0/Windows 95

C. Novell 3.12

D. Windows 3.11/WFW/NT 3.51

5. What are the two most common caching problems users encounter? (Select the two best answers.)

A. Increased network I/O

B. Stale data

C. Decreased network I/O

D. Excess use of hard drive space

6. When subscribing to a Web page, what optional items can you choose to download?

A. Graphics

B. Sound

C. Video

D. Java applets

7. How do you customize the order in which channels are displayed on a user's desktop?

A. With the IEAK Profile Manager.

B. With the Channel Wizard.

C. With the remote control.

D. You can't set a custom channel order.

8. Where do CDF files reside?

A. User's system

B. Server

C. InterNIC

D. DNS

9. What is the cost for subscribing to a channel for a year?

A. $100

B. $50

C. Varies from channel to channel

D. Nothing

10. What is the effect of using a proxy server to access the Internet from your local intranet if active caching is enabled? (Select the best answer.)

A. The client can only view sites not located in the proxy server cache.

B. A proxy server slows down Internet access times.

C. A proxy server speeds up Internet access times.

D. You can only view sites located in the proxy server cache.

11. Select two of the operation modes of the IEAK.

A. Corporate Administrator mode

B. Internal User mode

C. Internal Server mode

D. Internet Content Provider/Developer mode

12. Which operational mode provides the ability to create a single-floppy deployment?

A. Internet Service Provider mode

B. Corporate Administrator mode

C. Internet Content Provider/Developer mode

D. None

13. The Corporate Administrator mode allows an administrator to customize which of the following? (Select all that apply.)

A. Single-floppy deployment

B. Set security levels for sites

C. Configure the desktop

D. Install using a silent mode

14. What does the Active Desktop component provide to a user?
    A. Better integrated desktop that provides the same user interface for local resources and Internet-based resources.
    B. A new look to the My Computer window.
    C. A new desktop toolbar.
    D. A new Control Panel.
15. When upgrading Netscape, what will IEAK import?
    A. Plug-in components
    B. Bookmarks
    C. Proxy server settings
    D. You cannot upgrade Netscape to IE 4.0
16. Which security level in your security zone configuration will not allow any content that could harm your computer software?
    A. High
    B. Medium
    C. Low
    D. Custom

17. You have a network that uses a proxy server to access the Internet and cache Internet sites for faster access. You also have an intranet that provides access to local resources. You want local resources to be accessed directly, and Internet sites to go through the proxy server. How would you configure this in the IEAK Wizard?
    A. Configure a new proxy zone.
    B. Place a check in the Enable Proxy Settings box.
    C. Add a second NIC to call client for access to the local resources.
    D. Place a check in the Do Not Use Proxy Server for Local (Intranet) Addresses box.
18. What is the best way to make changes to the settings you have made with the IEAK Wizard?
    A. Edit the `.INS` file manually.
    B. Rerun the IEAK Wizard and start from scratch.
    C. Run the IEAK Profile Manager and make the changes to the `.INS` file.
    D. Modify the `.INF` file.

19. You are preparing to deploy IE 4.0 on 100 Windows NT workstations that will access the Internet through a proxy server for most sites, but that will bypass the proxy server for sites located on the local network. The sites are listed in a script file that is updated frequently. How would you configure the settings in the IEAK Wizard to automatically implement updates to the script files every half hour?
    A. Configure an autoproxy URL with the URL and script files and then set the autoconfigure option to 30.
    B. Implement a proxy that all clients reboot their machines every half hour to get the updates.
    C. Modify the `.INS` file.
    D. Use the scheduler to schedule the update.

20. What does the `.INS` file contain?
    A. Configuration information about the user's computer.
    B. Configuration information for the browser.
    C. Configuration information for the active desktop.
    D. It is the primary installation file.

21. You want to view the settings for the IE 4.0 subscriptions using a text editor such as Notepad. What file would you view?
    A. `Subs.adm`
    B. `Inetres.adm`
    C. `Subs.Inf`
    D. `Inetres.inf`

22. What is the template file used to help reduce Outlook Express mail and news support cost?

   A. `oe.inf`

   B. `oe.ins`

   C. `oe.adm`

   D. `oe.cfg`

23. You have a network of 200 Windows 95 computers running Netscape Navigator 3.0, accessing the Internet through a proxy server. You are configuring a custom deployment package to upgrade all your users to IE 4.0. Can you import current proxy settings?

   A. No, proxy server settings cannot be imported.

   B. No, proxy server settings can only be imported from Netscape Communicator.

   C. Yes, proxy settings can be imported from Netscape Navigator 3.0.

   D. No, proxy server settings can only be imported from IE 3.0 browsers.

24. You have a network of 50 Windows NT Workstation computers running IE 3.01, accessing the Internet through a proxy server. You are configuring a custom deployment package to upgrade all your users to IE 4.0. Will your users' favorites be preserved?

   A. No, favorites settings can only be imported from 2.x browsers.

   B. Yes, favorites will be preserved from IE 3.01.

   C. No, favorites settings cannot be imported from IE 3.01.

   D. No, bookmark settings can only be imported from Netscape Navigator 3.0.

25. You have a network of 50 Windows NT Workstation and 125 Windows 95 computers running IE 3.01, accessing the Internet through a proxy server. You are configuring a custom deployment package to upgrade all your users to IE 4.0. What can you import as part of the upgrade process?

   A. Proxy settings

   B. Favorites folders

   C. Cookies

   D. Plug-ins

26. You have a network of 75 Windows 95 computers running Netscape 3.0, accessing the Internet through a proxy server. You are configuring a custom deployment package to upgrade all your users to IE 4.0. You want to configure all new plug-ins for use with the new deployment, and you don't want any other plug-ins from the previous version of Internet Explorer imported. What must be done?

   A. Select Do Not Import Plug-ins when creating the custom package.

   B. A script file must be run by each user before the upgrade is run to uninstall the plug-ins.

   C. Nothing. Plug-ins will be imported. You will have to go to each user and uninstall the plug-ins after the upgrade is complete.

   D. Nothing. Plug-ins are not imported when an upgrade is performed.

27. You have a network of 80 Windows NT Workstation computers running IE 3.01, and you want to use only the plug-ins configured with your custom deployment. What must be done?

   A. Nothing. Plug-ins will be imported. You will have to go to each user and uninstall the plug-ins after the upgrade is complete.

   B. Select Do Not Import Plug-ins when creating the custom package.

   C. Nothing. Plug-ins are not imported when an upgrade is performed.

D. A script file must be run by each user before the upgrade is run to uninstall the plug-ins.

28. You have a network of 135 Windows NT computers running Netscape Communicator, accessing the Internet through a proxy server. You are configuring a custom deployment package to upgrade all your users to IE 4.0. What would you do to save a user's bookmarks?

A. Nothing. The upgrade will import the bookmarks from Netscape Communicator.

B. Save all the bookmark information before deploying Internet Explorer 4.0 and then import the bookmarks after the deployment is complete.

C. Upgrade from Netscape Communicator to Internet Explorer 3.01, and then upgrade from IE 3.01 to IE 4.0.

D. Nothing. Bookmarks are incompatible with IE 4.0 favorites.

29. How do you create a custom welcome and help display message at the bottom of the Outlook Express window, providing the help desk's extension number?

A. Turn on the Tip of the Day feature and create a custom tip with the help desk's phone number.

B. Nothing. This cannot be done.

C. Use the infopane feature to display a one-inch pane at the bottom of the Outlook Express window with the help desk's phone number.

D. Create a custom toolbar bitmap with the help desk's phone number.

30. How do you configure your users to use Secure Password Authentication to log on to your local mail server? (Select the best answer.)

A. Enter each user's username and password during the installation of Outlook Express.

B. Select Use Secure Password Authentication when configuring the Internet Mail Services in your custom deployment package.

C. After the custom package is deployed, go to each user's computer and configure for Secure Password Authentication.

D. Select Encrypted User Authentication. Have the user provide the username and password when prompted.

31. You have a network of 180 Windows 95 computers running Netscape 3.01 and using Eudora Light as the email program. You are preparing to deploy IE 4.0 and make Outlook Express the default mail and news client. Some of your users are concerned that they will lose their mail messages and address entries. What information will be imported into Outlook Express?

A. Address book entries

B. Email messages

C. Plug-ins

D. Add-ons

32. A user calls wanting to configure her POP3 mail server information. Your mail server is named `UPS`, which is part of the `Diamond.com` domain. What would you tell the user to put for the mail server name?

A. `UPS`

B. `Diamond.com`

C. `UPS.Diamond.com`

D. `Diamond.com/UPS`

33. You want to disable the user's ability to share applications in NetMeeting. How can you do this? (Select the best answer.)

A. Under Restrict the Use of File Transfer, select Prevent User from Receiving Files.

B. Under Restrict the Use of Application Sharing, select Disable All Application Sharing Features.

C. Disable NetMeeting on the user's computer.

D. In User Manager for Domains, remove the user from the Collaborative local group.

34. You want to disable the user's ability to change the My Information options you configured before deploying IE 4.0 with the NetMeeting components. How would you do this?

A. Under Restrict the Use of the Options Dialog, select Disable the 'My Information' Options Page.

B. Set the default directory server to a domain controller and remove the user from the Collaborative local group.

C. Set the directory server to a member server and remove the user from the Power Users group.

D. Under Restrict the Use of the Options Dialog, select Disable the 'General' Options Page.

35. Can you limit the user's ability to send files when configuring NetMeeting? (Select the best answer.)

A. No, you can only limit a user's ability to both send and receive files.

B. Yes, by configuring the enabling the application sharing feature.

C. No, you can limit the user's ability to receive files only.

D. Yes, you can limit the user's ability to send files only.

36. You want to disable the user's ability to change the General options you configured before deploying IE 4.0 with the NetMeeting components. How would you do this?

A. Set the default directory server to a domain controller and remove the user from the Collaborative local group.

B. Set the directory server to a member server and remove the user from the Power Users group.

C. Under Restrict the Use of the Options Dialog, select Disable the 'My Information' Options Page.

D. Under Restrict the Use of the Options Dialog, select Disable the 'General' Options Page.

37. When selecting the multiple-floppy deployment method, what deployment packages are created? (Select all correct answers)

A. Multiple floppy

B. Single floppy

C. Network connection path

D. `Download` directory

38. You want to view the `.CAB` files created in your download directory to get an idea of how big the files are because you are expecting to create a deployment package for your Asian office. The directory you stored the deployment package in is `C:\Deploy`. What directory stores the `.CAB` files for a custom deployment?

A. `C:\Deploy\Ie4site\En`

B. `C:\Deploy\IE4Site`

C. `C:\Deploy\Download`

D. `C:\Deploy\Download\En`

39. What role must you select to specify the single floppy, multiple-floppy, and CD-ROM deployment method?

A. None of the roles will provide you with that ability. You must have the IEAK Extra to have all options available.

B. Corporate Administrator role.

C. Internet Service Provider role.

D. Content Provider/Developer role.

40. You have Windows NT on a client computer and want to use the single-floppy method to install IE 4.0. The deployment package you have configured has a custom ICM profile included. You have a modem, but haven't configured dial-up networking. What must you do to configure the connection? (Select two.)

A. Run the single-floppy deployment.

B. Run the Dial-Up Networking Wizard.

C. Run the Internet Connection Wizard.

D. Run the Windows NT installation. When it asks for custom programs, insert the floppy disk.

41. What folder is the floppy set stored in when the multiple-floppy deployment method is selected and the download folder is `c:\Deploymf` and the deployment language is English? (Select all correct answers.)

A. `c:\Deploymf\Mfloppy\Win95\En`

B. `c:\Deploymf\Mfloppy\Win95_NT\En`

C. `c:\Deploymf\Mfloppy\WinNT\En`

D. `c:\Deploymf\Mfloppy\En`

42. You are creating a custom deployment package and have selected CD-ROM as a deployment media. How can you add a custom background with your company's logo as part of the package?

A. In the Custom Background Bitmap location, provide the filename only to the bitmap file.

B. In the Custom Background Bitmap location, provide the path and filename to the `.BMP` file.

C. In the Custom Background Bitmap location, provide the path and filename to the `.JPG` file.

D. In the Custom Background Bitmap location, provide the path and filename to the `.GIF` file.

43. What are the minimum requirements for installing IE 4.0 on a Windows 95 computer? (Select all correct answers.)

A. 386/33 processor or greater

B. 16M of RAM

C. 486/66 processor or greater

D. 8M of RAM

44. What are the minimum hardware and software requirements for deploying IE 4.0 on a Macintosh system?

A. System 6.1 or later

B. Macintosh PowerPC processor or Macintosh 68030

C. 4M of RAM

D. 7M to 37M of free hard disk space

45. You are deploying Microsoft Internet Explorer 4.0 on a Windows 3.1 computer. The computer has an Intel 486/33 processor, 8M of RAM, and 100M of free disk space. Select the components that have to be upgraded before you can install IE 4.0.

A. Processor subsystem

B. RAM memory subsystem

C. Hard drive subsystem

D. Nothing has to be upgraded

46. A UNIX user calls wanting to install Internet Explorer 4.0. The user asks what the minimum requirements are to install IE 4.0 on the UNIX system. What do you tell the user? (Select all correct answers.)

A. 64M of RAM

B. 65M of free disk space

C. A SparcStation 2 or greater

D. None, you can't install IE 4.0 on UNIX.

47. You are attempting to run the IEAK Wizard on a Pentium computer with 64M of RAM and 1 gigabyte of free disk space. The computer has a fresh install of Windows NT 4.0 Server and Service Pack 3 has been applied. The IEAK Wizard appears to run properly, but the custom packages don't work. What would you try doing first to fix this problem?

A. Install Proxy Server 2.0

B. Install IIS 2.0 or newer

C. Install IE 4.0

D. Reinstall the IEAK

48. You are attempting to install the IEAK on a Pentium 200 computer with 64M of RAM and 180M of free disk space, running Windows NT 3.51, but you seem to be having problems. What would need to be upgraded to allow the IEAK to be installed?
    A. Operating system
    B. Hard drive subsystem
    C. RAM memory subsystem
    D. Processor subsystem

49. You are deploying Microsoft Internet Explorer 4.0 and will need to configure four different custom packages each on two different platforms for your users. How much free disk space should you plan on having on your download server? (Select the best answer.)
    A. 400M
    B. 650M
    C. 800M
    D. 320M

50. A user wants to install Microsoft Internet Explorer 4.0 with desktop components on a Windows NT 4.0 Workstation. The computer has an Intel 486/33 processor, 16M of RAM, and 90M of free disk space. Select the components that have to be upgraded before you can install IE 4.0.
    A. Processor subsystem
    B. RAM memory subsystem
    C. Hard drive subsystem
    D. None of the above

51. You are attempting to install the IEAK on a Pentium 133 computer with 64M of RAM and 200M of free disk space, running English Solaris 2.6, but seem to be having problems. Of the items listed below, which are most likely causing the problem? (Select all that apply.)
    A. Processor subsystem
    B. RAM memory subsystem
    C. Hard drive subsystem
    D. Operating system

52. You are attempting to run the IEAK Wizard on a Pentium computer with 64M of RAM and 1 gigabyte of free disk space. The computer has a fresh install of Windows NT 4.0 Server and Service Pack 3 has been applied, and you have installed IE 4.0. This is your notebook computer and you are attempting to configure the IEAK Wizard from your house. You have a modem and can attach to your network at work, which will provide you with Internet access. When running the IEAK Wizard, you do not have any Web sites to select from for component synchronization, and the wizard fails. What would you try doing first to fix this problem?
    A. Use the modem to connect to your network at work.
    B. Remove IE 4.0.
    C. Reapply the service pack.
    D. Reinstall the IEAK.

53. You are deploying Microsoft Internet Explorer 4.0 on a Windows for Workgroups 3.11 computer. The computer has an Intel 486/66 processor, 160M of RAM, and 125M of free disk space. Select the components that have to be upgraded before you can install IE 4.0.
    A. Processor subsystem
    B. RAM memory subsystem
    C. Hard drive subsystem
    D. None of the above

54. You are deploying Microsoft Internet Explorer 4.0 on a Windows 3.1 computer. The computer has an Intel 486/66 processor, 12M of RAM, and 100M of free disk space. The user needs to be able to run Java applications through IE 4.0. Select the components that must be upgraded before you can install IE 4.0.
    A. Processor subsystem
    B. RAM memory subsystem

C. Hard drive subsystem

D. Nothing would need to be upgraded

55. You are deploying Microsoft Internet Explorer 4.0 on a Windows 95 computer. The computer has an Intel Pentium 133 processor, 8M of RAM, and 25M of free disk space. Select the components that have to be upgraded before you can install IE 4.0 with the Windows Desktop Update.

A. Processor subsystem

B. RAM memory subsystem

C. Hard drive subsystem

D. None of the above

56. You are attempting to run the IEAK Wizard on a Pentium computer with 64M of RAM and 1 gigabyte of free disk space. The computer has a fresh install of Windows NT 4.0 Server and Service Pack 3 has been applied, and you have installed IE 4.0. This is your notebook computer and you are attempting to configure the IEAK Wizard from your house. You do not have a modem and are not attached to your network, which provides you with Internet access through your company proxy server. When running the IEAK Wizard, you do not have any Web sites to select from for component synchronization, and the wizard fails. What would you try doing first to fix this problem?

A. Install Proxy Server 2.0.

B. Install IIS 2.0.

C. Install a modem and connect to the Internet.

D. You cannot run IEAK on a notebook computer.

57. A user on your network wants to upgrade to Internet Explorer 4.0 with Windows Desktop Update. The user has a Pentium 166 with 12M of RAM and a 1 gigabyte hard drive with 250M of free space. The computer is running Windows 95. What components have to be replaced to perform the upgrade?

A. Processor subsystem

B. RAM memory subsystem

C. Hard drive subsystem

D. Nothing would need to be upgraded

58. Your company is preparing to deploy Internet Explorer 4.0, and you have to select a computer to run the IEAK Wizard on. A download server will be used to deploy the custom packages. Select the computers on which the IEAK can be installed.

A. A 486/100 computer with 32M of RAM and 70M of free disk space running Windows 95 with the most current service packs applied.

B. A SparcStation 2 with 128M of RAM and 2 gigabytes of free disk space.

C. A Pentium 200 computer with 128M of RAM and 500M of free disk space running Windows NT Workstation 3.51.

D. A 486/66 computer with 24M of RAM and 75M of free disk space running Windows NT Workstation 4.0 with Service Pack 3 applied.

59. You are deploying Microsoft Internet Explorer 4.0 on a Windows NT 3.51 computer. The computer has an Intel 486/33 processor, 12M of RAM, and 20M of free disk space. Select the components that have to be upgraded before you can install IE 4.0 and be able to run Java applications.

A. Processor subsystem

B. RAM memory subsystem

C. Hard drive subsystem

D. None of the above

60. Your company is preparing to deploy Internet Explorer 4.0, and you have to select a computer on which to run the IEAK Wizard. The system will also act as the download server, and you will install a fresh copy of Windows NT 4.0 Server before installing the IEAK. Select the best computer to use.

A. A 486/33 computer with 16M of RAM and 70M of free disk space running Windows 95 with the most current service packs applied.

B. A SparcStation 2 with 128M of RAM and 2 gigabytes of free disk space.

C. A Pentium 200 computer with 128M of RAM and 500M of free disk space running Windows NT Workstation 3.51.

D. A 486/66 computer with 32M of RAM and 175M of free disk space running Windows NT Workstation 4.0 with Service Pack 3 applied.

61. You entered your customization code and then discovered that the Corporate Administrator role is not available to you. What could the problem be?

A. You are not running the IEAK on a fast-enough computer.

B. Restart the IEAK Wizard, this time using the `/CA` switch in the command line.

C. The computer on which you are running the IEAK Wizard does not have enough free disk space to allow you to store a custom package.

D. You did not register for a license that provides the Corporate Administrator role.

62. Select the answer that best describes the function of the Automatic Version Synchronization (AVS) check box.

A. When checked, a Microsoft-defined download site will be used to verify that you have the most current of each of the components of IE 4.0.

B. When checked, a Microsoft-defined download site will not be used to verify that you have the most current of each of the components of IE 4.0.

C. When checked, the versions of each of your components will be recorded on the IEAK registration site for licensing registration.

D. When checked, the versions of each of your components will not be recorded on the IEAK registration site for licensing registration.

63. You are starting Stage 2 of the IEAK Wizard. In Stage 1, you could not select any languages, and now you have no download sites available. What could the problem be?

A. You were not connected to the Internet when you started the IEAK Wizard.

B. You are running in Corporate Administrator mode.

C. You are running in ISP mode.

D. You didn't provide a language in Stage 1, so you cannot see the download information.

64. While configuring a custom component, you are prompted to register the Uninstall key. What does the Uninstall key do?

A. Allows you to uninstall the custom component through the Add/Remove Program applet located in the Control Panel.

B. Registers the custom component with Microsoft.

C. Registers each user with the corporate administrator.

D. When combined with the GUID, provides a password for access to the custom component.

65. You are almost sure that at least some of the components listed on the AVS screen are current, but they all show up with a yellow exclamation icon. What could be causing this?

A. You are running in CA mode.

B. You are running in ISP mode.

C. AVS was not selected in Stage 1 of the IEAK Wizard.

D. AVS was selected in Stage 1 of the IEAK Wizard.

66. What are the dimensions that a custom bitmap for the Active Setup Wizard can be?

A. 120×200 (pixels)

B. 200×120 (pixels)

C. 256×200 (pixels)

D. 200×256 (pixels)

67. What's the easiest way to install IE 4.0 for all your computers in a folder called `Explorer`?

A. Select Install in the specified folder within the Windows folder.

B. From the Specify Where You Want Your Browser screen in the IEAK Wizard, select Specify Full Path of Custom Folder, and type the path in which you want IE 4.0 installed.

C. Select Install in the specified folder within the Program Files folder.

D. Give each of the users directions for installing IE 4.0 manually, and explain how to select the installation path.

68. In which mode do you want to run the IEAK to be able to select the Install Package Silently option?

A. Content Provider/Developer mode

B. Service Provider mode

C. Corporate Administrator mode

D. This option is only available with the IEAK Extra package

69. How can you place a custom title in the title bar of IE 4.0 and add a custom bitmap to appear behind the toolbar?

A. Configure a custom URL that has the information you want displayed, and configure that as the home page in your custom package.

B. Run the IEAK Wizard in Content Provider mode and create a custom Web site in Stage 1 that has the information you want in the title bar.

C. In Stage 4 of the IEAK Wizard, you can customize the title displayed in IE 4.0. You can also provide a path to a custom bitmap that will be displayed behind the toolbar.

D. This cannot be done from the IEAK Wizard.

70. Where in the IEAK Wizard are you able to configure it so that users do not see the default welcome page when IE 4.0 is launched the first time?

A. Support Configuration screen

B. Favorites Folder and Links

C. Home Page Configuration screen

D. Welcome Message Customization screen

71. You have a Web site that allows users in by reading the user agent string, and you want to add a code to the end of the string. How can you do this?

A. From the User Agent String Customization option, add your custom string.

B. From the Software Update Channels screen, select Security Codes and add your custom string.

C. From the Active Channel Bar Customization screen, add a special access header string.

D. This cannot be done from the IEAK Wizard.

72. You want updates that you configure through the IEAK Profile Manager to

occur only when the user restarts his or her system. How can you do this? (Select two answers.)

A. On the Automatic Browser Configuration page, leave the AutoConfig Every box blank.

B. On the Automatic Browser Configuration page, set the AutoConfig Every box to `-1`.

C. On the Automatic Browser Configuration page, set the AutoConfig Every box to `reboot`.

D. On the Automatic Browser Configuration page, set the AutoConfig Every box to zero.

73. You want all your users to use HOTBOT to perform searches by default. How can you do this?

A. From the Customize the Start and Search Pages screen, type the name of the site under Search Page URL.

B. From the Customize the Start and Search Pages screen, type the name of the site under Home Page URL.

C. From the Customize the Start and Search Pages screen, click the Test URL button.

D. From the Customize the Start and Search Pages screen, type the name of the site under Home Page URL, type **`search`**, and click the Test URL button.

74. You want all your users to use Outlook Express as their default mail and news client. How can you configure this?

A. On the Specify Internet Mail Servers and News Servers, select Make Outlook Express Your Default Mail Client and News Client.

B. For the incoming mail server, configure the entry for IMAP instead of POP3.

C. For the incoming mail server, type **`Outlook.servername`**, where *`servername`* is your mail server's computer name.

D. This has to be configured at the mail server.

75. How can you configure everyone to append the same signature to all new mail messages?

A. From the Include a Signature screen, select Append the Following Signature to Each Mail Message, and add the signature text.

B. From the Include a Signature screen, select Append the Following Signature to Each News Message, and add the signature text.

C. From the Include a Signature screen, select Append the Following Signature to Each News Message.

D. From the Include a Signature screen, select Append the Following Signature to Each Mail Message.

Answers and Explanations

1. **C** `IPCONFIG` only gives you your adapter information. `IPCONFIG /all` gives you all available TCP/IP information. The `WINIPCFG` command is used for Windows 95 systems.
2. **B** Inability to ping the loopback address usually means that TCP/IP is not installed correctly or that it did not bind to the NIC.
3. **A, C** The `tracert` command can be use to gather information about where a router is failing or is slow and can indicate why a Ping command might fail. It will not return any useful information on a loopback address.
4. **B** IEAK version 4.0 only supports the creation of deployment packages for Windows 95 and Windows NT 4.0. Although newer versions do exist that can create deployment packages for other platforms, the MCSE exam is based on version 4.0.
5. **B, D** When caching information, the information is stored locally using hard disk space. When a request is made for the URL, the local copy is delivered (unless the browser is configured to check for the most current version), which could provide stale data.
6. **A, B, C, and D** All answers are correct. You make your choices from the download page.
7. **D** Setting a custom channel order is not an option.
8. **B** CDF files reside on the server and are not pushed to the user.
9. **D** There is no cost to subscribe to a channel.
10. **C** If caching is enabled, the client should benefit from quicker access times when accessing the Internet.
11. **A, D** The three operational modes the IEAK can be run in are Corporate Administrator, Internet Service Provider, and Internet Content Provider/Developer modes.
12. **A** The only operational mode that provides the ability to create single-floppy deployment media is the Internet Service Provider mode.
13. **B, C, and D** Only the Internet Service Provider mode allows single-floppy deployment.
14. **A, B, C, and D** Active Desktop provides all these features.
15. **B, C** Plug-ins and add-on components must be reinstalled.
16. **A** The high security level does not allow downloading of anything that can harm your local system.
17. **B, D** By enabling proxy server settings, clients will access Internet sites through the proxy server. By setting the client to bypass the proxy for local sites, the client will access local sites directly.
18. **C** The IEAK Profile Manager can be used to automatically make the necessary changes to the `.INS` file and allow you to test the URL for the home page.
19. **A** By setting the URL for the script file, the client gets the update at each reboot. By setting the autoconfigure option to 30, updates will occur every 30 minutes.
20. **B** The auto configuration option allows the corporate administrator to create an `.INS` file that contains configuration information for the browser.
21. **C** Using a text editor, you could look at the `Subs.inf` file to view information about subscriptions.
22. **C** `oe.adm` is the template used to define policies for reducing mail and news support cost.
23. **C** Proxy server settings are preserved when upgrading from IE 3.x and Netscape Navigator 3.0.
24. **B** Favorites from IE 3.x and bookmarks from Netscape are imported into the new IE 4.0 favorites area.
25. **A, B, and C** Plug-ins and add-ons cannot be imported; you must reinstall these features.

26. **D** Plug-ins are not imported from Netscape browsers. You must reinstall the plug-ins after the upgrade is performed.
27. **C** Plug-ins are not imported from IE 3.x or Netscape Navigator when upgrading to IE 4.0.
28. **A** Bookmarks from Netscape are imported and added to the Favorites folder.
29. **C** The infopane option provides the ability to create a one-inch pane at the bottom of the Outlook Express window.
30. **B** Selecting SPA will force the user to provide a valid username and password.
31. **A, B** The information that can be imported to Outlook Express includes mail settings, address book entries, and all mail messages.
32. **C** The POP3 setting uses the FQDN to define the mail server.
33. **B** You can restrict the user's ability to share applications.
34. **A** You can restrict the user from modifying the General and My Information options pages.
35. **D** There are two file transfer options for NetMeeting, one for sending files and one for receiving files.
36. **D** You can restrict the user from modifying the General and My Information options pages.
37. **A, D** The `Download` directory is created every time a custom deployment package is created.
38. **A** The `.CAB` files for the deployment are stored in the `\I4site\`*language* directory, where *language* is the language selected for the custom deployment package.
39. **C** The only role that provides the single-floppy deployment method is the Service Provider role.
40. **A, B** You must install dial-up networking before the single-floppy installation can take place.
41. **A, B, and C** Floppy disk sets are created under `Win95`, `Win95_NT`, and `WinNT` directories in the `En` folder if the deployment language is English.
42. **B** Provide the path and filename to the custom bitmap file. The bitmap will be included in the deployment package that is created.
43. **B, C** The requirements for IE 4.0 are greater than the requirements for the Windows 95 operating system.
44. **B, D** The minimum requirements for a Macintosh computer include System 7.1 and 8M of RAM.
45. **A, B** The processor must be a 486/66 or greater, and a Windows 3.1 computer requires 12M to 16M of RAM.
46. **B, C** 64M RAM is recommended but not required; only 32M RAM is required.
47. **C** IE 4.0 must be installed on the computer before the IEAK Wizard will create good packages.
48. **A** The IEAK can only be installed on Windows 95 or Windows NT 4.0.
49. **C** There are really eight custom installs here, four for each platform. You should plan on 100M for each custom package configured.
50. **A, B** The processor must be a 486/66, and you must have 24M of RAM if you are including the desktop components, 16M of RAM for a regular installation.
51. **D** IEAK can only be installed on Windows 95, Windows NT, and Macintosh operating systems.
52. **A** You must have an active Internet connection for the wizard to work.
53. **D** The computer meets all requirements.
54. **B** To support Java, 16M of RAM is required.
55. **A, B, and C** For Windows 95, the processor must be a 486/66, and the computer must have 12M of RAM and between 43M and 78M of free disk space.

56. **C** You must have Internet connectivity to run the IEAK Wizard.
57. **B** 16M of RAM is required to run IE 4.0 with the Windows Desktop Update.
58. **A, D** Operating systems that can run IEAK are Windows 95 and Windows NT 4.0.
59. **A, C** Processor requirements are a 486/66 with a minimum of 12M of RAM and 43M to 78M of free disk space.
60. **D** Only answer D meets all the requirements.
61. **D** You must specifically register for the roles in which you want to run.
62. **A** AVS will verify that you have the most current components available by comparing them with a Microsoft-defined Web site.
63. **A** You must be connected to the Internet for the IEAK to function properly.
64. **A** Configuring the Uninstall key registers an uninstall program in the Registry and allows the component to be uninstalled using the Add/Remove Programs applet located in the Control Panel.
65. **C** If AVS is not selected during Stage 1 of the IEAK Wizard, all components will show up with yellow icons because the wizard cannot verify whether the version is current.
66. **A** The custom bitmap must be 120×200 (pixels) with up to 256 colors.
67. **B** You can specify the folder in which IE 4.0 will be installed while running the IEAK Wizard.
68. **C** You must be running in Corporate Administrator mode to have the silent install option.
69. **C** In Stage 4 of the IEAK Wizard, you can configure custom IE 4.0 title bars and bitmaps for the toolbar.
70. **D** The Welcome Message Customization dialog box allows customization of the welcome screen and messages.
71. **A** User agent string customization can be configured through the IEAK Wizard. The data is appended to the end of the string.
72. **A, D** By leaving the update interval blank or set to zero, updates occur only at system restart.
73. **A** To configure the default search page, you would provide the URL in the Search Page dialog box.
74. **A** Select Outlook Express as your Default Mail and News Server.
75. **A** To include a signature on every mail message, select Append the Following Signature to Every Mail Message. You must type something in the signature box before you can continue if this option is selected.

Practice Exam 2: Implementing and Supporting Microsoft Internet Explorer 4.0 by Using the IEAK

You will have 105 minutes to complete 75 questions. The passing score is 703 out of 1000. There will be two types of questions:

- Multiple choice: Select the correct answer.
- Multiple multiple choice: Select all answers that are correct.

At the end of an actual exam, you will be notified immediately whether you passed or failed. You will also receive a printed Score Report that states your score and your results by section. Do not lose this Score Report.

1. What is the best definition of the site subscription crawl depth?
   A. How many levels down in the site's hierarchical structure you will update.
   B. How many levels up in the site's hierarchical structure you will update.
   C. How many levels across in the site's hierarchical structure you will update.
   D. How many levels down in the site's hierarchical structure you will not update.

2. How can you configure NetMeeting so that users cannot send files?
   A. From System Policies and Restrictions, select Microsoft NetMeeting and then select NetMeeting Settings. Place a check in the Prevent User from Receiving Files box.
   B. From System Policies and Restrictions, select Microsoft NetMeeting

and then select NetMeeting Protocols. Place a check in the Disable TCP/IP box.

C. From System Policies and Restrictions, select Microsoft NetMeeting and then select NetMeeting Protocols. Place a check in the Prevent User from Sending Files box.

D. From System Policies and Restrictions, select Microsoft NetMeeting and then select NetMeeting Protocols. Remove the check from the Disable TCP/IP box.

3. What authentication type selections are available for LDAP? (Select all correct answers.)

   A. Anonymous

   B. Clear Test

   C. Password

   D. Secure Password

4. How can you configure nonproxy clients to receive updates without having to reinstall constantly?

   A. Select Enable Automatic Browser Configuration and under Autoproxy URL, provide the URL site on which the `.INS` file resides.

   B. Select Enable Automatic Browser Configuration and under Autoconfiguration URL, provide the URL site on which the `.JS` or `.PAC` file resides.

   C. Select Enable Automatic Browser Configuration and under Autoproxy URL, provide the URL site on which the `.JS` or `.PAC` file resides.

   D. Select Enable Automatic Browser Configuration and under Autoconfiguration URL, provide the URL site on which the `.INS` file resides.

5. How can you add a company information site to all of your users' Favorites folders?

   A. From the Favorites Folder and Links Customization screen, click Test URL and provide the URL to your company information site.

   B. From the Favorites Folder and Links Customization screen, click Add Folder and provide the URL to your company information site.

   C. From the Favorites Folder and Links Customization screen, click Add URL and provide the URL to your company information site.

   D. From the Favorites Folder and Links Customization screen, click Import and provide the URL to your company information site.

6. How would you delete an existing IE 4.0 channel configuration so that you could create a custom channel selection for your company?

   A. From the Customize Active Channel Bar, select Delete Existing IE 4.0 Channels.

   B. From the Customize Active Channel Bar, select Do Not Customize Channels.

   C. Click the Launch Channel Guide button. From IE 4.0, remove the current channels from the Channel Search Web page.

   D. This cannot be done. By default, certain channels always have to be displayed.

7. You have a help desk Web page to which you want your users' browsers to point. How can you configure your custom package to point to your custom help page?

   A. In Proxy Server Settings, set the Help selection to reflect your custom Web site.

   B. Set the Search Page URL to point to your custom help Web page.

C. Set the user's home page to point to your custom Web page.

D. Set the Support Page URL to point to your custom site.

8. You selected Install Package Silently during Stage 2 of the IEAK Wizard. What options are available on the Windows Desktop Update screen?

   A. Yes, No, and User Choice

   B. Yes and User Choice

   C. No and User Choice

   D. Yes and No

9. What would cause a user to not be able to choose whether or not to use the Windows Desktop Update?

   A. On the Integrate the Web Desktop Update screen, you selected Yes rather than User Choice.

   B. You are running in Content Provider mode.

   C. You are running in ISP mode.

   D. You are running in Corporate Administrator mode.

10. Select the best definition for Globally Unique Identifier (GUID).

   A. The name of a custom component that a user selects to install that custom component.

   B. A `.CAB` file that, when expanded, contains the executable code for a custom component.

   C. The executable code for a custom component.

   D. A unique identifier that helps distinguish one program or object from another.

11. What does a red check mark in the AVS window of NetMeeting indicate?

   A. You do not have a sound card, and it is required.

   B. There is not a valid copy of NetMeeting available on the download server you selected.

   C. You do not have a copy of NetMeeting available locally.

   D. You have a more current version of NetMeeting than is available on the download site.

12. You want to be able to specify the single-floppy, multiple-floppy, and CD-ROM deployment methods. What role must you select to have all of these options available to you?

   A. Content Provider/Developer role

   B. Internet Service Provider role

   C. Corporate Administrator role

   D. None of these roles will provide you with that ability. You must have the IEAK Extra to have all options available.

13. What would cause the language list to be blank while you are running the IEAK Wizard?

   A. You are not connected to the Internet.

   B. Nothing. The language option should be blank.

   C. The language is taken from the computer on which you are running the IEAK Wizard, and it is not English.

   D. You have to type in the language you want to use.

14. Your company is preparing to deploy Internet Explorer 4.0, and a download server will be used to deploy the custom packages using the IEAK Wizard. Select the computer on which the IEAK can run with no modifications.

   A. A SparcStation 2 with 128M of RAM and 2 gigabytes of free disk space.

B. A Pentium 200 computer with 16M of RAM, 500M of free disk space, running Windows NT Workstation with Service Pack 3 applied, and running IE 4.0.

C. A 486/33 computer with 16M of RAM and 60M of free disk space running Windows NT 3.51 Server.

D. A 486/66 computer with 16M of RAM and 40M of free disk space running Windows 95 with the most current service packs applied.

15. A user wants to install Microsoft Internet Explorer 4.0 with the Windows Desktop Update on a Windows NT system. The computer has an Intel 486/66 processor, 12M of RAM, and 30M of free disk space. Select the components that do not have to be upgraded before you can install IE 4.0. (Select all correct answers.)

A. Processor subsystem

B. RAM memory subsystem

C. Hard drive subsystem

D. All of the above

16. One of your Macintosh users wants to install IE 4.0 on her computer. She has a Macintosh PowerPC running System 6.8 with 12M of RAM and 40M of free disk space. She wants to know what she has to upgrade before she can install IE 4.0. What would you tell her to upgrade?

A. Processor subsystem

B. RAM memory subsystem

C. Hard drive subsystem

D. Operating system

17. A user wants to install Microsoft Internet Explorer 4.0 with the Windows Desktop Update on a Windows NT 4.0 workstation. The computer has an Intel 486/66 processor, 32M of RAM, and 30M of free disk space. Select the components that have to be upgraded before you can install IE 4.0.

A. Processor subsystem

B. RAM memory subsystem

C. Hard drive subsystem

D. Nothing has to be upgraded

18. You are deploying Microsoft Internet Explorer 4.0 on a Windows 3.11 computer. The computer has an Intel 486/33 processor, 8M of RAM, and 75M of free disk space. Select the components that have to be upgraded before you can install IE 4.0.

A. Processor subsystem

B. RAM memory subsystem

C. Hard drive subsystem

D. Nothing has to be upgraded

19. You are deploying Microsoft Internet Explorer 4.0 and will need to configure three different custom packages for your users. How much free disk space should you plan on having on your download server? (Select the best answer.)

A. 400M

B. 80M

C. 200M

D. 300M

20. One of your Macintosh users wants to install IE 4.0 on his computer. He has a Macintosh 68030 processor and is running System 7.1. The computer has 8M of RAM and only 50M of free disk space. He wants to know what he has to upgrade before he can install IE 4.0. What would you tell him to upgrade?

A. Processor subsystem

B. RAM memory subsystem

C. Hard drive subsystem

D. Nothing has to be upgraded

21. You are attempting to run the IEAK Wizard on a 486/66 computer with 24M of RAM and 200M of free disk space. The computer has a fresh install of Windows NT 40 Workstation and Service Pack 3 has been applied. The IEAK Wizard appears to run properly, but the custom packages don't work. What would you try doing first to fix this problem?
    - A. Upgrade the processor subsystem.
    - B. Install IE 4.0.
    - C. Upgrade the RAM memory.
    - D. Reapply Service Pack 3.

22. Your company is preparing to deploy Internet Explorer 4.0, and you have to select a computer on which to run the IEAK Wizard. Select the computers on which you can run the IEAK without upgrading the hardware.
    - A. A 486/33 computer with 16M of RAM and 70M of free disk space running Windows 95 with the most current service packs applied.
    - B. A SparcStation 2 with 128M of RAM and 2 gigabytes of free disk space.
    - C. A Pentium 200 computer with 128M of RAM and 500M of free disk space running Windows NT Workstation 4.0.
    - D. A 486/66 computer with 12M of RAM and 45M of free disk space running Windows NT Workstation 4.0 with Service Pack 3 applied.

23. You are deploying Microsoft Internet Explorer 4.0 on a Windows NT 3.1 computer. The computer has an Intel Pentium 75 processor, 12M of RAM, and 100M of free disk space. Select the components that have to be upgraded before you can install IE 4.0.
    - A. Processor subsystem
    - B. RAM memory subsystem
    - C. Operating system
    - D. None of the above

24. You are deploying Microsoft Internet Explorer 4.0 on a Windows NT 4.0 computer. The computer has an Intel 486/33 processor, 12M of RAM, and 100M of free disk space. Select the components that have to be upgraded before you can install IE 4.0 with the Windows Desktop Update.
    - A. Processor subsystem
    - B. RAM memory subsystem
    - C. Hard drive subsystem
    - D. None of the above

25. One of your users wants to install IE 4.0 on her computer. She has a NetWare 3.12 client running on Windows 95 with 12M of RAM and 70M of free disk space. She wants to know what she needs to upgrade before she can install IE 4.0. What would you tell her to upgrade?
    - A. Processor subsystem
    - B. Operating system
    - C. Hard drive subsystem
    - D. Nothing has to be upgraded

26. Your company is deploying Internet Explorer 4.0, and your Internet team has asked you which computer meets the minimum requirements to run the IEAK Wizard. A download server will be used to deploy the custom packages. Select the computer on which you can run the IEAK with no modifications.
    - A. A 486/66 computer with 16M of RAM and 70M of free disk space running Windows NT 4.0 with Service Pack 3 applied.
    - B. A SparcStation 2 with 128M of RAM and 2 gigabytes of free disk space.
    - C. A Pentium 200 computer with 128M of RAM and 500M of free disk space running Windows NT 4.0 Workstation with no service packs applied.
    - D. A 486/33 computer with 16M of RAM and 60M of free disk space running Windows for Workgroups.

27. You have a network of 100 Windows NT 4.0 Workstation computers running IE 3.01 and 250 Windows 95 computers running Netscape 3.0, accessing the Internet through a proxy server. You are configuring a custom deployment package to upgrade all your users to IE 4.0. Can you import current proxy settings as part of the upgrade process?
    A. Yes, proxy settings can be imported from IE 3.01 and Netscape 3.0.
    B. No, proxy server settings cannot be imported.
    C. No, proxy server settings can only be imported from IE 2.x browsers and earlier.
    D. No, proxy server settings can only be imported from Netscape Navigator 3.0.

28. You have a network of 100 Windows NT Workstation computers running IE 3.01, accessing the Internet through a proxy server. There is also an IIS server on your intranet to which users connect for confidential company information. A cookie is used to help keep track of how often users are connecting to the site. You are configuring a custom deployment package to upgrade all your users to IE 4.0. Will the user's cookies be imported when the user upgrades to IE 4.0?
    A. No, cookies cannot be imported.
    B. No, cookies are imported only from IE 2.x browsers.
    C. No, cookies are imported only from Netscape Navigator 3.0.
    D. Yes, cookies will be imported from the IE 3.x configuration.

29. You have a network of 40 Windows NT 4.0 Workstation computers running Netscape Navigator 3.0. You want to use only the plug-ins configured with your custom deployment. What must be done?
    A. A script file must be run by each user before the upgrade is run to uninstall the plug-ins.
    B. Nothing. Plug-ins are not imported when an upgrade is performed.
    C. Select Do Not Import Plug-ins when creating the custom package.
    D. Nothing. Plug-ins will be imported. You will have to go to each user and uninstall the plug-ins after the upgrade is complete.

30. Your company has a network of 40 Windows NT Workstation computers running IE 3.01. You will be using the IEAK Wizard to create a custom deployment package and want all your users to use Outlook Express for email. The company wants a signature appended to the end of each email message your users send. How do you configure this in the IEAK Wizard?
    A. A script file must be run by each user to configure the signature portion of Outlook Express.
    B. Nothing. The signature cannot be configured by using the IEAK Wizard.
    C. In the Include a Signature dialog box, select Append the Following Signature to Every Mail Message and enter the text to append to the end of each mail message.
    D. In the Include a Signature dialog box, select Use Mail Signature Also as News Signature.

31. You are upgrading from Eudora Pro to Outlook Express and want to create a custom welcome and help display message on the bottom of the Outlook Express window, providing the help desk's extension number. How would you do this?
    A. Use the infopane feature to display a one-inch pane at the bottom of the Outlook Express window with the help desk's phone number.
    B. Create a custom toolbar bitmap with the help desk's phone number.

C. Turn on the Tip of the Day feature and create a custom tip with the help desk's phone number.

D. Nothing. This cannot be done.

32. Your company has a network of 40 Windows 95 computers running Netscape 3.0. You will be using the IEAK Wizard to create a custom deployment package and want all your users to use Outlook Express as their email and news client. The company wants a signature that has the company name and slogan appended to the end of each email and news message your users send. How do you configure this in the IEAK Wizard? (Select two.)

A. A script file must be run by each user to configure the signature portion of Outlook Express.

B. Do nothing. The signature information will automatically be configured for you.

C. In the Include a Signature dialog box, select Append the Following Signature to Every Mail Message and enter the text to append to the end of each mail message.

D. In the Include a Signature dialog box, select Use Mail Signature Also as News Signature.

33. You have a network of 40 Windows 95 computers running IE 3.x and want to configure Outlook Express to be the default mail and news client. How can you do this? (Select two.)

A. While creating the custom deployment package, select Make Outlook Express the Default Mail and News Client.

B. Do nothing. Outlook Express will automatically become the default mail and news client.

C. While creating the custom deployment package, select Make Outlook Express the Default Mail Client.

D. While creating the custom deployment package, select Make Outlook Express the Default News Client.

34. Can you limit your users' ability to send and receive files in NetMeeting? (Select the best answer.)

A. Yes, you can limit the user's ability to send files or receive files.

B. No, you can limit the user's ability to receive files only.

C. No, you can limit the user's ability to send files only.

D. Yes, you can limit a user's collaboration ability.

35. How can you review the settings you used when you created a custom deployment package? (Select the best answer.)

A. Use the System Policy Editor to view the `Install.INS` file for the custom deployment package.

B. Run a test deployment and view the settings.

C. Use the IEAK Profile Manager to view the `Install.INS` file for the custom deployment package.

D. Use the IEAK Profile Manager to view the `Install.INF` file for the custom deployment package.

36. How can you allow a user to share applications but disable the user's ability to collaborate? (Select the best answer.)

A. Under Restrict the Use of File Transfer, select Prevent User from Receiving Files.

B. Disable NetMeeting on the user's computer.

C. In User Manager for Domains, remove the user from the Collaborative local group.

D. Under Restrict the Use of Application Sharing, select Prevent the User from Collaborating.

37. You want to disable the user's ability to change the General options you configured before deploying IE 4.0 with the NetMeeting components. How would you do this?
    A. Under Restrict the Use of the Options Dialog, select Disable the 'My Information' Options Page.
    B. Under Restrict the Use of the Options Dialog, select Disable the 'General' Options Page.
    C. Set the default directory server to a domain controller and remove the user from the Collaborative local group.
    D. Set the directory server to a member server and remove the user from the Power Users group.

38. When configuring NetMeeting on your local network, how do you prevent users from using the audio features?
    A. Configure the Set Limit for Audio/Video Throughput setting.
    B. Configure the Restrict the Use of Video/Bandwidth setting.
    C. Select the Prevent the User from Using Audio Features setting.
    D. Configure the Restrict the Use of Audio/Bandwidth setting.

39. While running the IEAK Wizard, you selected the multiple-floppy deployment method. What deployment packages were created?
    A. `Download` directory
    B. Multiple-floppy
    C. CD-ROM
    D. Single-floppy

40. You created a deployment package and selected the single-floppy for deployment media. What deployment methods were created?
    A. CD-ROM
    B. Multiple-floppy
    C. Single-floppy
    D. `Download` directory

41. You want to be able to specify the single-floppy, multiple-floppy, and CD-ROM deployment methods. What role must you select to have all these options available to you?
    A. Content Provider/Developer role.
    B. Internet Service Provider role
    C. Corporate Administrator role
    D. None of these roles will provide you with that ability. You must have the IEAK Extra to have all these options available.

42. What information is stored on the floppy set when a multiple-floppy set is created for deployment of IE 4.0?
    A. The floppy set stores all the information needed to deploy IE 4.0, with the exception of the `.INS` files.
    B. The floppy set stores all the information needed to deploy IE 4.0, with the exception of the `.CAB` files.
    C. The floppy set stores all the information needed to deploy IE 4.0, with the exception of the `.INF` files.
    D. The information stored on the floppy set can completely install IE 4.0 without connecting to perform a download.

43. In which folder is the floppy set stored when the multiple-floppy deployment method is selected and the download folder is `c:\Multiple` and the deployment language is English? (Select all correct answers.)
    A. `c:\Multiple\Mfloppy\Win95\En`
    B. `c:\Multiple\Mfloppy\Win95_NT\En`
    C. `c:\Multiple\Mfloppy\WinNT\En`
    D. `c:\Multiple\Mfloppy\En`

44. You have created a custom deployment package and selected CD-ROM as a

deployment media. You want to change the title bar for the Autorun dialog box. What file would you edit?

A. `Title.INI`

B. `Iecd.INI`

C. `Autorun.INF`

D. `Install.INI`

45. You have been tasked with deploying Internet Explorer 4.0 on all your company's computers. Your company has very strict security requirements, and you must have as much control over each user's configuration as possible. What mode would you select?

A. Content Provider mode

B. Internet Service Provider mode

C. Corporate Administrator mode

D. All modes provide the same configuration options

46. You are running the IEAK Wizard and must have the ability to create a single floppy for installation. What mode must you be running in?

A. That option is always available

B. You must run in Content Provider mode

C. You must run in ISP mode

D. You must run in CA mode

47. You have been tasked with deploying Internet Explorer 4.0 on all your company's computers. You have to be able to configure proxy settings. What mode must you run in?

A. Content Provider mode

B. ISP mode

C. CA mode

D. All modes provide the same configuration options

48. You are in Corporate Administrator mode configuring a custom package for deployment using the IEAK Wizard. You have to configure the security zone settings so that the user will not be prompted for a user name and password when accessing local sites but will be prompted for this information for Internet-based sites. What is the most appropriate security level?

A. Low security

B. Medium security

C. High security

D. This is not configurable through the IEAK Wizard

49. How can you prevent users from changing the security levels after the deployment of IE 4.0?

A. In Stage 4 of the IEAK Wizard, select Disable Modifications in the Security Zone dialog box.

B. In User Manager for Domains, remove the user from the Domain Users global group.

C. During Stage 3 of the IEAK Wizard, set the browser for Read Only.

D. In Stage 5 of the IEAK, set the System Policies for Internet Restrictions, Security to not allow users to add or delete sites from the Security zone.

50. There is a site on the Internet your users access on a regular basis that uses Java applications and ActiveX controls. To which zone would you add this site to allow the site to function properly on your users' computers, assuming that you trust the site?

A. Internet zone

B. Local Intranet zone

C. Trusted Sites zone

D. Restricted Sites zone

51. You want to route all FTP traffic through a proxy server with a host name of `PublicFTP`. You want all other Internet traffic to use a proxy server with a host

name of `Publicproxy`. How would you configure the proxy server settings? (Select two.)

A. Remove the check mark from the Use the Same Proxy Server for All Addresses check box. For the FTP protocol, type **`http://PublicFTP`**.

B. Remove the check mark from the Use the Same Proxy Server for All Addresses check box. For the FTP protocol, type **`http://proxy`**.

C. Remove the check mark from the Use the Same Proxy Server for All Addresses check box. For all other protocols, type **`http://Publicproxy`**.

D. Remove the check mark from the Use the Same Proxy Server for All Addresses check box. For all other protocols, type **`http://ftp`**.

52. You need to quickly view the configuration settings for a custom package you created using the IEAK Wizard. Which file would you view?

A. `Install.INS`

B. `Deploy.INS`

C. `Install.INF`

D. `Deploy.INF`

53. You are the corporate administrator for a small company with an installed base of 50 Windows 95 computers and 50 Windows NT computers. All your users need Internet access. Your users all need to set the corporate Web site as the browser's home page, but the site address changes about every two weeks. You have decided to use the IEAK Wizard to deploy IE 4.0 on all the users' desktops, but don't want to go to each user's desktop and change the home page information every few weeks. How can you automate the update process? (Select two.)

A. Modify the master `.INS` file.

B. Modify the user's logon script to download the new file with each logon.

C. Modify the master `.INF` file.

D. Add the users to the Power Operators group.

54. How can you modify the proxy server settings in your deployment package after it has already been created?

A. After deploying IE 4.0, send an email to each client explaining how to set proxy server access.

B. Edit the `.INS` file manually.

C. Run the IEAK Wizard again and change the proxy server settings.

D. Run the IEAK Profile Manager to make the change to the `.INS` file.

55. You are preparing to deploy Microsoft Internet Explorer 4.0 on 50 Windows 95 computers and 125 Windows NT Workstations that will access the Internet through a proxy server for most sites, but will bypass the proxy server for a list of sites that change daily. The sites are listed in a script file that is updated every night at midnight. Your users are forced to log off nightly. How would you configure this in the IEAK Wizard?

A. Define the URL and filename under Autoproxy URL.

B. Define only the URL under Autoproxy URL.

C. Define only the filename of the script.

D. Define the URL and filename under Autoconfigure URL.

56. How can you implement changes on the browser for your clients using IE 4.0 without manually reconfiguring each user's computer?

A. Enable automatic browser configuration. Provide the filename for only the `.INS` file.

B. Enable automatic browser configuration. Provide the URL for only the `.INS` file.

C. Enable automatic browser configuration. Provide the URL and filename for the `.INF` file.

D. Enable automatic browser configuration. Provide the URL and filename for the `.INS` file.

57. You are preparing to deploy Microsoft Internet Explorer 4.0 on 100 Windows 95 computers. They will be deployed to two different groups. The Sales group needs a different browser configuration than does the Human Resources group. Both configurations will change on a regular basis, and you want to be able to provide automatic updates to each of the groups. How can you do this? (Select two.)

A. Use the IEAK Profile Manager to create two different `.INS` files, one for the Sales group and one for the Human Resources group.

B. Use the IEAK Wizard to create two custom packages, one for each group, each enabling automatic browser updates; the Sales group should point to one `.INF` file and the Human Resources group should point to a different `.INF` file.

C. Use the IEAK Profile Manager to create two different `.INF` files, one for the Sales group, one for the Human Resources group.

D. Use the IEAK Wizard to create two custom packages, one for each group, each enabling automatic browser updates; the Sales group should point to one `.INS` file and the Human Resources group should point to a different `.INS` file.

58. You want to view the IE 4.0 Advanced settings using a text editor. What file would you view?

A. `Inetset.INS`

B. `Inetset.CAB`

C. `Inetset.INF`

D. `Inetset.ADM`

59. You want to view the NetMeeting policies for users and computers using Notepad. What file would you view?

A. `Conf.CAB`

B. `Conf.INS`

C. `Conf.INF`

D. `Conf.ADM`

60. What is the template file used to help define Active Desktop settings?

A. `Shell.INF`

B. `Shell.ADM`

C. `Shell.INS`

D. `Shell.CAB`

61. Which statement is true of `.CAB` or `.INF` files?

A. `.CAB` files define parameters in `.INF` files.

B. `.INF` files are the same as `.CAB` files.

C. `.CAB` files are stored in `.INF` files for distribution to clients.

D. `.INF` files are stored in `.CAB` files for distribution to clients.

62. You are having trouble accessing your favorite Web sites. You want to check the IP settings on your Windows NT 4.0 system. What utility would you use?

A. IPCONFIG

B. WINIPCFG

C. Help

D. Network Monitor

63. You are running a Windows 95 client system and you cannot access any Web pages. What tool would you use to view your IP configuration, and how would you access it?

A. IPCONFIG from a DOS prompt.

B. IPCONFIG from the Start, Run window.

C. WINIPCFG from a DOS prompt.

D. WINIPCFG from the Start, Run window.

64. You issue the `ping 127.0.0.1` command and the request times out. What can cause this? (Select two answers.)

A. You forgot to install a loopback connector.

B. The NIC card could be bad.

C. The cable from your system to the network hub could be defective.

D. TCP/IP is not installed properly.

65. You are having problems gaining access to the Internet. You issue `ping 127.0.0.1` and get four successful replies. You ping several local hosts, some successfully and some not successfully. You cannot ping any remote hosts. What is the most likely cause of your problem?

A. You have an incorrect gateway.

B. You have an incorrect TCP/IP address.

C. You have an incorrect subnet mask.

D. There are no remote hosts available right now.

66. You are able to ping your proxy server by using the IP address, but you cannot ping it by using the FQDN. What is the likely cause of the problem?

A. WINS

B. Incorrect gateway

C. DNS

D. The proxy server is down

67. You are experiencing intermittent problems getting to your corporate headquarters' main Web page from your house by using an ISDN connection. What utility could you use to help determine what the problem is with the connection?

A. `tracert`

B. Ping

C. IPCONFIG

D. FTP

68. You issue a Ping command to an FQDN and receive a `Request Timed Out` message. What could you try next?

A. Issue the same Ping command except use the `-v` (verbose) switch.

B. Issue the same Ping command except use the `-r` (route) switch.

C. Issue a `tracert` command to the same FQDN.

D. Issue a Ping command from the original destination node and see whether you can ping yourself (the original source node).

69. Version 4.01a of the IEAK Wizard allows you to build customized IE 4.0 deployment packages for which platforms? (Select all correct answers.)

A. Windows 95/NT 4.0

B. Windows 3.11/WFW/NT 3.51

C. UNIX

D. Macintosh

70. You began experiencing an increased amount of network traffic over the last week. What utility can you use to monitor network traffic and specifically look for who or what is generating the additional traffic?

A. IPCONFIG

B. WINIPCFG

C. `tracert`

D. Network Monitor

71. You have a network that spans multiple subnets. You need to configure Network Monitor to span all subnets. Where do you get a copy of Network Monitor that will span multiple subnets?

A. The `microsoft.com` Web page for download

B. NT Server Installation CD-ROM

C. System Management Server (SMS)

D. You cannot configure Network Monitor to span several subnets

72. You are attempting to run the IEAK Wizard on a Pentium computer with 64M of RAM and 1 gigabyte of free disk space. The computer has a fresh install of Windows NT 4.0 Server and Service Pack 3 has been applied, and you have installed IE 4.0. This is your notebook computer and you are attempting to configure the IEAK Wizard from your house. You have a modem and can attach to your network at work, which will provide you with Internet access. When running the IEAK Wizard, you do not have any Web sites to select from for component synchronization, and the Wizard fails. What would you try doing first to fix this problem?

A. Use the modem to connect to your network at work.

B. Remove IE 4.0.

C. Reapply the service pack.

D. Reinstall the IEAK.

73. Your company is preparing to deploy Internet Explorer 4.0, and you have to select a computer on which to run the IEAK Wizard. A download server will be used to deploy the custom packages. Select the computers on which the IEAK cannot be installed.

A. A 486/100 computer with 32M of RAM and 70M of free disk space running Windows 95 with the most current service packs applied.

B. A SparcStation 2 with 128M of RAM and 2 gigabytes of free disk space.

C. A Pentium 200 computer with 128M of RAM and 500M of free disk space running Windows NT Workstation 3.51.

D. A 486/66 computer with 24M of RAM and 75M of free disk space running Windows NT Workstation 4.0 with Service Pack 3 applied.

74. You have a network of 100 Windows NT Workstation computers running IE 3.01, accessing the Internet through a proxy server. There is also an IIS server on your intranet to which users connect for confidential company information. A cookie is used to help keep track of how often users are connecting to the site. You are configuring a custom deployment package to upgrade all your users to IE 4.0. Will the user's cookies be imported when the user upgrades to IE 4.0?

A. No, cookies cannot be imported.

B. No, cookies are imported only from IE 2.x browsers.

C. No, cookies are imported only from Netscape Navigator 3.0.

D. Yes, cookies will be imported from the IE 3.x configuration.

75. You have a network of 60 Windows 95 computers running Netscape Navigator 3.0, accessing the Internet through a proxy server. You are configuring a custom deployment package to upgrade all your users to IE 4.0. Can you import current proxy settings as part of the upgrade process?

A. Yes, proxy settings can be imported from Netscape Navigator 3.0.

B. No, proxy server settings cannot be imported from any browser.

C. No, proxy server settings can be imported only from IE 2.x browsers and earlier.

D. No, proxy server settings can be imported only from IE 3.x and later browsers.

Answers and Explanations

1. **A** The crawl depth is how many layers down a site you will update.
2. **A** Under NetMeeting Settings, you can disable the user from sending or receiving files.
3. **A, C, and D** Clear Test is not a listed option.
4. **D** Nonproxy clients use an `.INS` file for updates. The Autoconfiguration dialog box points to the location of the `.INS` file.
5. **C** You would select Add URL. The entry you provide would point to the site desired.
6. **A** You can delete the current IE 4.0 channel settings by selecting Delete Existing IE 4.0 Channels.
7. **D** You would configure the Support Page URL to point to your custom information site.
8. **D** User Choice is not available in silent installation mode because the user is not prompted for any information.
9. **A** There are three options for the Windows Desktop Update: Yes, No, and User Choice.
10. **D** A GUID is a unique identifier that helps identify programs or objects. An algorithm is used to help ensure uniqueness.
11. **C** You do not have any version of NetMeeting installed on the computer on which you are running the IEAK Wizard.
12. **B** The ISP role will present you with all the deployment methods.
13. **A** You must be connected to the Internet for the IEAK Wizard to run properly.
14. **B** This is the only computer that needs no modifications to run the IEAK Wizard.
15. **A** The processor is the only component that does not have to be upgraded.
16. **D** The minimum operating system that will support IE 4.0 with Macintosh is System 7.1.
17. **C** The minimum free disk space needed to install IE 4.0 on Windows NT is 56M.
18. **B** The minimum amount of RAM needed is 12M.
19. **D** You should figure about 100M of disk space for each custom package.
20. **D** The system meets the minimum requirements.
21. **B** IE 4.0 must be installed on the computer that is running the IEAK Wizard.
22. **C** Only this computer will work without upgrading any hardware.
23. **C** IE 4.0 will not run on a Windows NT 3.1 computer; you must have at least Windows NT 3.51.
24. **A, B** The processor and memory subsystems have to be upgraded to run Windows Desktop Update.
25. **D** Because the actual operating system is Windows 95, all minimum requirements are met.
26. **A** This is the only computer that will work.
27. **A** Proxy settings can be imported from both browsers.
28. **D** Cookies can be imported.
29. **B** Plug-ins must be reinstalled.
30. **C** You can configure a signature file to append to every mail message sent.
31. **A** The infopane option provides the ability to create a one-inch pane at the bottom of the Outlook Express window.
32. **C, D** Options are available to make Outlook Express the default mail client and/or the default news client.
33. **C, D** Options are available to make Outlook Express the default mail client and/or the default news client.
34. **A** There are two file transfer options for NetMeeting, one for sending files and one for receiving files.
35. **C** You can use the IEAK Profile Manager to view the `Install.INS` file for a custom deployment package.

36. **D** You can allow a user to share an application but disallow collaboration.

37. **B** You can restrict the user from modifying the General and My Information options pages.

38. **C** You can prevent the user from using the audio features by using the Restrict the Use of Options dialog box.

39. **A, B** The `Download` directory is created every time a custom deployment package is created.

40. **C, D** The `Download` directory is created every time a custom deployment package is created.

41. **B** The only role that provides the single-floppy deployment method is the ISP role.

42. **D** The information stored on the floppy set allows a user to do a complete installation of IE 4.0.

43. **A, B, and C** Floppy disk sets are created under `Win95`, `Win95_NT`, and `WinNT` directories in the `En` folder if the deployment language is English.

44. **B** The file that stores the custom bitmap and title bar information is the `Iecd.INI` file.

45. **C** The Corporate Administrator mode provides the most flexibility in configuring user options.

46. **C** ISP mode is the only mode that will allow single-floppy installation media.

47. **D** Proxy server settings are available in all IEAK modes.

48. **B** Medium security allows the user to log on automatically in the Local zone.

49. **D** You can allow or disallow the user from changing Security zone settings in the System Policy settings during Stage 5 of the IEAK Wizard.

50. **C** By default, the security level for the Trusted Sites zone is set to low.

51. **A, C** The host name can be used to configure proxy settings, and different proxy servers can be configured for each of the Internet protocols.

52. **A** The configuration information is stored in the `Install.INS` file and can be viewed with any text editor.

53. **A, B** You can automate updates by modifying a master copy of the `.INS` file and appending the user's logon script to download the `.INS` file when logging on.

54. **D** To modify a deployment package you have already created, use the IEAK Profile Manager.

55. **A** A script file can be used to define domains that will bypass the proxy server. The script file is run each time a user requests a site.

56. **D** You would want to enable automatic configuration and then provide the URL and filename for the `.INS` file.

57. **A, D** You would configure two deployment packages. Both would have automatic browser configuration update enabled. You would set one group to obtain updates from one `.INS` file and the other group to obtain updates from a different `.INS` file.

58. **C** You could use a text editor to view the IE 4.0 Advanced settings, which are stored in the `Inetset.INF` file.

59. **C** NetMeeting configuration information is stored in the `Conf.INF` file.

60. **B** `Shell.ADM` is the template file that stores Active Desktop settings.

61. **D** `.INF` files are organized into `.CAB` files for distribution.

62. **A** IPCONFIG with the `/all` switch will give you information about your DNS search order.

63. **C, D** WINIPCFG is the command for viewing TCP/IP information on Windows 95. D is the best answer because it is a GUI utility for Windows 95. There is no need to go to a DOS prompt.

64. **B, D** If TCP/IP did not bind to the NIC, or if you have a bad NIC, you would get this type of error. The cabling does not have to be connected because the loopback ping does not go out to the physical media.

65. **C** Although answers A and B could be correct, the most likely cause is an incorrect subnet mask. Pinging several local hosts with different results means that there is a subnet mask problem. A faulty gateway would not affect local hosts. An incorrect IP address would affect all the hosts you tried to ping.

66. **C** Because you have a success ping with the IP address but not with the host name, it is a DNS problem.

67. **A** `tracert` is a useful utility to troubleshoot slow or faulty router connections.

68. **C** A `tracert` command will give you some detail about where the Ping command failed.

69. **A, B, C, and D** All answers are correct.

70. **D** Network Monitor will allow you to view packets and determine what is causing the excessive traffic on the network.

71. **C** SMS has a complete version that allows you to configure across several subnets. The copy on the Windows NT Server CD-ROM allows you to capture packets only on a single machine.

72. **A** You must have an active Internet connection for the IEAK Wizard to run properly.

73. **B, C** The IEAK can be run only on a computer running Windows 95 or Windows NT 4.0.

74. **D** Cookies are imported when an upgrade from IE 3.x to IE 4.0 occurs.

75. **A** Proxy server settings are imported when an upgrade is performed from IE 3.x or Netscape Navigator browsers to IE 4.0.

APPENDIX **A**

Review of Additional Concepts

Because the Microsoft certification exam for the IEAK requires knowledge beyond the implementation of the product, this appendix serves as a review of some additional concepts. On the exam, you will be expected to operate within the Windows NT domain structure and solve problems related to TCP/IP configuration. This appendix presents a brief review of domain structures, user accounts, and TCP/IP troubleshooting concepts.

This appendix is by no means a comprehensive guide to IP troubleshooting. You should already be accomplished with all the troubleshooting methods described here. If you are not, it would behoove you to study these concepts in some depth. Also, you should read and understand the IE 4.0 White Paper available on TechNet or the Microsoft Web site before attempting to take this test.

Domain Structure

The way a domain is structured has a lot to do with how it is administered. You might encounter several different domain models. Microsoft acknowledges only four official domain structures; however, many people have created their own hybrids of these models. Be sure that you pay attention to the trust relationships and access paths when working with domain structures.

Single Domain

The Single Domain model is probably the easiest to deal with when troubleshooting or diagramming a network. The Single Domain model has no trust relationships, and the access paths are maintained within the domain.

Single domains usually have fewer than 15,000 users and aren't as difficult as the other domain models to administer. A network using this structure consists of a single Primary Domain Controller (PDC) plus any number of Backup Domain Controllers (BDCs). Users can be easily granted access to any resource on the domain.

Master Domain

The Master Domain model provides one level of separation between the users and the resources. In the Master Domain model, there can be many trust relationships, but all point toward the master domain. That is to say, all other domains trust one domain, called the *master domain*. The trust relationships from the other domains (resource domains) are one way: Resource domains trust the master domain.

Master domains usually have fewer than 25,000 users. The separation between users and resources simplifies user account and computer account management. The access path always flows from the master domain to the resource domains. This means that users in the master domain can easily be granted access to resources in any of the resource domains.

All the user accounts in the Master Domain model are supposed to reside in the master domain. In this way, administrative tasks for managing the users can easily be separated from the tasks of managing the actual workstations, printers, file servers, and so on. Centralized Information Technology departments favor either the Master Domain model or the Multiple Master Domain model (described in the following section).

Master domains are often referred to as *account domains* because they hold user accounts.

Multiple Master Domain

The creation of the Multiple Master Domain model is an extension of the Master Domain model. The useful limit on a Master Domain model is about 25,000 users. If the domain grows much larger than that (sometimes well before that time), the creation of another domain should be considered. When the multiple master domain is created, you literally have multiple master domains. Just as with the Master Domain model, the individual resource domains trust the master domain.

Each resource domain must trust each master domain. In addition, the master domains have two-way trust relationships between them. This configuration allows administrators in any given master domain to control the entire domain. Because there is virtually no limit to the number of master domains that can form a multiple master domain, there are no real limitations on the number of users. This is a good configuration for large, centralized IS teams.

Complete Trust

Complete Trust domain models allow for access paths in all directions. When working with Complete Trust models, you don't really have to worry about whether or not someone has an access path. Instead, you can spend time verifying that person's resource permissions.

The Complete Trust model allows for computers and accounts to be mixed in each and every domain. There is no real limit on the number of users a complete trust can handle.

User Management

Several options are available to administrators for managing user accounts. When choosing how to set up user accounts, one of the most important items to consider is how to organize accounts in a logical fashion.

Several types of accounts affect user management: user accounts, global group accounts, local group accounts, and computer accounts. Each of these types is covered in the following sections. Management techniques for user accounts are also discussed in the text that follows.

User Accounts

User accounts represent users. Instead of identifying user accounts only by user name, Windows NT creates a Security Identifier (SID) for each account type. The SID is a unique alphanumeric identifier specific to each account.

User accounts can be given access to a system and its resources directly or through group memberships. The primary purpose of most user accounts is to provide computer and network access to an individual user.

Global Group Accounts

Global groups were designed to hold user accounts. These groups are maintained only on domain controllers. Global groups aren't available in networks without domain controllers.

Local Group Accounts

Local groups were designed to hold user accounts or global groups. In a workgroup, users are placed into local groups to obtain permissions. In a domain, the global groups are placed into local groups.

Normally, resource permissions and system access rights are assigned to local groups. Users gain resource permissions and system access based on their membership in local groups.

Computer Accounts

Because Windows NT computers have native file and logon security, each computer also has its own database to track access permissions. On a domain, the individual databases of all the Windows NT computers must be linked to the domain controllers to provide access paths from one computer to the other. Adding a computer account to the domain creates these access paths.

Essentially, a computer account is a link to a certain computer's database. When a workstation or server joins the domain, the databases are registered with the domain; the domain administrator and the domain users' global groups are granted administrative and user-level access, respectively, in the joining computer's database.

AGLP

The initials AGLP stand for Accounts, Global Groups, Local Groups, Permissions. It is a recommended strategy for implementing accounts in a domain structure. The administration mantra is as follows:

> Place user **A**ccounts into **G**lobal groups, which go into **L**ocal groups, where users gain their **P**ermissions.

This method provides a separation between the user and the permission that allows the administrator to manage groups instead of users. Global groups are used to represent classes or categories of users (such as Accountants, Sales, Managers, and so on). Local groups provide a place to group access rights (such as First Floor Print access, Top Secret File permissions, or Backup Operator rights). When global groups are added to local groups, users get the correct permissions. Administrators shouldn't have to manage the individual user once he or she is assigned to the appropriate groups.

System Policies

The Windows NT administrator can control the user's operating environment using System Policies. The administrator can create system policies using the Windows NT 4.0 System Policy Editor (`POLEDIT.EXE`), which is located in the Administrative Tools section of the Start menu.

The Policy Editor is a type of Registry editor that is a little more user friendly than `REGEDIT.EXE` or `REGEDT32.EXE`. Instead of presenting hives, keys, and subkeys, the Policy Editor uses template files (`*.ADM`). These template files provide a structured view of the Registry by category, such as Windows NT Network, Windows NT Printers, Windows NT System, and so on. You can change these settings by clicking check boxes (as opposed to changing hex values in REGEDIT or REGEDT32).

> **The basic templates that come with the System Policy Editor are `WINNT.ADM`, `WINDOWS.ADM`, and `COMMON.ADM`. `WINNT.ADM` provides settings specific to Windows NT. `WINDOWS.ADM` provides settings specific to Windows 95. `COMMON.ADM` provides settings available in both Windows 95 and Windows NT.**

You can use the Policy Editor to edit the local system Registry, or you can create a file that will edit the policies of domain clients. This is part of the "zero administration initiative." You can create default settings for the computer, users, or groups. Group settings can be placed in priority order by selecting Options|Group Priority in the Policy Editor. If you create a policy for a specific user, that policy is used instead of any group policy for that user. Computer settings apply to the system and are implemented no matter who logs on.

The Microsoft Zero Administration Kit, downloadable from `www.microsoft.com/windows/zak`, provides a set of examples that show Information Technology (IT) professionals how to use Windows system policies to reduce support, management, and end-user operation costs on Windows NT Workstation 4.0 and Windows 95. Using the Zero Administration Kit, a corporation can increase the manageability of Windows-based systems by centralizing functionality.

If you are saving policies to be implemented on computers throughout the domain, you must save the policies as `NTCONFIG.POL` for Windows NT clients and as `CONFIG.POL` for Windows 95 clients. These files must be placed into the `netlogon` share on every domain controller in the domain. The physical directory that is shared as `netlogon` is the `scripts` directory under `%systemroot%\system32\repl\import`.

> **Even if you use the `COMMON.ADM` template to create the policy, you must save it as `CONFIG.POL` *and* `NTCONFIG.POL` if you want it to be used by both Windows NT and Windows 95 clients on your network.**

Proxy Server Overview

In addition to domain administration issues, you should understand how a proxy server can be employed on your network to control access.

The main application for the Microsoft Proxy Server is to provide access and control for your users to the Internet. The proxy serves as a single gateway to the Internet so that you can monitor, control, and provide access to the Internet from that single point.

With the Microsoft Proxy Server, you can do the following:

- Keep all or some of your internal clients from accessing the Internet.
- Allow or disallow Internet clients from accessing your internal network.
- Limit the Internet sites to which your users can connect.
- Provide a single connection point for your clients to the Internet.
- Provide Internet file caching for internal clients; this speeds user access to frequently used resources. The proxy cache can even be active, which means that it will update its cached Internet files in anticipation of client access. In that way, clients get the latest files from the local proxy cache.
- Keep a log of sites visited by proxy clients.
- All proxy clients use one IP address for Internet access.
- Reverse hosting allows clients to create Web sites accessible from the Internet.

TCP/IP Basics

You can use many different utilities to troubleshoot an IP network. When troubleshooting IP connections, probably the most important item to understand is the nature of the problem. Understanding the IP architecture is one of the keys to properly troubleshooting it.

IP is divided into four layers. From the bottom to the top, these layers are Network Interface, Internet, Transport, and Application. The following sections look at IP problems, their respective layers, and how to handle them.

Network Interface Layer

The IP Network Interface layer includes the network card and the drivers used to merge data frames onto the wire. The problems that can occur at this layer are driver corruption and configuration errors, MAC address problems, and physical connection problems.

One of the first items you should check when you find that a computer cannot communicate on the network is the physical attachment to the network. If the cable is not attached to the card, the data cannot be transferred.

If you have the wrong NIC driver, or the driver is corrupt, your computer cannot communicate on the network. You should see configuration errors in Windows NT if you have the wrong driver, the wrong I/O address, or the wrong IRQ. All of these items are covered under the category of basic network troubleshooting. Usually, the Windows NT Event Viewer can identify the problem; then it is up to you to consult the manufacturer's documentation, specifications, and utilities to set the card and load the proper driver.

Another item that can cause problems is the MAC (Media Access Control) address. MAC addresses are assigned by the network manufacturer and are designed by the IEEE to be unique. However, some manufacturers have failed to follow IEEE guidelines, so you may occasionally find network cards with duplicate MAC addresses.

Usually, the Windows NT Event Viewer will report an error if Windows NT finds a duplicate MAC address on the network. There are several ways to view the MAC address, but the two most popular methods are to use `NETSTAT` and `ARP`.

ARP (Address Resolution Protocol) gives you a list of MAC addresses it has resolved. When communications are sent over the wire, they are always sent from one MAC address to another. If you are sending a packet to a remote computer, the packet is sent to the MAC address of your router and forwarded from there. Inbound packets from remote segments will have the MAC address of your local router because that is the last host to handle the packet before your computer gets it. You can check your ARP cache by typing the following at the Windows NT command prompt:

```
ARP -c
```

This command shows you the local IP to MAC address resolutions. Remember that if the IP is remote, you will see only the MAC address of your local router.

Another command you can use to determine MAC addresses is the **`NBTSTAT`** command, which stands for NetBIOS over TCP/IP statistics. If you enter ***`Nbtstat -a IP_address`***, where ***`IP_address`*** is the actual IP address of a host on your network, you will see that computer's name table and MAC address.

You can see your own MAC address and IP configuration by typing **`IPCONFIG -all`** at a command prompt. With Windows 95, you should use the command `WINIPCNFG` to see your IP configuration. This utility is also available for Windows NT in the Windows NT Resource Kit. You can also look at the properties for the IP protocol through the Network icon in the Control Panel (in both Windows 95 and Windows NT). Although `WINIPCNFG` and `IPCONFIG` are available for both Windows 95 and Windows NT, the certification exam is testing your knowledge of which utilities are available with a basic installation of Windows 95 or Windows NT with the TCP/IP protocol installed.

If you want to monitor and open the actual packets transmitted on the wire, you should use the Windows NT Network Monitor. You can capture, collect, and analyze network packets with this utility.

Internet Layer

The Internet layer contains components such as IP (Internet Protocol), ICMP (Internet Control Message Protocol), and IGMP (Internet Group Message Protocol).

IP is the addressing scheme of the Internet and any IP internetwork. Each IP address (host ID) must be unique on the network, but hosts on the network should share the same network identification if they are expected to communicate with one another on the network.

The subnet mask separates the network ID from the host ID. For example, IP address `192.168.1.1` with subnet mask `255.255.0.0` has a network ID of `192.168` and a host ID of `1.1`.

> **It is beyond the scope of this text to enter into a complex subnet masking discussion. Because knowledge of TCP/IP is a requirement for the exam, if you have forgotten or never learned this information, it would behoove you to study it before taking the exam.**

Clients on the same physical segment should have the same network ID but different host IDs. When they need to communicate outside of the local segment, the clients must also be configured with a default gateway (a.k.a. a *router*). The default gateway sends any information that goes outside the local segment to the correct segment or on to its own default gateway.

Local clients and routers maintain routing tables that allow them to properly route packets on the network. You can view the routing table of your local computer with the `ROUTE PRINT` command from the Windows NT command prompt.

If your routing table is incorrect, packets can be sent to the wrong place (misrouted). In this situation, you may be able to communicate with some clients (probably on your local segment) but may not be able to communicate with other clients. You should also check the default gateway to ensure that it is set correctly.

Ping is an excellent utility for diagnosing connectivity problems. If you can ping a client, you know you have a physical connection. Ping uses ICMP messages (relayed from one host to another) to find a client on the network. If you cannot ping a remote host, try to ping your local router. If you cannot ping the local router, ping your own IP address. If all of your ping attempts fail, ping the loopback (`127.0.0.1`) to see whether your IP configuration is valid. If the ping succeeds anywhere along the way, you should suspect that the problem lies beyond the location of your last successful ping.

Another diagnostic utility that uses ICMP messages is Trace Route (`TRACERT`). Trace Route actually follows your message from host to host as it navigates the network. If you have a problem along the way, the trace will fail to get to the next host. This can be a quick way to identify a downed router.

Transport Layer

The Transport layer is usually not the place where you will find an IP error. The Transport layer includes the TCP (Transmission Control Protocol) and the UDP (User Datagram Protocol). Unless someone has configured a Web server to operate on a port other than TCP 80, you shouldn't have too much trouble with the Transport layer.

You can check the status of your Transport layer ports and sockets by issuing the `NETSTAT` command at the Windows NT command prompt. This command reports back on all your active Transport layer ports and sockets.

A socket is the combination of the IP address and TCP/UDP socket number.

To learn more about the options of the `NETSTAT` command, type **`NETSTAT /?`** at the Windows NT command prompt.

Application Layer

The problems that can occur at the Windows NT Application layer are quite extensive. Most Application layer errors have to do with IP to host name resolution problems. When people enter something like `PING www.hudlogic.com`, the `www.hudlogic.com` part must be resolved to an IP address. On the Internet, name resolution is the job of a DNS (Domain Name System) server. Microsoft networks that have DHCP or WINS (Windows Internet Name Service) enabled will also have WINS servers working to resolve computer names to IP addresses.

If a DNS server is incorrectly configured, you won't be able to type the host name into a browser (or any other utility for that matter) and pull up the site. Other than going to the actual DNS server, you can use the `NSLOOKUP` command to check this configuration. `NSLOOKUP` queries the DNS server about the specific IP address it has mapped to the computer name. Another way to find out which IP address is configured in the DNS server for a particular host is to ping the computer name. The Ping utility will tell you which IP address it is attempting to ping. You will obviously have to know what the correct IP address for the computer name is before you can make the determination that the DNS server is incorrectly configured.

You can also troubleshoot the WINS server by seeing which address it gives to the Ping utility. Other than that, you can check the WINS server itself for proper configuration. Sometimes, it takes a purge of the database to correct problems. Because WINS clients register with the WINS server every time they boot, clearing the database shouldn't cause any lasting problems.

Glossary

The following are terms with which anyone taking the *Implementing and Supporting Microsoft Internet Explorer 4.0 MCSE* exam should be well acquainted.

128-bit encryption—The size of the key used to encrypt the message or data. The 128-bit encryption optional component is available for the IEAK from the Microsoft Web site and can be used only in the United States at this time.

Active Channel—A Web site enabled for "smart pushes" with the addition of a CDF file.

active content—Information requiring frequent updates.

Active Desktop—An integration of the Web and the desktop.

Active Setup—The setup utility on which IE 4.0 is based. Active Setup is based on the ActiveX engine.

ActiveX—An open, cross-platform standard that enables developers to create interactive content for the World Wide Web.

add-on—An optional component of IE 4.0. This type of component is not an integral part of IE 4.0 and can be installed by the user at a later date to provide additional functionality.

`.ADM` file—An administrative file used to configure users' rights and restrictions. This creates the same type of file as the System Policy editor in Windows NT 4.0.

ASP—Active Server Pages.

autorun—The utility that automatically runs a file on a CD-ROM when the disc is inserted in the drive.

AVS—Automatic Version Synchronization.

baseline—Basic indicators that are gathered and archived when a product is operating normally. The baseline is typically compared to current indicators on a system as an aid in tuning and troubleshooting.

bookmark—In Netscape Navigator, a bookmark is used to store the location of a URL. Bookmarks are comparable to the Favorites folder in IE 4.0.

browser (a.k.a. Web browser)—Software that displays content from the World Wide Web on your computer's desktop. Two examples are Netscape Navigator and Microsoft Internet Explorer 4.0.

`.CAB` file—A cabinet file that organizes `.INF` files. The `.CAB` file is downloaded to the client and expanded, freeing all the little `.INF` files.

cache—Temporary storage location. When Web objects are cached locally, they are stored on the hard disk.

.CDF file—The file added to Web sites that differentiates a channel from a typical site.

CDF—Channel Definition Format.

channel subscription—A special kind of site subscription in which the site contains a .CDF file resulting in smart pulls and smart pushes of information.

channels—*See* Active Channel.

Chat—A text-based program used to communicate while using NetMeeting.

client/server architecture—A network and application design that divides processing between clients and servers. The opposite of peer-to-peer.

CMAK—Connection Manager Administration Kit. CMAK is used to automate the client's modem connection information.

collaborate (or collaboration)—To work together. With IE 4.0, the group of products allows users to work on the same document simultaneously across a network or the Internet.

conferencing—A term typically associated with NetMeeting; when two or more users communicate using audio or video.

Content Advisor—A tool used to adjust the caution rating of Web content.

content rating—A caution rating for Web content based on four things: language, nudity, sex, and violence.

Corporate mode—One of the three configuration and customization options in IEAK.

crawl depth—How many links deep a site subscription will go looking for updated content.

customization code—A 10-digit code number assigned by Microsoft for accessing your IEAK CD-ROM.

desktop—How your screen looks when you log in to your system. *See also* Active Desktop.

DHTML—Dynamic HTML.

directory structure (directory tree)—The hierarchical structure of the file system.

distribution media/methods—The way a custom IE 4.0 kit will be distributed: CD-ROM, multiple floppy disks, and single disk (single disk is for ISPs only).

DLS—An industry-standard format for packaging instrument sounds.

DNS—Domain Name System (or Server).

ECMA-262 specification—The ECMA standard defining the ECMAScript scripting language.

ECMAScript—The European Computer Manufacturers' Association scripting language. JScript and JavaScript are two implementations of this standard.

event—Something that causes something else to take place. For example, an event is something that would cause a program to branch.

event viewer—A Windows NT utility for viewing events. The information is stored in one of three log files: system, security, or application.

Favorites folder—In IE 4.0, favorites provide a way to create markers or links to sites that the user will visit on a regular basis.

firewall—A hardware or software device used to isolate an internal network from an external network, such as the Internet.

folder—A term used to describe a directory or subdirectory on a hard disk.

FQDN—Fully Qualified Domain Name. This is the descriptor used to identify Internet locations.

FTP—File Transfer Program/Protocol.

full subscription—*See* site subscription.

GUI—Graphical User Interface.

History folder—The location in which pointers to the most recent Web pages are kept.

home page—A Web site (or file) to which your browser goes when you open the browser or click the Home button.

hop—A direct link from one computer to another. It usually requires several hops to get from point A to point B on the Internet.

HTML—Hypertext Markup Language.

HTTP—Hypertext Transport Protocol. The protocol used to connect to servers on the World Wide Web. Web site addresses begin with the characters `http://`.

HTTPS—Secure HTTP.

hyperlinks—Locations on Web sites that point to other sites.

hypertext—A link between related text.

IE4—Internet Explorer 4.0

IEAK—Internet Explorer (IE4) Administrator Kit.

`.INF` file—Stores component configuration information for individual IE 4.0 components.

infopane—A one-inch pane at the bottom of the Outlook Express window that can be customized using the Profile Manager. This window can contain HTML data.

`.INS` file—Holds custom settings used to deploy IE 4.0.

Internet (the Internet)—It is very hard to define the Internet in a way that is either meaningful or easy to grasp. To say that the Internet is the world's largest computer network is to trivialize it.

Internet Locator Service (ILS)—A "white pages" for NetMeeting. When you come online, you register with the ILS and can access other users listed in the ILS.

Internet zone—*See* security zones.

intranet—A company's internal network structure that can communicate using Internet-based tools.

IP—Internet Protocol. This is part of the TCP/IP protocol suite.

IP configuration—The group of settings affecting TCP/IP transmissions and the TCP/IP protocol suite.

IPCONFIG—A Windows NT utility used to view the TCP/IP configuration.

ISDN—Integrated Services Digital Network. ISDN allows higher speed communications than current analog modems.

ISP—Internet Service Provider.

Java—A programming language used on the Internet to write small programs or applets that perform specific functions when activated. Java programs are stored in script files.

JavaScript—A way of providing active content using the Java programming language.

JScript—Microsoft's implementation of the ECMA 262-language specification.

LAN—Local Area Network.

LDAP—Lightweight Directory Access Protocol. A software protocol used for locating resources such as people, files, and devices in a network.

Local Intranet zone—*See* security zones.

MAN—Metropolitan Area Network.

Microsoft FrontPage Express—A Web page editor packaged with IE 4.0.

Microsoft Internet Explorer—A Web browser from Microsoft. This browser is comparable to Netscape Navigator or Mosaic.

Microsoft NetMeeting—A multimedia conferencing tool packaged with IE 4.0.

Microsoft NetShow—A component of the IE 4.0 package that allows users to deliver streaming audio/video over the Internet or an intranet.

Microsoft Outlook Express—A messaging product available with the IE 4.0 package.

MIME—Multipurpose Internet Mail Extensions.

multimedia—A combination of text, graphics, sound, and animation.

Netscape Communicator—A browser used to view Web information. This browser is comparable to Microsoft Internet Explorer.

network—A grouping of computers connected through network interface cards and some form of transport media (cable). The Internet is a large, public domain network.

Network Monitor—A network analyzer utility available with Windows NT Server used to view frames of data that travel across a network.

newsgroup—A discussion forum popular with Internet users. A newsgroup is typically hosted by an individual or group, and everyone is allowed to add entries to the newsgroup. The entries are stored at various locations on the Internet.

NSLOOKUP—Name Server LOOKUP. A Windows NT TCP/IP utility used to help troubleshoot name resolution problems.

object—A programming term roughly meaning a collection of functions that implement a capability.

ODBC—Open Database Connectivity.

OLE—Object Linking and Embedding.

page (a.k.a. Web page)—Any site on the Internet or an intranet. A page can contain several objects such as wave files and pictures.

partial subscription—*See* site subscription.

peer-to-peer—A communication architecture in which all parties are equals, as opposed to the client/server architecture.

Ping—A TCP/IP utility for testing network connectivity.

plug-in—Netscape's term for an add-on.

POP3—A standard protocol for receiving email.

PPP—Point-to-Point Protocol. This is a protocol used by modems.

protocol—A set of rules or conventions relating to the format and timing of data transmission between two devices.

proxy—A way to send or receive items on behalf of another user. A proxy server can be used to "hide" or provide a level of separation between an internal user and the Internet.

proxy server—A server that isolates internal network users from external network objects. The proxy server receives requests for information from the user. The proxy server then handles the external communications and provides the information back to the user.

pull—A means of information dissemination in which the user has to take the initiative to "pull" information. *See also* smart pull.

push—A means of information dissemination in which the content provider has to take the initiative to "push" information to users. *See also* smart push.

RealPlayer—A streaming video player option packaged with IE 4.0.

Restricted Sites zone—*See* security zones.

script—A small program executed by the shell.

scripting language—A programming language used for writing scripts.

search engine—Software that searches for data based on some criteria. AltaVista, Yahoo!, and Magellan are three Internet search engines.

search page—Special Web pages used to search for information on the Internet or an intranet.

security zones—IE 4.0 has four preassigned security zones used for determining what access and restrictions apply to Web sites. The four zones are Internet, Local Intranet, Trusted Sites, and Restricted Sites.

Service Pack—Microsoft occasionally releases patch kits for products. The patch kits are referred to as Service Packs.

SGML— Standard Generalized Markup Language. *See also* WYSIWYG.

silent installation—A way of installing IE 4.0 on a user's system without requiring any interaction on the part of the user.

site certificate—An ID card of sorts for a commercial Web site.

site subscription—Users can subscribe to any Web site, resulting in their automatically receiving updated site content (full subscription) or just receiving notification of updated content (partial subscription).

smart pull—The automated pulling of information by users based on some criteria. With IE 4.0, the terms *smart pull* and *smart push* are being used in relationship to channels.

smart push—The automated pushing of information to users based on some criteria. With IE 4.0, the terms *smart pull* and *smart push* are being used in relationship to channels.

SMTP—Simple Mail Transfer Protocol.

software distribution channel—A way of using channels to provide software updates.

SSL—Secure Sockets Layer protocol.

subscription—*See* site subscription, full subscription, partial subscription, and channels.

TCP/IP—Transmission Control Protocol/Internet Protocol.

Telnet—An Internet protocol. Also a remote login program that uses the Telnet protocol.

Temporary Internet Files folder—Web sites are downloaded to your Temporary Internet Files folder before you can view them. Also referred to as a *cache*.

`tracert`—Trace Route. A TCP/IP utility for troubleshooting connectivity problems.

Trusted Sites zone—*See* security zones.

URL—Uniform Resource Locator. An address on the Web.

user agent string—A way of identifying a user when he or she browses the Web.

video conferencing—A component of Microsoft NetMeeting that allows audio/video communications.

Visual Basic Script—A scripting language provided by Microsoft that is similar to a subset of the Visual Basic programming language.

VPN—Virtual Private Network.

VRML—Virtual Reality Modeling Language. A language for writing 3D HTML applications.

WAN—Wide Area Network.

Web site—Any location on the Web.

Webcasting—A relatively new term that encompasses the push updating of selected information on a user's desktop through inconspicuous distribution over the Internet or an intranet at prearranged times.

whiteboard—A component of Microsoft NetMeeting.

WINIPCFG—A Windows 95 TCP/IP utility.

World Wide Web (a.k.a. WWW, W3, or the Web)—The total collection of information available from the Internet. An Internet service that links local and remote content. (Originally, documents were the only form of content.)

WYSIWYG—What You See Is What You Get. A term for word and presentation editors with which the final product is always displayed. The opposite of SGML.

Index

A

B

C

D

E

F

G-H

I

N

O

P

T

U

V

W

Z

MCSE Training Guide: Core Exams (BUNDLE)

New Riders Development ISBN: 1-56205-821-5 $149.99 US/$208.95 CDN 3000 pp.

This bundle covers all four core exams for only $149.99. CD-ROM's TestPrep software hyperlinks test questions to book's text immediately: readers can find complete explanations for any study question. The *only* study materials you need to pass *all* core exams, and it's approved by Microsoft.

Covers: Certification—MCSE

MCSE Training Guide: Internet Information Server 4

Emmett Dulaney, MCSE ISBN: 1-56205-823-1 $49.99 US/$70.95 CDN 500 pp.

IIS 4 is covered by objective; each objective is broken down into manageable chunks and explained so that readers can easily study and find what they need to know for that objective. Following each chapter is a series of review questions that relate to the chapter. The New Riders test engine completes the package by including practice exam questions in a format very similar to that of the actual certification exam. Offers insider tips and information from a distinguished MCSE.

Covers: Certification—MCSE, MCSE+I, MCP

MCSE Training Guide: Windows 95 70-064 Exam

Ed Tetz, MCSE ISBN: 1-56205-880-0 $49.99 US/$71.95 CDN 864 pp.

Utilizing the successful *Training Guide* approach, this book covers the *new* Windows 95 core exam: Exam #70-064—Implementing and Supporting Windows 95 (Exam 70-63 was retired April 98). Study test questions and practice taking the exam with the exclusive TestPrep test engine on the CD-ROM. Approved by Microsoft as Microsoft Certified Professional study material.

Covers: Certification—MCP, MCSE, MCSE+I

MCP+I Training Guide: Internet Exams

Emmett Dulaney, MCSE ISBN: 1-56205-879-7 $99.99 US/$143.95 CDN 1584 pp.

MCP+I Training Guide: Internet Exams instructs exam takers on the details they need to pass each of the exams leading to the popular new Internet certification in an efficient, effective manner. This comprehensive book covers each of the three exams: Internetworking with Microsoft TCP/IP on Microsoft Windows NT 4.0 (70-059), Implementing and Supporting Microsoft Windows NT Server 4.0 (70-067), and Implementing and Supporting Microsoft Internet Information Server 4 (70-087). Our exclusive TestPrep test engine software provides the realistic simulation of the exams and allows users to link back to chapters in an electronic version of the book to review incorrect responses. Each exam section is organized by the Microsoft exam objectives.

Covers: Certification—MCP+I, MCSE+I, MCP

MCSE Training Guide: TCP/IP

Anthony Tilke, et al. ISBN: 1-56205-747-2
$49.99 US/$70.95 CDN 670 pp.

MCSE Training Guide: TCP/IP is the most comprehensive, cost-effective, and efficient way to pass the Internetworking Microsoft TCP/IP on Microsoft Windows NT 4.0 (Exam 70-059) elective. Organized in a concise, easy-to-read manner, this book is the only study material readers will need to pass one of the most popular and challenging MCSE electives! Written by a professional team of Microsoft Certified Systems Engineers and Microsoft Certified Trainers. Includes practice test questions, lists, table, notes, tips, and tricks to completely prepare users for the exams. CD-ROM contains TestPrep test engine software: a realistic simulation of the actual exams. It enables users to link back to chapters in an electronic version of the book for review of incorrect responses. Each exam section is organized by the Microsoft exam objectives.

Covers: Certification—MCSE, MCSE+I, MCP+I, MCP

MCSE Training Guide: SQL Server 6.5 Administration

Brad McGehee, et al. ISBN: 1-56205-726-X $49.99 US/$70.95 CDN 704 pp.

MCSE Training Guide: SQL Server Administration provides users with all of the latest information they need to pass this popular exam and covers all the intricacies of SQL Server 6.5. Utilizing the knowledge of MCSDs, MCSEs, and MCTs, this book contains all the insider tips, notes, and strategies readers need to take a step closer to becoming an MCSE. The book contains test questions, lists, tables, notes, tips, and tricks to completely prepare readers for the exam. It's organized in a concise, easy-to-read manner to give users the most valuable information efficiently. It contains complete coverage of the Exam (70-026) objectives. Provides readers with more than just exam basics—offers extra information on the technology itself! Hundreds of practice test questions and hands-on lab exercises allow readers to apply what they've learned—right away! CD-ROM features TestPrep test simulator, with practice questions, study cards and flash cards features, and links to electronic copy of the entire book.

Covers: Certification—MCSE, MCSE+I, MCP

MCSE Training Guide: SQL Server 6.5 Design and Implementation

Sean Baird, MCSE, et al. ISBN: 1-56205-830-4 $49.99 US/$70.95 CDN 553 pp.

MCSE Training Guide: SQL Server 6.5 Design and Implementation provides users with all of the latest information they need to pass this popular exam and covers all the intricacies of SQL Server 6.5. Utilizing the knowledge of MCSDs, MCSEs, and MCTs, this book contains all the insider tips, notes, and strategies readers need to take a step closer to becoming an MCSE or MCSD. The book contains test questions, lists, tables, notes, tips, and tricks to completely prepare readers for the exam. It's organized in a concise, easy-to-read manner to give users the most valuable information efficiently. *MCSE Training Guide: SQL Server 6.5 Design and Implementation* contains complete coverage of Exam 70-027. Hundreds of practice test questions and hands-on lab exercises allow readers to apply what they've learned—right away! CD-ROM features TestPrep test simulator, with practice questions, study cards and flash cards features, and links to electronic copy of the entire book.

Covers: Certification—MCSE, MCSE+I, MCSD, MCP

REGISTRATION CARD

MCSE Test Prep: Internet Explorer 4

Name ______________________ Title ______________________

Company ______________________ Type of business ______________________

Address ______________________ Email ______________________

City/State/ZIP ______________________

Have you used these types of books before? ☐ yes ☐ no

If yes, which ones? ______________________

____

How many computer books do you purchase each year? ☐ 1–5 ☐ 6 or more

How did you learn about this book? ______________________

Where did you purchase this book? ______________________

Which applications do you currently use? ______________________

____

Which computer magazines do you subscribe to? ______________________

____

What trade shows do you attend? ______________________

____

Comments: ______________________

____

____

Would you like to be placed on our preferred mailing list? ☐ yes ☐ no

☐ **I would like to see my name in print!** You may use my name and quote me in future New Riders products and promotions. My daytime phone number is: ______________________

New Riders Publishing 201 West 103rd Street ◆ Indianapolis, Indiana 46290 USA

Fax to 317-581-4663

Fold Here

NO POSTAGE
NECESSARY
IF MAILED
IN THE
UNITED STATES

BUSINESS REPLY MAIL

FIRST-CLASS MAIL PERMIT NO. 9918 INDIANAPOLIS IN

POSTAGE WILL BE PAID BY THE ADDRESSEE

NEW RIDERS PUBLISHING
201 W 103RD ST
INDIANAPOLIS IN 46290-9058